The Paraglyph Mission

This book you've purchased is a collaborative creation involving the work of many hands, from authors to editors to designers and to technical reviewers. At Paraglyph Press, we like to think that everything we create, develop, and publish is the result of one form creating another. And as this cycle continues on, we believe that your suggestions, ideas, feedback, and comments on how you've used our books is an important part of the process for us and our authors.

We've created Paraglyph Press with the sole mission of producing and publishing books that make a difference. The last thing we all need is yet another tech book on the same tired, old topic. So we ask our authors and all of the many creative hands who touch our publications to do a little extra, dig a little deeper, think a little harder, and create a better book. The founders of Paraglyph are dedicated to finding the best authors, developing the best books, and helping you find the solutions you need.

As you use this book, please take a moment to drop us a line at feedback@paraglyphpress .com and let us know how we are doing - and how we can keep producing and publishing the kinds of books that you can't live without.

Sincerely,

Keith Weiskamp & Jeff Duntemann
Paraglyph Press Founders

4015 N. 78th Street, #115
Scottsdale, Arizona 85251
email: feedback@paraglyphpress.com
Web: www.paraglyphpress.com
Phone: 602-749-8787

"*Monster Gaming* is that geek gaming buddy we all wish we had when we needed some advice on the future of personal entertainment. I've been a dedicated gamer for twenty years and I have plenty of things to learn from this loaded tome. It is the ultimate book for the modern gamer. It's filled with a lot of love, a ton of info, and the best guidance an aspiring game geek could ever want."

– Justin Hall, links.net and gamegirladvance.com

ABOUT THE AUTHOR

Ben Sawyer, Author

Ben Sawyer is a well-known and successful technical author and unapologetic hardcore gamer. Sawyer owns four consoles, a GameBoy advance, four PCs, and a 50" TV to play them all on. He has written and produced over 10 books ranging in topics from MP3 to game development. Ben is the President of Digitalmill, an interactive development and tech market research company based in Portland, Maine. Currently he is working with a division of the U.S. Government to adapt addictive game technology and design ideas to public policy planning and training. He can be contacted via email at bsawyer@dmill.com or visit his Web site at www.dmill.com.

Paul Steed, Cover Artist

Paul Steed has been making art for computer games since 1991. He is a regular speaker at the Game Developers Conference in San Jose, CA. Best known for his work on id Software's Quake series, he is the author of *Modeling a Character in 3ds Max* (Wordware Publishing) and *Animating Real-time Game Characters* (Charles River Media). He can be contacted via email at st33d@nak3d.com.

This book is for Olivia Cabot for loving the kid in me that isn't going away...

ACKNOWLEDGEMENTS

This is my twelfth book. I have so many people to thank for getting me to this point. I want to start with thanking my mother because she bought me every game system imaginable until I started buying my own. Who'd have thought it would have amounted to something huh ma? I guess you did. Let that be a lesson to all the mothers out there. Let your sons play video games and one day they might actually make some money because of it and thank you for it!

I want to also thank Keith Weiskamp, my publisher, and friend. Not many authors have a relationship as close with their publisher as I do. I'm happy to know what started with an offer to give some punk his first book contract back in 1993 would have gotten him so far ten years later. You have no idea how many games I've bought with my book money over the years although I guess you do now. Thanks for all the support and help.

While on the subject of publishers let me also thank Cynthia Caldwell and Steve Sayre at Paraglyph as well. Small teams can do big things and Steve and Cynthia prove that. I also want to thank the artist, Paul Steed, for the cover of this book. Paul gave us much of his time and effort amidst a busy schedule. I can't think of an artist who fits the monster gamer profile more than Paul.

There are also the many people who gave me some input or encouragement, either explicitly or implicitly during the creation of this book that I would like to thank including Justin Hall, Erin Puariea, Mike McShaffry, Robin McShaffry, Joe Cataudella, Matt Barker, Jason Della Rocca, Alex Dunne, John Lundy, Stephen Chan, Veso, Swen Vincke, David Laprad, Noah Fahlstein, Brian Clair, David Cole, Matthew Bellows, Miyuki Jane Pinckard, Channel Summers, Johnny Wilson, Jason Grimm, the members of the Serious Game mailing list, and the many authors of articles, books, fan sites, and more that have informed me over the years.

I want to especially thank Angel Munoz of The CPL and Avault.com for writing the foreword to this book, and providing input into the chapter on competitive gaming.

I thank all my co-workers at Digitalmill who handled everything while I had plenty of days at home writing: Beth Bryant, Doug Briggs, Lucky, Elgin, and Adam Mattessich.

CONTENTS AT A GLANCE

CONTENTS

FOREWORD

Hi, my name is Angel Munoz and I am a hardcore gamer.

Thank God I never have to say that in some sort of perverse Gamers Anonymous meeting. Instead, I can relish a life that is filled with games, gaming peripherals, gamers, and "Monster Gamers." And what a life it has become. If someone had told me when I was growing up in New York City that someday people would win tens of thousands of dollars, automobiles, and other merchandise prizes from being good at games I'd have told them to double up on the medication they were taking. Today, after founding the Cyberathlete Professional League (**www.thecpl.com**) in 1997, the notion doesn't seem so crazy. Last year the CPL gave out over $200,000 in cash prizes to teams and individuals who proved in standardized competitive play that they were the best in the world. Given that, it's clear we've come a long way since the first days of pong.

In just thirty years the gaming industry has gone from offering games that some thought were a fad to the point where it's arguably bigger than the movie industry. This growth wasn't built on the backs of only those who create the games—it is the entire community of developers and players that make it happen. The developers get tons of books published for them, and now we have one for us—the hardcore gamers! Monster Gaming isn't a hint-book, it's a manual for gamers. Some might argue that we don't need an entire book to tell us how to become hardcore gamers. I would just say, "Isn't it cool that now there is so much to know about gaming that a book like this actually makes sense? In fact I think this will be one of many books covering gamers, not just games or game development. That means something to me—it means gaming has grown into more than just the games themselves.

At the very center of the recent explosion in interactive entertainment is the community of gamers. Show me any other industry where people are so involved in its economic life-blood aside from using their own hard-earned money or allowance to buy the industry's products? Stop trying... it's not that easy. The sports industry may be one of the closest and I know something about both, sports and gaming. Certainly the movie, music, or publishing industries cannot make this claim. How many people get to legally redo Star Wars into their own movie? When was the last time a book author allowed readers to rewrite the ending? And the last time I checked, the best competitive component the music industry could provide was Karaoke and American Idol. Like I said, stop trying.

Gamers don't just play games; they build entirely new games through modding. Gamers don't just talk about games; they found entire communities on the Web. I did that with The Adrenaline Vault in 1995 and since its launch, AVault.com has grown exponentially (as the CPL does now). We didn't do it for the money. We did it because we love games. Today Avault.com is one of the top game information and review sites on the Web. Fan sites are nothing new on the Internet, but go visit any gaming fan site, and you'll experience a community that is much more vibrant and interactive than any Britney Spears site or even most movie sites.

Gamers also don't just hang out with their friends; they throw entire parties, inviting dozens of people from around their region to participate in friendly competitions. Gamers are also increasingly international. People compete together from around the world, and bonds build around the communities formed from online games, fan sites, modding and more. At this year's CPL Counter-Strike World Championship in Dallas, Texas, at least twenty teams will be from outside the U.S., including markets people might not expect such as Japan, Sweden, Denmark, Germany, Turkey, Chile, Venezuela, and Brazil. Gaming is a global phenomenon. Since it's founding in 1997 the CPL has grown to support a European branch, and soon will support a branch in Asia as well. In Korea there are entire networks devoted to showing games and tournaments on TV. One of last year's surprise hit games came from Cro-Team based in Croatia. The globalization of gaming is a powerful trend that is shaping the industry in unexpected new ways and creating opportunities worldwide.

So for the better part of a decade my life has been transformed, first personally by games, and now professionally. I'm certainly not alone. Everyday I meet people who are building entire lives around what could be called the "meta-gaming" industry, a scene that exists on top of and around the existence of great games like Halo, Quake, Half-Life, StarCraft, and more. The culture of gaming is interactive, it requires you to take action to finish a game, so it's no wonder that the community itself is made up of people who want to interact and want to take the bull by the horns. That is the real strength of games, that we aspire, as gamers, for it to be so much more. And it will be. In just the few short years that The CPL has been active, it has already outstripped some of the early growth of other major sports. Far be it for me to think that we'll be bigger than the MLB or NFL, but we're already paying out more in real dollars for our first tournaments than the PGA did with their first tournaments. That's nothing to discount.

And we're just getting started. Games are getting better, more people are modding, and the PC hardware industry wants gamers to acknowledge their components as the best. Intel, NVIDIA and others aren't calling up standard corporate CEOs asking them to label their next products as "the next big thing"—they're calling us! In fact, Intel and NVIDIA aren't sponsoring teams of spreadsheet masters who can out-add the rest of the world. They're sponsoring teams of gamers to travel the world and participate in gaming tournaments; and they're sponsoring the tournaments themselves.

We've just scratched the surface of what games will be. In a piece that best-selling author Ben Sawyer wrote for the Adrenaline Vault he said it well:

> "Unlike some other forms of media, game development in its emerging form is still dealing with a huge technical ramp-up that brings dramatic changes every several years— if not every year. Movies were originally small, silent, black and white films, but other than the addition of sound, color, and numerous improved special effects, how much has the film medium changed? Other than the form of delivery and new electronic genres, how much has technology changed recorded music? Guttenberg invented moveable type in the 1400's, but books remain relatively unchanged regardless of changes in the underlying production technology. As a media form, games have perhaps the closest relationship between advancement of the medium and advancement of its underlying technology and production processes."

In short, more cool stuff is on the way! I would add that we've only just begun expanding the "meta-gaming" industry too. Tournaments will get bigger; there will be more gaming TV networks like G4 and Gamer.tv. We'll see great gamers respected, as other athletes are, for mastery of their own game. We'll see games permeating our society even more. We might even get to watch a good gaming movie someday (ok maybe I'm stretching things a bit).

So where do you fit into all this? Well, you've taken the first step by having this book in your hands. It's not just some cute story—it's a call to arms, to join the legion of gamers who are taking things to another level and are building a new global culture centered on games. So now you are one of the not so few anymore, a "Monster Gamer" or at least a "Monster Gamer to be." Real gamers don't just play games; they live by them. And this book will show you how to join the fun. I did, and unquestionably it's been one of the most enjoyable experiences of my life.

Hi, my name is Angel Munoz and I am a hardcore gamer.

Angel L. Munoz,
Cyberathlete Professional League Founder and President
May 2003

INTRODUCTION

I wrote this book because I love people who love games and in my opinion no one has written a book for real game lovers. Of course, you can find clue books and books written for fans of specific games or even consoles but no one has written a book for hardcore gamers, showing them how to get the most out of their passion. Today gaming involves so much more than just grabbing a controller and firing away. It's a lifestyle and a great one at that. So my mission is to provide you with the guidebook that screams out, "If you want to be the ultimate hardcore gamer, a true monster gamer, here's the stuff you really need to know."

Goals for this Book

When I write a book I usually plan a few small goals as to what I want readers to take away from the book. These goals are usually different for different groups. With this book I had three major goals in place:

1. I wanted a book that presented game culture from a how-to perspective.

2. I wanted to create a book that could show experienced gamers something they didn't know and help less knowledgeable gamers master the basics to become really knowledgeable.

3. I wanted a book that would be fun to read and serve as a sort of "badge of honor" for gamers.

So, after 300+ pages of writing night after night, you have the first iteration of my effort to create a guidebook for gamers. Is it perfect? Yes, and no. It's perfect because it is what I set out to create. But it's also not perfect because game technology and gaming culture are a moving target and are so vast I'm bound to have forgotten or missed something. I hope you won't crucify me like the way we gamers crucify unfinished games that promise patches for buggy features. Patches notwithstanding I do promise to keep adding to the book on my web site, **games.dmill.com**.

Meta-Gaming

Call me crazy but 2003 in my opinion will be the year that gaming really breaks out. The rise of competitive gaming, the creation of G4—the North American cable channel, the debut of America's Army, the growth of Machinima, the growing dominance of modding, and other factors are taking gaming to heights we've never seen. All of this is due to the growth not only of technology and the games themselves, but the growth of gamers. A book like this really couldn't have been written up until now.

Games are now almost embedded everywhere in our world but it's the way games are driving things that really makes the difference. The mobile industry is bracing for a huge fight around gaming, car designers are consulting with game designers, gamers are now a demographic of choice like hip snowboarders and skate punks. Computer makers owe much of the demand for progressing desktop technology to gamers. Our insatiable appetite for bigger, faster, and better technology is dwarfing the needs of IT guys who've shut their wallets the past two years. So everywhere I look I see not only games and game developers driving the marketplace, but gamers as well. The generation of gamers has grown to become a force, economically and socially. Among the several game projects I'm working on now is an effort called Serious Games **www.seriousgames.org**. A play on words (because in my opinion all games are serious ideas and fun), the project has as its aim to improve the way people think and learn about policy decisions and other management functions. The government is getting ever more serious about games in the right ways here by following through on the premise that a better world can be created using games.

I hope that this book will help you further develop your passion for everything related to gaming.

Ben Sawyer
Portland, ME

HELP ME!

Despite this book, I'm not the world's foremost expert in all things gaming. And though I think this book is great, it is not the end-all be-all. This is where you the reader come in. I want to hear from you. Write me, send me ideas for the next edition, give me stuff to put on my site. *Son of Monster Gaming* will come someday and with your help I can make it even better.

Write me at **bsawyer@dmill.com**.

And don't forget to visit **games.dmill.com** as well to get updates, news, and more for this book.

chapter 1

WHAT EVERY MONSTER GAMER NEEDS TO KNOW

It all began with Pong...

I can still vaguely recall the day my mother brought Pong home. We played it at camp and I got so good I started playing my parents' friends who would come by to lose quarters. (Those suckers!) I had a little piggybank right next to the machine and when I won I'd take the quarter and put it in the piggybank in case anyone would want it back thinking they'd been hustled (which they had been). This began my love affair with gaming. Since those profitable days of growing up lakeside in Maine, I've owned or played tons of games. Games changed my life and became a huge part of it, both personally and professionally. I love video games and everything remotely related to them.

I'm suspecting those of you reading this book also have the same love of games. Unfortunately, very little has been written about the lifestyle of being a hardcore gamer. ("Monster gamer" is the name I think is better suited.) As games have gotten more complex, and game culture has gotten richer and more diverse, there is much more to know about games than how to swindle friends at Pong. It takes serious skills to be a top-notch monster gamer. Monster gamers eat, sleep, and breathe gaming. Gaming is a passion monster gamers never give up, and can never get enough of.

In this book I'm going to cover every aspect of being a monster gamer. I want to give you the tools and advice so that you can have the most tricked out PC, know more about games than anyone you hang out with, become the most competitive gamer you can be, and join the community of other monster gamers. So, read this book, pass it on to all of your friends, and help spread the knowledge of monster gaming. (And don't forget to tell your friends to buy a few extra copies so that I can make a little dough and buy a few more games!)

Getting Your Start

To be a real monster gamer you need to acquire a lot of knowledge. To start, we'll run through some basic material. You can think of this knowledge as the foundation for any monster gamer's education. If the rest of this book is college, consider this chapter prep school.

The History to Learn

I'm a big believer in knowing history, so let's start with a quick gaming history lesson. Some of you may have been born yesterday, so you'll have more to catch up on. Knowing a little about the history of gaming is important to being a monster gamer. After all, without knowing the various games that started different crazes, where Sega came from, or that Microsoft was never a big gaming powerhouse until the late 1990s, you won't be able to hold your own with other gamers. The next time you go to a LAN party or other gaming event, you'll feel like a fish out of water unless you have some cool gaming facts stuffed in your brain. For example, if someone mentions that Freelancer is basically a souped-up Wing Commander, or that such and such a game reminds them of Elite, or that Ultima Online goes all the way back to a game called Akalebeth, you'll be lost. If you're still not convinced, ask yourself what film buff hasn't at least read or seen something by Orson Wells, Buster Keaton, Charlie Chaplin, or Francis Ford Coppola?

So how do you catch up on your gaming history? Aside from the chapter in this book on retro gaming, there are several books and several sites you should check out. Table 1.1 lays out the major books you can read to learn more about the earlier days of gaming and Table 1.2 summarizes the best sites that can help.

TABLE 1.1
Books on the history of gaming.

BOOK TITLE	AUTHOR	SUMMARY
Arcade Fever ISBN: 0762409371	John Sellers	No, this isn't a John Travolta spin-off here. We're talking gaming, not disco. This guide covers the major games and history of the arcade era.
Electronic Plastic ISBN: 3931126447	Jaro Gielens, Büro Destruct, Robert Klanten	A book about the history of handheld games before the likes of GameBoy, Lynx and N-Gage, Simon, Mattel Football, and others.
Game Over Press Start To Continue ISBN: 0679736220	David Sheff, Andy Eddy	A well praised look at how Nintendo reinvigorated the entire game industry after the industry's first collapse.
Hackers ISBN: 0141000511	Steven Levy	Not totally about games but it provides a lot of early history of some of the early pioneers of the games business.
High Score: The Illustrated History of Electronic Games ISBN: 0072224282	Rusel DeMaria, Johnny L. Wilson	An illustrated guide with dozens of photos and scans of games we all should remember coupled with great stories and anecdotes by two people who witnessed much of he industry first hand.
Masters of Doom ISBN: 0375505245	David Kushner	An entire book devoted to the sometimes contentious story behind how John Carmack and John Romero created Doom and Quake.
Opening the Xbox ISBN: 0761537082	Dean Takahashi	A journalistic overview of how Microsoft became so interested in games that it decided to gamble big-time into the console wars.
Phoenix: The Fall & Rise of Videogames ISBN: 0964384825	Leonard Herman	Considered by many to be one, if not the most definitive look at the history of video games.
Power Up: What Video Games Have to Teach Us About Learning and Literacy	James Paul Gee	A controversial look at the positive things that can be learned from video games by a well known professor of education.
Software People ISBN: 0671509713	Gary Carlston	An old book (1985) most likely found through Abebooks.com. It details the early formation of the computer game industry. Written by one of the founders of Broderbund Software.
Supercade ISBN: 0262024926	Van Burnham, Ralph H. Baer	A great visual book about arcade gaming. Visit the book's site at www.supercade.com.
The Ultimate History of Video Games ISBN: 0761536434	Steven L. Kent	Kent, a well known game journalist, covers a lot of ground in this 600 page tome. Well worth having. Between this and *Phoenix* you'll have a great set.

(CONTINUED)

TABLE I.1 (CONTINUED)
Books on the history of gaming.

Book Title	Author	Summary
Zap!: The Rise and Fall of Atari ISBN: 0738868833	Scott Cohen	A dated book (1984) that is interesting because of its historical focus on Atari. It has not been updated and doesn't even have a complete view of Atari itself giving short-shrift to key products.
Digital Press Video Game Collector's Guide ISBN: 0970980701	Joe Santulli	For anyone interested in the history of games, as well as retro collecting, this guide covers every 8-bit system and comes with complete cartridge lists, pictures, scarcity ratings, production notes, and pricing guidelines.

TABLE I.2
Sites on the history of gaming.

Name	The Skinny
Classic Gaming www.classicgaming.com	A great site that covers the entire classic/retro gaming movement.
Brookhaven National Laboratory www.osti.gov/accomplishments/videogame.html	Did video games begin there? Well yes they did…see the site for more details.
Digital Game Archive www.digitalgamearchive.org	A major effort to preserve games and gaming history.
Gamespot Guide to Videogame History www.gamespot.com/gamespot/features/video/hov	Four expert authors on game history compiled a guide to video gaming's past.
Moby Games www.mobygames.com	A great database with full credits and info on many games past, present, and future.
Museum of Video and Computer Games www.computerspielemuseum.de	This museum in Germany also offers a 76-page booklet on games for ordering too.
Ralph Baer's Essay www.ralphbaer.com	The original inventor of pong and video game systems shares his firsthand history.
Stanford's Game History Course www.stanford.edu/class/sts145	The Web component of one of the most popular courses offered at Stanford.
Videotopia www.videotopia.com	Covers a traveling exhibit on game history.

Magazines to Read

When it comes to getting news, monster gamers turn to one of two sources: traditional magazines and online Web sites. Other than the occasional trip to a .plan (**www.quakefinger.com** is the best place to read various .plan files) or an IRC exchange, these two sources are the places to get news. It's easy to go down to the local magazine stand and pick up a few magazines about gaming but monster gamers need to know *everything* about games and that means obtaining magazines and news outside the scope of their home market. The problem with magazines is that it's a brutal business. New rags come and go and only a few seem to stick around. Table 1.3 lists the major magazines and sources to get them. The biggest three markets are Europe, Japan, and the U.S. but there are magazines in Australia, Singapore, and Taiwan as well.

TABLE 1.3
Magazines for real gamers.

MAGAZINE(S)	PUBLISHER	REGION	SUBSCRIBE@
Famitsu Xbox Weekly Famitsu Famitsu PS2 Famitsu Cube+Advance Arcadia E-Login Tech Gian	Enterbrain	Japan	www.enterbrain.com You will have to try some of the import stores, and anime import stores to find copies of these. Arcadia covers arcade titles, and Weekly Famitsu is the bible for Japanese Gaming News.
Computer Games	Strategy Plus, Inc.	North America	www.cgonline.com
Electronic Gaming Monthly Official U.S. PlayStation Magazine Computer Gaming World GameNOW Xbox Nation GMR Magazine	Ziff Davis	North America	www.zdmcirc.com/zdmcirc/misc/gamerstop.html
Game Informer Magazine	Gamestop	North America	www.gameinformer.com
Game Pro	IDG	North America	www.gamepro.com
Official Xbox Magazine PC Gamer PSM Magazine	Future Network USA	North America	www.futurenetworkusa.com

---

(CONTINUED)

TABLE 1.3 (CONTINUED)
Magazines for real gamers.

Magazine(s)	Publisher	Region	Subscribe@
Play	Fusion Publishing	North America	www.playmagazine.com
Total Gamer	Canada Computer Paper. Inc.	North America	www.totalgamer.ca
101 PC Games PC Gamer PC Format Edge Gamesmaster NGC Official UK Playstation Magazine Official UK Netgamer Playstation 2 Magazine Playstation 2 Official Tips Magazine UK PSM2 Max Xbox Gamer	Future Publishing	UK/Europe	www.futurenet.co.uk/futureonline/magazine.asp
Games PLAY+ CUBE Total Advance XBM P2	Paragon Publishing	UK/Europe	www.totalgames.net
Hype>> GBA World PC GameZone PC GameGuide PC PowerPlay Nintendo Gamer PSW	Next Media	Australia/NZ	www.publishing.next.com.au

I definitely recommend *IGN Insider*, an electronically distributed magazine from the folks behind IGN.com, *PC Gamer*, and the *Official Xbox Magazine* (U.S.). It's especially good for English speaking readers because it offers some good reports from what's going on in Japan. It costs $29.95 a year to subscribe. Find out more at **http://insider.ign.com**.

Sites to Visit

The world-wide nature of the Internet and the sheer breadth of sites makes the task of finding the best game sites almost impossible. There are hundreds of gaming sites around the world but I'll try to break out some leaders and build from there. Table 1.4 gives you the quick low-down on 30 of the best sites for basic gaming news, view, reviews, downloads, and more. I've also starred my top eleven.

TABLE 1.4
Add these hot gaming sites to your favorites now!

SITE	URL	SITE	URL
Adrenaline Vault*	www.avault.com	Heaven Games*	www.heavengames.com
Aus Gamers	www.ausgamers.com	Homelan*	www.homelan.com
Blues News*	www.bluesnews.com	Loaded Inc	www.loadedinc.com
Eurogamer	www.eurogamer.net	Mad Gamers	www.madgamers.net
Evil Avatar	www.evilavatar.com	PC Game World	www.pcgameworld.com
Game Axis	www.gameaxis.com	PC Gaming	www.pc-gaming.com
Game Planet	www.gameplanet.co.nz	Rebel's Gamespot	www.rebels-gamespot.com
Gamers.com*	www.gamers.com	Robs Gaming	www.robsgaming.com
Games Domain*	www.gamesdomain.com	ShackNews*	www.shacknews.com
Games Xtreme	www.gamesxtreme.net	Telefragged	www.telefragged.com
GameSpot*	www.gamespot.com	UkGamer	www.ukgamer.net
GameSpy Network*	www.gamespy.com	United Gamers Online	www.ugo.com
Gamesxtazy	www.gamextazy.com	Video Game Review	www.videogamereview.com
Happy Puppy	www.happypuppy.com	Voodoo Extreme*	www.voodooextreme.com
Game Faction	www.gamefaction.com	Total Games	www.totalgames.net
Fragland	www.fragland.net	Wired Play	
Gone Gold	www.gonegold.com	Gaming Illustrated	www.gamingillustrated.com
PC vs. Console	www.pcvsconsole.com	GamerFeed	www.gamerfeed.com
IGN*	www.ign.com	Game Guru	gameguru.box.sk
Game	www.game.co.uk	Game Planet	www.gameplanet.co.nz
PC Powerplay	www.pcpowerplay.com.au	Hyperactive 3.1	www.hyperactive.com.au
ForGamer	www.forgamer.net	GameTab	www.gametab.com

Getting Inside the Industry

Some monster gamers might want to go further than all of the key user and history sites as well as magazines and understand the industry itself even more. I recommend you check out the five sites presented in Table 1.5 that track the development and business side of the industry.

TABLE 1.5
Web sites that track the industry.

SITE	URL	SITE	URL
Gamasutra	www.gamasutra.com	MCV	www.mcvuk.com
Game Developer Magazine	www.gdmag.com	Develop Magazine	www.developmag.com
Games Industry (UK)	www.gamesindustry.biz	GIG News	www.gignews.com

Women Play Games Too

Much too often some jackass thinks games are only a "guys" thing. Anyone who has played a lot of Quake or other games knows this isn't true. Sure, gaming is a male-dominated scene but there are a lot of women who are into games, and many of them are quite accomplished. Here's a piece of infamous gaming lore: John Romero and Stevie "Killcreek" Case initially met when she kicked his ass at Quake. At E3 (the leading gaming and entertainment tradeshow) for many years GameSpy used to have female Quake master Kornelia playing all comers. She rarely, if ever, lost.

So where do you go on the Web to participate in the women/girl gaming scene? Table 1.6 lists the best sites around, which regardless of the gender slant, are some of the better sites to begin with.

TABLE 1.6
Web sites for monster women gamers.

SITE	URL	SITE	URL
Game Gal	www.gamegal.com	Digital Girl	www.digital-girl.com
Game Girlz	www.gamegirlz.com	Game Girl Mania	www.ggmania.com
Cali Girl	www.caligirl.net	Girlz Clan	www.girlzclan.com
Lady Gamers	www.ladygamers.com	Women Gamers	www.womengamers.com

Where to Go to Think about Games

Once you get "schooled" in the past and the present, you'll need to acquire some higer, more philosophical gaming knowledge. To help with that I've provided the resources in Table 1.7 to show you the best sites to find deep thought and

TABLE 1.7
Get really smart by checking out these gaming resources.

Site	Comments
Digiplay www.digiplay.org.uk	Two universities in the U.K. run the Digiplay Initiative. The site provides news, and lots of resources concerning game research, technical, and cultural studies.
DIGRA www.digra.org	The Digital Games Research Association is working to help organize academic and non-academic researchers of games, game culture, game theory, design, and technology.
Game Culture www.game-culture.com	A site devoted to discussions about the entire culture of gaming and the study of that culture. Features a discussion list and a number of articles on gaming culture.
Game Girl Advance www.gamegirladvance.com	Run by a group of great writers, this site has some of the best up-to-date commentary on games, the gaming scene, game culture, and more. Do me a favor too when you go by there, drop a few bucks in their online donation box!
Game Research www.game-research.com	Covers the "art, science and business of computer games."
Game Studies www.gamestudies.org	Describes itself as a "crossdisciplinary journal dedicated to games research." It publishes several times a year and is focused on the "aesthetic, cultural and communicative aspects of computer games."
Greg Costikyan's Blog www.costik.com/weblog	Greg is one of the more deeper and provocative thinkers in the industry and his blog is interesting as a result.
Joystick101.org www.joystick101.org	This site is sort of modeled after Slashdot. Forum leaders like University of Wisconsin's Kurt Squire post topics to spur conversation and then you're allowed to chime in.
Links.net www.links.net	The personal blog of Justin Hall who travels the world to bring us unique personal insights about life and games.
Ludology.org www.ludology.org	Maintained by Gonzalo Frasca, this is a fairly well kept site on a number of video game theory topics. Well recommended.
Play Research www.playresearch.com	Based in Sweden, this research group covers interactive issues including games and "game like" technologies.

(CONTINUED)

TABLE 1.7 (CONTINUED)
Get really smart by checking out these gaming resources.

SITE	COMMENTS
Games, Gamers and Gaming Culture www.knowledge.hut.fi/ projects/games/gamelinks.html	Not sure how much often it is updated but the site features a good set of links.
Games To Teach cms.mit.edu/games/education	The home page for Henry Jenkin's Games To Teach research project that is exploring how to use games to teach a wide variety of topics.
The Serious Games Initiative www.seriousgames.org	Run by yours truly. A project with The Woodrow Wilson Center for International Scholars that discusses how games and game developers can help improve the future of management and government.

provocative writing about games. By frequenting these sites and Weblogs, you'll be able to talk on a higher-plane about gaming than the minions who toil away at just a sport game or two, or the latest racing game for the PS2.

Where to Go to Watch Games

Music fans have MTV but gamers are also getting their own TV networks both online and through cable. Shows have been produced about gaming before but never entire networks. Table 1.8 covers all you need to know to be able to tune in to gaming TV around the world.

Tools Every Monster Gamer Should Have

I will talk about many tools in other chapters so let me be brief here and focus on a few tools that are fundamental to art of being a monster gamer.

✔ **Instant Messenger**: If you don't have at least one instant messenger then something's wrong. I use three of the damn things (see my intro for my addresses) and probably should upgrade to Trillian or Jabber which can let me talk to different IM systems using a single client.

✔ **IRC Client**: I have to admit, I'm just not a huge IRC guy. But there is no denying how much IRC is part of the gaming scene. Most people use mIRC, a Windows client, which you can get at **www.mirc.com**. Mac users can check out Ircle at **www.ircle.com** while Linux users can check out bitchx.com.

✔ **Screenshot Creation and Photo Editor**: Lots of gamers like to take screen shots, and build Web sites. So a good Photo editor is useful. For screenshots, get Hypersnap DX.

TABLE 1.8

Show/Network	Type	How to Get
G4 TV www.g4tv.com	Cable Network	You must have G4TV on your cable system, or get DirectTV or Dish Network.
Gamer TV www.gamer.tv	Online Video Network Show	Supplies shows and content to various channels like G4 and streams it out over the Web. See site for more info.
Extended Play www.techtv.com/extendedplay	Show	Must have TechTV on your system, or get DirectTV or Dish Network. C-band satellite dish: GE Americom Satcom C4 transponder 12135 degrees west 40 degrees elevation.
MBC Game mbcgame.intizen.com *On Game Net* www.ongamenet.com *ITV Game* www.itvgame.net	Korean TV Network	All of these sites have paid video-on-demand capability but you have to be able to read or navigate the Korean language site to get access. If I figure out how to do it I'll put the information on games.dmill.com. You also might try emailing them as well.

✔ **Server Searching Tool**: See Chapter 8 for more on this topic. GameSpy, All Seeing Eye, and so on are essential tools for l33t competitive gamers.

Monster Gaming—A World Beyond Your PC and Console

What I find to be the most simulating over the past few years is the reality that the gaming scene has grown to encompass much more than just games. Think about it. All of a sudden we have a rich history to write about, we have professional gaming tournaments and professional gamers, gamers build their own games and modifications, and others are making entire animated movies using game engines. The entire PC industry is in a massive slump bigger than we've ever seen in our lifetimes. But there is one bright spot—gaming. After all, where is the industry now turning for inspiration and salvation—games and gamers. The entire arena of skins and PC mods has its roots in gaming. Major car manufacturers are asking designers of games like Ridge Racer and Gran Turismo to consult on their actual new cars. Even the government is getting involved using titles like America's Army to recruit new soldiers and projects like Serious Games (**www.seriousgames.org**) to find new ways to solve problems. All of this is proof that gaming is not only transcending the entire media and technology space but also education, industrial design, and much more. I can't think of a better time to be a monster gamer.

Sony, which makes billions of dollars, recently had three quarters of its profits attributable to games. This from a company that makes half of the world's TVs, owns a movie studio, and a record label. Now if only we could get a decent game movie from these guys!

In the 21st century, monster gamers are leading the way. Those pocket-protector engineers of the previous century are old news. Monster gamers represent such a coveted demographic that the world wants to know what we think, what we're doing, and how we're doing it. This is perhaps one of the most important lessons you can take from this book in total. And I hope after these few short pages you're as motivated as ever to become the best monster gamer you can.

chapter 2

How to Become a Better Gamer

The real title for this chapter was "Never Stop Running and Avoid Straight Lines" but my publisher changed it when I wasn't looking. Screw that; what does he know about monster gaming, anyway? He probably thinks Quake is a course on disaster planning for middle managers. As gamers, we need to focus on what we really must master to become real monster players—a pursuit that involves dedication to thinking out of the box and all of that other crap. Let's face it, getting good is not really about how fast your gamepad kung-fu is grasshoppa. The warrior who is intelligent, honorable, *and* fierce is better than the warrior who kills, but is neither honorable, nor disciplined. To become a better gamer you must do many things well and my goal in this chapter is to give you the real monster gamer roadmap (and some of the knowledge you need so that you can be smarter than your wannabe gamer friends). My program is actually an easy five-step one (but leave your coffee mug at home when you come to the meetings):

✔ Develop core knowledge of games and derivative issues
✔ Build a foundation approach to playing all games

✔ Become multifaceted by playing multiple genres of games well

✔ Improve your skills through disciplined practice

✔ Play with honor and respect

Developing Your Knowledge

It goes without saying that the more you know about the game industry in general, the types of games available, and the specific techniques for playing different games, the more you'll be a force to be reckoned with. Your mission as a monster gamer is to also know which games are good, when they're coming out, and more. In this chapter we're concerned with the critical elements of knowledge that make us better at playing games. We'll first explore the games themselves, delving into the categories of games available, and then I'll discuss general strategies and practices that you can apply across multiple titles or genres.

Basic Game Genres

To develop good overall knowledge of gaming, you should start by becoming fully aware of the game genres. Classifying this stuff, of course, is just as much wild-ass guess work as it is science. It is a little like trying to teach a person who's never spoken English the differences between the words "there," "their," and "they're." I've tried to create a definitive list of genres for this book to help us later discuss tips for dealing with different kinds of games. After all, I can't tell you how to become a better player at wargames if you think I'm talking about games that belong in the fighting genre. As Table 2.1 shows, there are 17 recognizable genres.

Of course now that I've defined the genres, we can have endless debates about which ones are best, and which games should be included in each genre. For example, should Dark Summit from THQ be classified as a sports game because it features snowboarding or should we put it in the arcade game category because of its approach? We also can talk about various sub genres of games like the text adventure vs. graphical adventure, or games that span multiple genres like GTA3, which is a driving/shooting/adventure/arcade game, not to mention kick ass fun! For the sake of this chapter (and my brain), the list is what Moses would have chiseled on his tablet and we're not going to worry about games than span multiple genres.

Building a Foundation Approach to Playing Games

Here is one rule we need to get out of the way: If you play games a lot and you don't get better, you probably suck and you should find another hobby like bowling or darts. My impression, however, is that you bought this book because you're

TABLE 2.1
The basic game genres every monster gamer should know.

SPECIFIC GENRE	POSTER CHILDREN
First Person Shooter	Doom, Quake, Unreal, Medal of Honor, Half-Life, CounterStrike
Driving/Racing	Nascar, F1, Need 4 Speed, Driver
Fighting	Virtua Fighter, Soul Caliber, Dead or Alive, Mortal Kombat, Tekken
Sports	Madden Football, NBA 2K3, Tiger Woods Golf, High Heat Baseball
Role Playing Game	Ultima, Final Fantasy, Dragon Quest, Morrowwind, Fallout
Wargame	Eastern Front 1941, Empire
Arcade	Joust, Pac Man
Puzzles	Tetris, Bejewelled
Gambling/Cards	Hoyles Casino, Microsoft Casino, FreeCell, Solataire, Bridge
Non-Electronic Adaptations	Chessmaster 9000, Monopoly, Magic The Gathering, Risk
Adventure	Kings Quest, Monkey Island, Zork
Platformer	Donkey Kong, Super Mario, Crash Bandicoot, Earthworm Jim, Sonic the Hedgehog
Strategic Management	SimCity, Capitalism, SimGolf, Civilization
Real Time Strategy	Age of Empires, Command and Conquer, Warcraft, Starcraft
Simulation	Janes Series, Flight Simulator, Crimson Skies
MMORPG	Everquest, Ultima Online, Asherons Call, Star Wars Galaxies, The Sims Online
Educational	Who cares!?!@@?

smart and talented so you only need to worry about my ten commandments for becoming a more skilled gamer:

1. An Edge is usually razor thin, so don't get cocky and miss the details.

In Olympic-level 100 meter races (track or swimming), the difference between gold and silver can be measured in milliseconds. In NASCAR, the challenge is not only about the fine line between winning and losing but also in just finishing the race in one piece. Hard core game playing is no different. The first principle for getting good is to realize that even things you might not normally give much thought too, such as how you sit, the lighting in your room, how tense you are, and so on, need to be considered. If you take the time to talk to good Quake players or read tips on Command and Conquer or WarCraft, you'll quickly realize how dedicated hardcore gamers are at finding every new edge they can. Your mantra for the next week should be, "consider everything." Tape this to your toilet seat if it helps you.

Some companies have started selling vitamin/chemical supplements targeted directly at gamers. No joke! They are marketed under the brand MindFX (**www.mind-fx.com**). These companies claim that taking their supplements will improve energy, reaction time, and relaxation. You'd have to shove this stuff down my throat to get me to take it. This is not the kind of edge you need. This stuff is not tested by the FDA and is barely, if at all, regulated. If your doctor says it's okay to take this crap, go for it but I don't think you'll be scaring anyone away at your next LAN party because of your monster gaming prowess. To get more energy and improve your reaction time, do what real athletes do (no don't take steroids): work out, run, lift weights, bike, or whatever else gets your heart pumping. Oh, and I forgot; also take a nap now and then.

2. All games are meant to be beat and won by most players so don't be a loser.
We often forget that most games aren't meant to deny us a sense of accomplishment. No game designer has a mandate to reduce you to a puddle of despair on the verge of going postal. In fact, their goal is usually quite the opposite. Games are meant to be conquered, although they shouldn't be too easy; otherwise, you wouldn't have fun. Almost every game deserves to be beat and won. That is a fundamental approach you must take when playing any game, and especially in those moments where you're not necessarily making headway as fast as you think you should.

Multi-player competitive games are the only exception to this rule I can think of. These games might seem as if they are designed to allow house bound acne-laden 14-year-old agoraphobes acquire some semblance of self-confidence as they pummel those of us with full-time employment and family responsibilities over-and-over until we're ready to quit. In reality, of course, multi-player games are meant to create an environment akin to sports where the person who is the most skilled, and most conditioned (physically and/or mentally), can reign supreme at some point.

3. Don't skimp on hardware and configs—they really make a big difference.
Thinking your hardware doesn't make a difference in your play is like a baseball player who thinks he doesn't need a good glove. Tiger Woods actually blamed

some poor golf on his equipment once. If Tiger Woods thinks his equipment choices can help his game, then your equipment choices can help your game too. This includes having the best configured PC you can get, as well as the best keyboard, mice, and gamepads to boot. In Chapters 4 and 11 I'll help you get the edge by telling you which gear is the best for setting up a monster gaming system.

Configs refer to the many configurable options that most games provide today, be they remapping of controllers, the ability to bind keys into various macros, or how you config your system overall. Great players learn to find the most optimal configurations for their games. In many cases you don't even need to experiment very much—gamers regularly post configurations that you can download and experiment with. When I first played FPSs I did little to remap the keyboard. It was easy enough with the default configuration to get through the single player versions. Once I shifted to playing against friends I was shown a bunch of different keymaps that made things much better. While everyone will have various opinions on what's best, definitely look at the keymap files for many first person shooters found at fan sites for help.

 Control remapping didn't exist when I was a kid! I remember seeing someone play Super Mario Brothers and Donkey Kong Jr. by reversing their hands. They played much better than the standard way. At first, I figured they were just left-handed. They just found their timing was better with those games if they switched hands. I tried the same thing, and viola my skill increased considerably. It just goes to show you the extent to which your configuration can help your play.

4. Set aside time to both practice and play games.

I can hear you saying duh!, but think for five seconds about the fact how practicing is quite different than playing. Any real musician knows this. When you play a game, you're either just having fun or you're competitively trying to beat the pants off of your opponent. You progress as you see fit and generally you are not in a perfectionist mindset. Practicing, on the other hand, is about perfecting a specific portion of your overall skill set. It is more systematic and isn't meant to be about progressing in the game itself. So how often do you see yourself (in an organized fashion) taking the time to practice a game? You can be sure that great players practice. People who get better at games are disciplined players. They play a game over and over and they systematically try different approaches to find the optimal solutions. An optimal solution is not always the first solution and good players develop the discipline needed to actually figure out the best way to play a game among a plethora of approaches that work.

5. Don't lose sight of the fact that most games are based on (or suffer) from patterns.
If someone showed you a sequence of numbers that went 3, 5, 9, 17, and 33 could
you determine the next number in the pattern? Many computer games work the
same way, and if you can solve the patterns that exist in them you become a better
player. A pattern is a *consistent, characteristic form, style, or method* and the essence of
computers is consistency. This is especially true of single player games. AI systems
usually revolve around basic rules and patterns that the game implements. You
can begin to pick up on the pattern after you play enough times. Patterns might be
a specific sequence of attacks a character uses in Mortal Kombat, or a particular
point where you can expect the computer to launch attacks at you in Command
and Conquer.

Elite players go to great depths to understand a game's patterns. For example, they
actually spend time practicing and timing the respawn intervals from picking up
powerups, armor, and weaponry in games like Quake, Unreal, and other FPS maps.
They can actually develop patterns of movement around a map that enables them to
continually replenish their supplies while strafing other players and racking up frags.
This is the mindset you need to develop and practice to become an elite FPS player.

Program controlled players don't think strategically; they obey rules in order to
mimic strategies. Most computer-controlled players are programmed with simple
AI techniques to make them a little more challenging. For arcade and sports games,
basic AI is used to keep opponents in front of players, or in pursuit of them properly, and so on. With strategic titles, things get more complex. For all the talk of
technologies like neural nets and other fancy techniques, don't count on it. Most
developers just use basic rules for their computer-controlled players.

Because you are smarter than the average bear, you should play in a manner to
actually test for patterns by following the same moves or routines yourself until
you're able to determine how the computer responds to your moves. The idea
is to put your scientist hat on and start isolating variables (in this case a specific
move). Soon enough the computer will reveal its secrets. Sucker! For example, keep
throwing kicks at a computer player until you can determine its standard series of
responses. You'll then be able to create or test for combinations that will result in
landing a critical hit. If only life were this easy! You will know you've decoded the
pattern when you can readily anticipate the computer's next move much as you
would figure out 65 was the next number in the sequence of numbers I gave you
earlier. (The formula, in case you're curious is: 2 * the preceding number -1.)

6. Human players are human so don't forget they are fun, unpredictable, and challenging.

Human players, on the other hand, aren't wired with AI algorithms. Good and competitive ones want your head on a stick and they'll take it if you let them. There's nothing like getting your butt wiped by a 13-year-old monster gamer in training (MGIT) half way around the globe to make you realize you're not as good as you think. The world is changing because of online game play. Gamers are used to playing with in-person opponents but online play adds an entirely new dimension. Your opponents aren't getting easier, they're getting much tougher. Sure, there are always a few newbies around to pick your teeth with, but they are getting harder to find. Besides, where's the challenge in that?

Because more gamers now play with other human players than just against "the machine," games are changing in three ways: their life cycle is extending, they are becoming more fun, and they are getting more challenging. Human players create their own sets of rules that drive their strategic thinking. They formulate more strategies than computers, and they are more apt to change them to better suit conditions. (They don't call it the half-time adjustment for nothing.) This means that your pattern matching skills won't solve all of your problems. You'll need to get really good at dealing with the unpredictability of real people.

Humans can think outside the box (unless they work for the same company you do) and they can formulate longer-term and complex strategies. So you should expect most players to do things that computer players *wouldn't do*. Expect them to play a game as they do to beat a computer, which you yourself should realize from your single-player experience. If beating the computer was easily done by always moving to the left, then you already know most players will do when facing off against you. This is until they start to realize that they're not playing a computer anymore.

One concept to think about when playing humans is the notion of "tells," which is a method for incorporating a psychological approach to playing. Tells comes from poker, where the strategy involves forcing people to guess wrong about when you're bluffing or playing it straight. If a player thinks you've got nothing and you have a straight flush, you'll likely clean up. Likewise, if a player thinks you've got something and you don't, they'll fold and you'll either win, or at least cut your risk. Tells are simple little things a player might do like crossing his legs every time he draws a good hand, breathing faster, or throwing his chips down on the table in a certain way. Tells are quick hints, and they tend to indicate moves about to happen.

Great players work at not establishing consistent tells while simultaneously figuring out their opponents' tells.

Tells also apply to computer gamers except the challenge is that you can't always see your opponents. You'll need to rely on other ways to spot a tell. For example, consider how your opponents play a game. Look for chat signals (which guarantees they are newbies), or standout moves that foreshadow events to come. For example, in Quake many newbie players learn to "head fake" when they are getting low on ammo by firing once at you with a shotgun then repeating this action. You charge in thinking this is an easy kill only to find out they've readied a BFG with your name on it. Of course experienced players see this setup coming a mile away. When playing with others, look for consistent signs or actions that tip future play. Expect people to bluff and factor that into your playing.

Another issue to consider is that most of us fall into various categories in the way we think despite how much we think we're different. Some of us are aggressive, some are slow but methodical, some are impatient, and others are impulsive. While it's hard to universally categorize player personality types, we can divide players into two basic psychological categories, extroverts and introverts. Extroverts are aggressive players who charge ahead and play in an offensive style, whereas introverts plan, probe, and think more about strategy. How you play against those two player types should be different. A quick scan of various game forums, articles on fan sites, and FAQs (research) will help you better identify the basic categories of players and how others deal with them.

7. You must read in order to be a better gamer.

It should go without saying that reading about games makes you a better player. However, this point is meant to highlight more than just reading the latest copy of GamePro or some stupid clue book. The most competitive games like Command and Conquer, Quake, Halo, and Unreal have huge fan sites, FAQs, and discussion boards devoted to them. These sites have discussion boards, major articles on strategy, interviews with the developers, and much more. You could spend at least two or three days reading about Quake tactics alone. (I did.) So don't assume you know everything until you get out there, find the sites, and read up!

8. You should talk too!

Vincent Cerf clearly helped create the Internet so gamers could talk to each other! The best gamers spend time interacting with each other using IRC, IM, and email. You can really learn from talking to other gamers. The best secrets sometimes don't make it into print. In addition, by interacting with other gamers you can join clans and guilds, which are important support groups for online games and MMORPGs. Because of the Internet, gaming is increasingly becoming a socialized culture. Just as major athletes share tips on how to bat and how to score in football, gamers share that information also.

9. You must be willing to endure better players to get better.

The only way to get truly better at many games is to play better players. If you're not willing to endure considerable embarrassment and butt kicking you will never get entirely better. Bots and tougher AI settings will only get you so far. Disciplined practice will also only get you so far. At some point you need to get in the ring and see what you're made of. It's an endurance test of another sort to improve against other players. There is always going to be a better player unless of course you're the best and even then the best don't always win. Michael Jordan lost even when they he was at his peak—you will too.

10. Learn to think like a game developer.

If you study game development or start to develop your own games, you'll eventually start to think like a developer. Thinking like a developer is a great abstract way to become a better player. As developers are making their games, they're playing them too (or others are), and they're actively designing stages, levels, segments, and so on with several possible ways to overcome them.

When you play a game try to put yourself in the developers' shoes and think about how they went through their design process. What were they thinking when they designed the portion of the game you're dealing with?

Mastering Games by Genre

Now that we've covered some of the universal truths about gaming, it's now time to dig a little deeper and look at some tips for mastering specific genres of games.

Driving/Racing Games

If you hang out with fanatics of these games you'll quickly discover that there are a few things they get all worked up about. First and foremost is hardware. The true monster gamers who enjoy driving and racing games have the best wheels, peddles, and other controller setups that they can afford. These devices really help you play better than you can with a lowly gamepad or keyboard. (See Chapter 4 for information on the best recommended racing peripherals available.)

In addition to getting the best hardware, there are a few tips you can out to work to make you a monster racing game player. First and foremost, you should always try to memorize the track. Next, learn to drive using the stick. Nearly every modern day racing game rewards those who manually shift with faster times. Using just the automatic mode is a recipe for losers. Starting on automatic is okay for learning the tracks and other nuances of the game, but the true pro eventually moves on to master manual shift to get the inevitable bonus that comes from that.

Another basic trick is to forget about using the break early in the process, and just lay off the gas to take turns. This is much easier than trying to coordinate both the acceleration and the breaking. Eventually you'll learn how to take the break so you never let up on the gas. I learned how to get over my propensity to not use the break by taping the acceleration button or key that affects the gas down so I could focus on regulating the speed of the car using downshifts and the break.

Fighting Games

Fighting games are all about combos, and once you memorize the combos you'll be way ahead of the game. The best and easiest way I've learned various combos (if I couldn't find them in the manual or I hadn't in total frustration gone to the FAQ online) is to play fighting games in two-player mode and just practice with one player until I've mastered everything I can.

Sports Games

Sports games are a little challenging to look at as a single genre because there are many varied products, covering a wide range of sports and each operating a bit differently. For example, the rules and strategies for soccer don't apply to baseball. However, there are still a number of basic strategies you should be aware of that span the range of sports games. The first is the *two-player practice mode* strategy. The key here is to play in two-player mode until you investigate and master all of the basic nuances of the game. For example, there's nothing like taking a player out of the game in FIFA or NBA 2K to help you spend more time figuring out tricks for passing, playing defense, and stealing bases. I've used this two-player practice strategy for years to develop my skills with nearly every sports game I've come across.

 For two-player practice I also advise that you get a really bad player to just play the other controller (select a kid sister, girlfriend, or a spare nephew who idolizes you) and just have them do what you tell them. It's a good thing that most games like Sega's excellent Virtua Tennis include lots of practice modes because I don't have a kid sister to boss around anymore or a nephew who idolizes me to be my practice dummies.

Another great way to get better at any sports game (especially if you're not a sports game junkie) is to incorporate what I call the "minimize your role on defense" strategy. Most sports games make the computer play defense for all of the players you don't control. Some defensive positions are harder to play initially than others. For example it's much harder to play a cornerback in football because if you don't stay with the receiver, which is easier said then done, you're going to be roasted by the opposing quarterback. Or in basketball if you're always covering the guy with the ball it's hard to stay on him until you get used to the game. Thus, you can start by focusing on the easiest places. In football consider playing a defensive lineman, and in basketball try picking the center and hang out near the basket. Let the computer deal with the hard stuff and whoever you are playing with your won't be able to shake and bake you as easily. Of course, the best defense does come from playing those harder positions so you'll want to learn to master them as once you get the basics down.

Role Playing Games and MMORPGs

You might not realize that there are strategies for getting better at RPGs other than spending hundreds of hours of time playing them. After all, RPGs are all about the work of building up your characters until they take on super deluxe powers. There are, however, some basics tips every monster gamer should know by heart. The first is to explore everything; no self respecting RPG guru leaves any pixel unexamined, any character not talked to, any monster not split into a million pieces. If you don't meticulously peruse everything you could stop your progress or slow it way down. Patience is a virtue with RPGs.

Another strategy for winning RPGs involves managing your inventory properly. Dungeon Siege is a great example of this. All players need to manage the "hand me down" life of party-based-RPGs. This means taking the time to evaluate the weaponry and armor you have on hand. You also should meticulously rearrange the weaponry and armor among the party so each person has the best opportunity to chop up dragons or two-headed post-apocalyptic zombies. Of course, this can get exhausting. The 40th time I rearranged swords, potions, and armor in Dungeon Siege I was about to lose it. But any second you short a character of better tools will definitely slow their progress and endanger their health.

Wargames

The monster wargamer is both a student of specific games, and the art of war strategy in general. To get great, you should consider reading about warfare and strategy in addition to playing. Fortunately, there are numerous books and Web sites on warfare that you can turn to for help. The biggest problem, of course, is that wargames are facsimiles of war, and thus every last strategic insight from war itself or from books about war won't necessarily polish your skills. I bet that even the best generals at the Pentagon might not beat you or I at games like Advance Wars and Panzer Elite.

Some of my favorite books that you should consider adding to your library include:

The Book of War : Sun-Tzu's "The Art of War" & Karl Von Clausewitz's "On War"
By Sun Tzu and Karl Von Clausewitz
Published by Modern Library
ISBN: 0375754776

This is a two-for-one tome that combines a couple of the most fundamental texts on total warfare. These texts serve as war 101 for many students of war strategy. Clausewitz is not an easy read but it's worth the effort.

The Complete Wargames Handbook: How to Play, Design, and Find Them
By James F. Dunnigan
Published by Quill
ISBN: 0688103685

James F. Dunnigan is a legend in the wargame industry and is one of the foremost authors on war tactics, strategies ,and politics. This out-of-print book can still be found here-and-there is also available online at:

www.strategypage.com/prowg/default.asp?target=wargameshandbook /contents.htm

Be warned: This book is a very dated work but is still of interest to hardcore war gamers.

How to Make War: A Comprehensive Guide to Modern Warfare for the Post-Cold War Era
By James F. Dunnigan
Published by Quill
ISBN: 0688121578

A much more recent (and still in print book) by the wargame legend. It covers modern war as seen through the eyes of the Persian Gulf War. It contains a number of strategic lessons, description of various armies, and their doctrine and much more.

Maneuver Warfare Handbook (Westview Special Studies in Military Affairs)
By William S. Lind
Published by Westview Press
ISBN: 086531862X

Considered by many to be one of the best books to read about maneuver warfare. A big time read.

One thing I've exeprienced with many wargames, especially ones where you can grow, add, and manage units like Alpha Centurai, Civilization, Empire, Advanced Wars, and so on, is that the computer AI has trouble dealing with the building up of forces. Most wargame AI focuses on attacking the player fast; otherwise, it wouldn't be as much "fun" for a while since the "fun" is in having units that square off against one another.

Another thing about wargames (and this also applies to real-time strategy games) is the inherent problems with the A* algorithm used to move units around a board. A* is the special "AI" routine programmers use to generate paths from one object (say the enemy base) to another (your base). In most cases, the goal is to use A* to determine the optimal route. (Optimal in this case means the route that requires the fewest number of moves.) Well, if Hannibal were alive today he'd pretty much kick most computer AI generals' asses because, as he proved, the path of least resistance is usually the longest path. This aspect of wargame AI introduces two big things. First, if enemies are coming from one direction you can expect more of them to constantly come from that direction. Secondly, you can assume that they will take the shortest route between two points, and you can move your units on longer and more winding paths to minimize potential contact with the enemy.

Platform and Arcade Games

When it comes to the basic arcade games, what is there to say other than practice makes perfect? Arcade games are like birds; they are simply wired for pattern matching. By design they tend to offer basic puzzles and patterns that you are asked to identify and then circumvent. Trial and error is the order of the day here. Of course there are some play strategies good platform and arcade game veterans follow to rack up buckets of points. I call this the three-tiered approach. First, your focus should always be on making progress (level eating I like to call it), where the goal is to advance to the end of play as fast as possible. Your job shouldn't be to explore every nook and cranny, just move forward as fast as you can unless the game forces you to do otherwise. Once you get good at this, you can go back through and truly explore every aspect of the game. Finally, the third and final stage involves focusing on "point perfection" whereby you utilize all your skills to perfect the perfect level, maximize points through exquisite play, find all secrets, and utilize all bonus capabilities in the scoring system.

Master players usually achieve some higher-level of play by playing some games for no other reason than to look for more perfect ways to do various tasks in an arcade game. If the game involves jumping, they may jump the same chasm 50 times in a row until they've got it down to a pixel-perfect science. That is really the arcade way to mastery!

Strategic Management Titles

Ah the corporate whore genre. The good news is that players can't kiss ass to get ahead in a strategic management game like they do in real life. In this sense, games are really better than life.

Most strategic management games revolve around resource management techniques and solving them is a matter of understanding how the resources work. To be good at these games you need to learn to parse the decisions you make into a good "flow." Most strategic management games include a lot of various moves, reports, and overall data. Initially, we all struggle with the flow of a game and it takes a while to develop a good one. This process usually starts by truly understanding the interface and reports that are generated. You never truly manage these titles until you manage each and every screen and understand exactly how they work.

The second aspect to good flow involves breaking up decision intervals. Almost every strategic management game has a set of moves that are long-term or short-term. The problem with flow is that you usually don't realize which decisions are which right away. Thus, in the first few games you play you won't realize how much a move made several turns ago would change the circumstances now. The first thing I do when playing these games is begin to break decisions into categories of intervals. I think about issues like, which decisions do I need to set at the outset of my game? Which ones need to be addressed every turn? And which decisions do I need to look at every few turns?

The final decision flow aspect is order. Even if you've parsed decisions into intervals, you need to decide a means of rapidly moving around the interface to impact your decisions. Figuring out the order of moves is the final task for decision flow management. One critical point to look for is what I would call *equilibrium states*. These are points where the entity you're managing isn't growing or contracting in size. However, it may be piling up resources during this time. For example, in early SimCity games it was easy to hit an equilibrium stage and just pile up tax revenue. I used to leave my machine on all night and come back in the morning ready to hit another build cycle.

Simulations

In the simulation camp, we find three types of games: flight simulators, ground vehicle simulators, and sea based simulators. In terms of the strategy for these games, I'll focus on the combat aspect of these simulations because there isn't a ton of strategy to these game other than learning the proper operation of the vehicle in question. How then, do you get better at combat simulation games? On the research side there are two things you can do. First you should visit Web sites or read books on flight tactics. I've compiled some good resources on these in Table 2.2 which I suggest you take advantage of if you want to improve your ability at any flying game be it Crimson Skies, Combat Flight Simulator, IL-2 Stormivik, or Earth & Beyond.

TABLE 2.2
Sites and resources on air combat tactics.

URL/COMMENTS

www.paul.fitzsimons.btinternet.co.uk/tactics.html#break

    Great site with pictures and all the info you need to learn basic dog fight tactics.

www.airattack.co.uk/club/aaguide/tactics/tactics.htm

    Alternative and better-designed version of the above.

BOOK/COMMENTS

Fighter Combat: Tactics and Maneuvering
By Robert L. Shaw
ISBN: 0870210599

    Well reviewed on Amazon and recommended by fans of flight sims.

How to Live and Die in the Virtual Sky
By Dan Crenshaw
www.flightsimcentral.com/fsc/howtolivandd.html

    A series of articles that is now a well reviewed self-published book by the author.

Real-Time-Strategy Titles

I'm making a wild-ass guess here (well, maybe not so wild) that with the exception of first-person shooters, no other genre of games has been written about like RTS gaming. The first real-time strategy game I ever played was Herzog Zwei for the Genesis (see Figure 2.1). This was a pretty amazing game (hard too) for its time and is widely considered the first real-time-strategy game. Although there are some who would say Ancient Art of War from Broderbund was the first RTS game, Herzog certainly influenced the "look and play" of games like Dune II (wrongly assumed by many to be the first RTS), Command and Conquer, Total Annihilation, and Warcraft.

If you're new to RTS games, expect a lot of pain and suffering as you adjust to their play mechanics as compared to the other more turn-based or slower-paced mechanics of war gaming titles. The mere real-time nature of these games really does change the entire structure of how you play them. It's easy for even great game players who haven't spent a lot of time playing RTS games to be frustrated for a while.

If you are inexperienced with RTSs, I can give you some first time advice that will really help. Playing an RTS game is very much like playing chess; you have to really

FIGURE 2.1
Herzog Zwei by Techno Soft is widely considered the first modern RTS game created and has legit cult status among hardcore RTS fans.

understand the strengths, weaknesses, and timing for each "unit" of the game. This includes the most critical factor: what combinations of units and their positioning relative to each other is used to achieve certain goals? This also goes for the inevitable resource management aspect most RTS games feature. Whether its base placements or resource allocations, your overall strategy should be based on what you emphasize and when. Each strategy game will be different although they all seem less so once you've memorized the units and built up the basic patterns you need to play good offense or suffocating defense.

This all leads to the heart of many RTS strategies, which is the combination of build orders and rushing. Build orders are strategies that people discuss that concern the order, combinations, and amounts of units that you build. Certain combinations of units and the time it takes to assemble them construct specific strategies. *Rushing* is the process of utilizing a certain type of combination of units by throwing them at an enemy in an attempt to overwhelm them in a fast move. True rushing usually involves a specific type of unit but can involve combinations. For most RTS fans, these moves are to be memorized much like Chess champions memorize all sorts of fancy named attacks and defenses. This combined with your real-time assessment of the opposition is what will drive your success in RTS games.

Be warned, however. Some higher-minded RTS fans think certain types of rushes (such as tank rushes in CnC) are cowardly acts or the acts of newbies. Others aren't offended by these acts and there are some specific articles that show you how to defend many of the common rushes opponents might use.

First Person Shooters

I saved the best for last. When it comes to strategies and techniques for achieving l33t status as a gamer, no group has gone to more extent to philosophize and prostletize then fans of first person shooters. Here is a summary of the most fundamental approaches to being a great FPS player:

✔ **Never stop running and avoid straight lines.** If you stand around or run in detectable patterns, you'll be toast. Players will pick you off before you've had a chance to switch weapons.

✔ **Strafing moves are key.** If you can't keep yourself perpendicular to your opponents while moving forward or backward you'll never end up scoring frags during a retreat or while properly staying on target. Although there are a number of special strafing moves, the most important is circle strafing. Circle strafing, as shown in Figure 2.2, is the practice (and you need to) of firing in

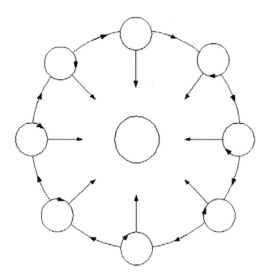

FIGURE 2.2
Viewing circle strafing from a top-down perspective.

strafing mode while moving your character in a circle around the opponent. This makes you a much harder target to hit while maintaining fire on your target. It is a key move most FPS players have to master to move up in the ranks. Some pros further suggest not only circling in one manner, but mixing it up by shifting from clockwise to counter-clockwise. Advanced players will also combine jumping with regular strafes and circle strafes creating—a very hard target to hit!

✔ **Memorizing maps and developing fast paths through which to retreat is critical to survival in deathmatches**. You should be able to recognize a map while running forward or backwards. Many maps also have natural choke points where the map forces players into closer quarters that are ripe for a grenade, rocket, or other weapon that would obliterate anyone caught in these natural traps. You should also avoid moving through the map in any sort of detectable pattern. At first this isn't much of an issue but as the field of players whittles down, it will produces a discernable pattern your opponents will take advantage of.

✔ **Listen closely during games, especially if you have a good sound system**. Headphones are critical for most good players because the amount of audio clues that can be decoded in an FPS is substantial. Games like Thief are designed to really take advantage of audio clues.

✔ **Stay away from walls when moving around in deathmatches**. Good players utilize walls when using rocket launchers (key weapons in most FPS games) because they can still inflict damage due to the blast radius of the rocket by hitting a wall near you. Walls also really limit your movement options.

✔ **Be careful how you aim your rockets**. When aiming a rocket look for players by walls, and if not aim the rocket at their feet so it will hit the floor near them as opposed to passing them by.

✔ **Try to get better bots to fight against**. The best bots page going right now is Randar's bot page located at **http://members.cox.net/randar/main.shtml** which contains all of the best bots available for downloading. You'll also find complete news and documentation on a wide range of bots. Since some bots serve different training purposes, you'll need to install a few that can help you.

✔ **Watch your back at all times**. On crowded levels in big deathmatch games some players fire spare ammo down hallways as they run by to catch unsuspecting players they don't even see who might be entering the hallway.

✔ **Stealth tactics are important in deathmatches**. Good players will actually notice weapons or items that have been picked up by you as a means of tracking you. This technique is used most when there are few players left on a level.

✔ **Utilize various bluffs as best you can**. Set off noises that might fool others into thinking you took a platform to a different level on a map. Other players roam with lower-end weapons taking potshots at others in hopes of drawing them out and then switching to better weapons once their enemy has flushed themselves out.

The extent to which people will look for an edge in games like Quake is truly amazing. One trick people write about is "The silent Quad trick." It actually exploited a bug in Quake's sound code to allow players to pick up the Quad Damage power-up without triggering the sound that is associated with it, which usually results in players seeking cover. For more on the silent quad see: **www.planetquake.com/fun/ dm4_tricks_silent.html#SILENT_QUAD**.

Specific Game Knowledge and Strategies

Good gamers research games, especially the games that have many strategies and tactics to learn and master. A great place to find specific game knowledge for many games is the GameFAQs database (see Figure 2.3) which is located at **www.gamefaqs.com**. This site has nearly 2000 FAQs, walkthroughs and guides covering consoles new and old, and a multitude of PC games. Aside from killer fan-sites, developer sites, and newsgroups this site is the best single source for game tips, tricks, and inside information.

FIGURE 2.3
The GameFAQs database.

Playing with Honor and Respect

Monster gamers have a reputation to withhold: They play hard and fair. They approach gaming with some level of chivalry that makes people respect them for the fun, and professionalism they bring to the art of destroying their opponents. Gaming, especially online gaming, is a community experience so you'd better play fair if you want to be accepted. You get better by playing with the best players who in turn have no interest in playing against whiny, snippy, cheating jackasses. As online games grow, activities like LAN parties become more common. And I promise you that there is a right way and a wrong way to play. If you misbehave, you'll be banned from servers, you'll lose respect from the best monster players, and your crappy rep will follow you to the gaming grave.

To help you play with honor and respect, I've compiled a unique guide to gaming etiquette to finish off this chapter. Hopefully, we can turn even the worst offenders into more respected gamers. If not, we'll continue to trash them online!

The Monster Video Game Etiquette Guide

I've seen a number of small essays and posts on gaming etiquette. I haven't, unfortunately, found an end-all, be-all guide on gaming etiquette. So, I decided to crank one out that combined a lot of the conventional wisdom of gamers with my own specific twist as "Joe" monster gamer. This guide includes the "10 Basic Rules of Monster Gaming Etiquette." I'll start with the rules and then I'll discuss some less-obvious tips. Table 2.3 provides a quick summary of the etiquette points I'll be discussing.

Rule 1: Gaming etiquette should follow regular etiquette.

Where was it ever written that basic politeness and the golden rule doesn't apply to gaming? I've seen normal people act like complete jackasses when someone puts a gamepad in their hands or they play anonymously online. Hey, it's okay to be a little wild in a virtual world but don't forget that you are playing with other humans and not a bunch of machines. There's no excuse for using taunts, nasty words, or actions that would be *vehemently* frowned upon in your day-to-day world, such as at work (especially when the boss is around). If you think I'm wrong, test this principal, and be prepared for the backlash. Gamers who practice good game etiquette do so at all times with all types of games, be they in arcades, at a LAN party, online, or in the living room with friends.

Rule 2: When joining a game always first double check the server rules.

Make sure you know the rules that apply to swearing, flaming, base-to-base fighting, and which characters are permitted on sniper only servers.

TABLE 2.3
Summary of good gaming etiquette.

Keep it reasonable

Practice etiquette everywhere

No one likes a quitter

Talk trash only among friends

Don't gloat; don't whine

Don't talk too much

Disconnects happen

Help others

Respect timeouts

Don't spawn kill

A team is a team

Play at your level

Rule 3: Don't be a quitter, unless you have a damn good reason.

Gamers really hate quitters. Face it, you've probably been a quitter yourself at one time or another. Remember the time you pulled the plug on your consoles in frustration or when you dropped out online? Quitting sucks for everyone who is playing because the other players are left holding the bag. Of course, there are good reasons why you might need to quit, like when you realize it's 10:00 p.m. and you promised your girlfriend or your spouse you were going to cook dinner. (Another night on the sleeper couch downstairs for your punishment really sucks.) If you're online, explain you need to go, thank others for the ass-whipping you've just been handed, and elegantly exit the action.

One of the more devious ways of quitting is the sneaky "disconnect" fake. You take yourself offline suddenly and then claim you were disconnected. Although net reliability is increasing, disconnects are still frequent enough that you can't be certain the person on the other end isn't being honest, unless it happens three or four times just as you're about to win.

Rule 4: Your trash talk must be in direct proportion to how well you know the others playing with you.

A friend once set up a LAN party back in the early days of deathmatching. I was an experienced player and I had played through Quake, Doom I, II, and all the other hot games. However, I wasn't much of a Quake deathmatch player. I talked major trash all week to my friend Matt about how I was going to kick his butt and wipe the floor with everyone. I showed up talking trash to everyone in the room. Needless to say, I got waxed heavily. Most of the players saw my trash talking for what it was, a distraction to hide my lame-ass playing skills. I talked myself into looking like a fool.

Trash talking is an art form. I'm pretty good at it, but I only use it on people whom I'm friendly with. These people can tell when I'm not talking down to them. Trash talking is essentially a friendly sport best practiced in close circles and only then in a tongue-and-cheek fashion. If you can't be funny talking trash, then shut the hell up!

Rule 5: Don't be a sore loser or a "gloater."

Remember the lesson Mr. Jockstrap taught you in fifth grade gym class? There's no place in the monster gamer world for people who who whine and pout or make constant excuses. On the other side of the coin, don't gloat. Sure, after you beat that friend of yours who talked trash all week and had beaten you four times in a row, it's ok to break out a little dance. In general, and especially with anonymous online opponents, the basic "gg" (good game), or "n1" (nice one) will suffice.

When you lose, don't make tons of excuses, like "Your cable modem gave you an unfair advantage!" Even if it did, so what, get over it. Get better; improve your net connection and stop whining. And most of all, don't blame lag—an action that draws special hatred. If you really are experiencing a bunch of lag, drop out of the game appropriately.

Rule 6: Talk at the right times and try to keep unnecessary chatter to a minimum. People hate incessant chatter during a game. This goes doubly as more games add voice capability. Most chat takes place at designated times in games like during a level load, or when a game match is over. When playing new games keep your trap shut and learn when the more experienced players begin chatting it up. You should also learn the basic chat shorthand, which is shown in Table 2.4. (For more on this topic see Appendix A for the complete glossary of game jargon and shorthand.) Cut this table out and put it by your computer. And don't ever commit chat sin: NO CAPS while chatting. That's like rooting for the Yankees at Fenway Park.

2

TABLE 2.4
The basic shorthand used for games you should know.

BBL	Be Back Later	K	OK
BRB	Be right back	LO	Hello
DM	Deathmatch	LOL	Lots of Laughs
FC	Flag Carrier	LPB	Low Ping Bastard
FF	Friendly Fire	N1	Nice One!
FFA	Free-for-all	NP	No Problem
FR	Flag Room	NS	Nice Shot
GG	Good Game	OMG	Oh My God
GL	Good Luck	PK	Player Killer
GR8	Great	PL	Packet Loss
GS	Good Shot	RJ	Rocket Jump
GTG	Go to go	ROFL	Rolling on Floor Laughing
HF	Have Fun	TP	Team play
HPB	High Ping Bastard	TX	Thanks
JK	Just Kidding	WTF	What the F**k?

Rule 7. Help other people because you might need help one day.

Newbies don't know what they're doing by definition so try to help them out now and then. The better they get, the more challenging it gets for you. Unless you want to be the grandmaster of the mediocre (that's an honorable goal), share some of your knowledge. That 29th level pro that smokes a thief trying to take you out may have been a newbie you helped six months ago.

Rule 8. Respect people who are in the game but not playing at the moment.

There are times when players are "in the game" but aren't "in the game," meaning they stopped for a bathroom break, ran to answer the phone, or went to pay a bill. Whatever the reason, gamers often have ways to communicate that they're pulling out of a game without dropping off the server. For example, in Quake players frequently point themselves into a corner facing a wall. As you play games, look for such practices (which could be different for each type of game), and try to respect the fact that even monster gamers have to take a bathroom break every now and then. Just hope the gamer you're playing with didn't get called away by the Marines to go fight the Iraqis or something.

Rule 9. Avoid spawn kills and killing team members.

A spawn kill is the first person shooter equivalent of goal hanging in basketball. Also called *spawn-camping* or just *camping*, a player just waits by common spawn points and attacks people right as they come out of the place. Spawn killing is considered the cheapest form of killing and is frowned upon by veteran Quake, Unreal, and Half-Life players. See how many l33t servers you get kicked from doing this.

Team games are difficult enough so don't make them harder by taking shots at someone who has just joined your team. In some games this isn't even possible, yet there are still ways to hurt your team such as not playing hard enough or otherwise causing problems. If you're on a team, act like it. Remember that there is no "jerk" in "team."

Rule 10. Pick on people your own size.

This rule of gaming etiquette cuts both ways. Newbie gamers should play at a level that's appropriate for their skill and knowledge, or at least identify themselves as such, and work at getting better. Experienced players should stay away from servers that cater to newbies. If they are playing in person, they should try to coach rather than dominate and bully. Games work best when each side is matched relatively well.

"In-Person" Etiquette

Most of the points of etiquette covered thus far are either general ones or relate to online gaming. This isn't the only form of gaming so we need to look at in-person and LAN specific etiquette.

Let Guests (or the Weakest Player) Chose Settings and Controller Types

Guests in my house always get to choose the controller they wish to use. If you have multiple controllers give your guest the option to choose his controller. Guests also get to choose teams and other game settings. This rule can be discarded if you are by far the inferior player. The point of this is to allow the inferior player to choose the options, which may raise their edge against you.

Share Your Gaming, but Don't Punish Good Gamers

This is one for the parents out there, or for kids who need to plead their case. I've heard many parents ration games between kids by setting a timer. Each kid gets a certain amount of time to play before he or she must relinquish control to the other player. This sucks. If I'm good, I should get to play a bit longer. Good gaming etiquette should be based on finding ways to share games that reward good play and competition. With the exception of saving games, arbitrary rules of allotted time don't do that at all.

If you must do something like this, a better tactic my sister and I used when we were kids was a gaming handicap. If I could play Robotron for one hour without losing, and she couldn't play ten minutes then she got three games for my every one.

Remember Sports Games Have Special Rules of Etiquette

In a column on IGN's Insider Web site, author Chris Carle came up with a few additional rules of etiquette that pertain specifically to sports games. They are really useful to remember:

✔ **Don't abuse instant replay**. A few instant replays when showing someone a game for the first time is okay; after that it's annoying. Always ask permission from other players if you really need to see an instant replay.

✔ **Respect the way the game is played in real-life**. One of Chris' main points that is worth following is that you should play the game the way it's played in real life. This is especially important to follow if you're a much better player than your opponent.

✔ **Never, ever pause a play in the middle of a play**. As Chris says, "That's just lame." If there is a worse thing to do, other than quit or knock off the power in a video sports game, I'm not sure what it is.

✔ **Acknowledge special trick plays, teams, or players**. In the Lakers vs. Bulls game on the Sega Genesis, Phoenix Suns forward Tom Chambers can score from a special place on the floor every time; it doesn't matter who is guarding him or that Tom Chambers was never this good in real life. You just hit the spot, press the shoot button, and he can throw down a double pumped two-handed jam. I remember playing him against my friend Amed one day just to embarrass him for a few minutes. Eventually, he caught on that something was screwy. We laughed about it for a few minutes and then the "Tom Chambers" rule of sports gaming etiquette was born: If there are unfair or unrealistic moves or players, we acknowledge them up front and ban such players, teams or play from the game.

LAN Party Etiquette

This book contains an entire chapter on LAN parties and competitive gaming; however let's look at the critical LAN Party Etiquette here:

✔ **Bring headphones because many LAN parties require them.** Even if you do bring speakers they're not to be set on 11 even if yours "goes to 11."

✔ **Don't touch anyone else's equipment without getting permission.** Don't ask don't use is the order of the day here, unless you want to experience punishment not of a virtual kind.

✔ **When setting up take your time**. Be careful not to cut off other player's power, or pull cables that aren't yours. When in doubt, ask everyone first!

✔ **Don't bring a PC with a virus on it and infect everyone**. Update your virus software and run a virus scan before attending.

✔ **Don't be a space hog**. Bring the minimal rig you need and keep your space needed to a minimum so all the people who show up can play.

✔ **Don't exclude junior's parents**. If you're hosting allow parents and even encourage them to attend if their kid wants to go

✔ **Stay off other player's machines even if they have open directories and shares**. You're not there to snoop or pilfer files from another person's machine. Some parties actually set aside time for this anyway.

✔ **Play games but keep Web surfing, email, IRC, etc. to a minimum**. If you need to do that so much, why are you at a LAN party in the first place? Don't act like a teeny-bopper at the mall with a cell phone.

✔ **Don't keep playing in single player game (unless you're out of the tournament at hand) when you should be playing what others are playing.**

✔ **Don't tip off other player's positions to others when you're not playing.**

✔ **Avoid peeking over at others screens when playing.**

Cheating at Games

Any discussion of becoming a better gamer should include something about cheating. Cheating is a *big* deal in the gaming world. For some reason, there are people who enjoy cheating at videogames, especially with online games or at LAN parties. Perhaps we should blame the hacker ethic of trying to do something people don't think can be done (i.e. cheating without getting caught), but I think there are people who think it's fun to ruin the fun others are having. Whatever the reason people cheat doesn't matter. The outcome is always the same—cheating hurts the game. Detecting cheaters, and knowing what forms of cheating exist is thus important insight to being a better gamer. Here is a overview of the more devious types of cheating and what you can do about them.

Aimbots

Aimbots are probably the number one scorn of established players, especially for first person shooter games. An *aimbot* is a program of various sorts that takes the skill out of aiming in an FPS. The result is perfect or near-perfect hits every time. What fun is that?

To avoid aimbots, you can frequent servers that police for them. As you might suspect, you'll find the most aimbots (and other cheats) being used during school holidays, weekends, and during times kids are playing. You can read much more about aimbots and other cheats from the Unreal Tournament perspective at **www.digdilem.org/ut/aimbot.html**. The site covers a lot of cheats and hacks that are common to FPS games.

Wall Hacks

These are specialized hacks that let people see or even shoot through walls. Some are created through video card configurations while others require mods to be installed. Both are forms of cheating and if detected during play will result in complaints and potential banning from a server.

Speed Hacks

These are hacks that change your speed relative to others in a game. Even a slight speed difference can be a big difference. Speed hacks have existed for FPS and RTS games.

Map Hacks

Map hacks are programs that people run that show them more about what's going on then they would see in the normal view of their game. They are used a lot by cheaters at RTS games. A few enterprising people have created them for MMOR-PG games like EverQuest as well.

Countering FPS Cheaters

There are several resources around today to deal with cheaters in first person shooter games. The first is Punkbuster, a server program which can be used to help server admins better protect their servers and players from cheaters. Their sister site, Punksbusters.com, is a community of server owners who share IDs of cheaters so they can be banned from a network of servers. Another good site is Counter Hack located at **www.counter-hack.net** (see Figure 2.4). If you play any of the major first person shooters you should visit this site and catch up on the various anti-cheating detection and prevention tactics and news.

Countering Cheaters in General

To counter cheaters in general you must be vigilant but fair. Just like the game etiquette guide says, you can't assume people are cheating. But if you suspect

FIGURE 2.4
Punkbusters.com is one of several sites and methods popping up to keep cheaters from ruining our fun.

someone, the best thing you can do is to leave the game. This deprives the cheater. Before leaving, try to gather as much information about the player that you can. If the cheat is plainly evident, try to take a screenshot and record the game session. Your best weapon is to let others know about the cheater by putting the word out on sites like punkbuster.com. Most cheaters get off by frustrating other people they play. Try not to be too frustrated in chat or by your actions, and move on with whatever information you can gather. The community of good players hates cheaters and the best way to get cheaters banned is to let good players know about the cheaters you encounter.

Cheat Codes, Cheats, Walkthroughs, and Web Searching

Monster gamers don't cheat and they don't read cheat books. They also don't use cheat codes to finish a game and they don't turn to walkthroughs on the Web to finish games unless they're really, really stuck. That doesn't mean that the best of us don't eventually look at cheat codes, or even peek at a walkthrough every now and then. However, this type of information is used mostly after we've finished a game and we want to use those tools to wring extended play out of a game, or see if there was something critical that we missed.

The Monster Gamer Ethic

Hopefully you've learned that there is a more formal and disciplined approach that you can take to getting really good. Monster gamers are like athletes in many ways. While our physical work may be limited to a few digits or some easy shifting in our chairs during play, the eye-hand coordination, the mental stamina, and neural reflexes have to be just as high as some athletes, or master players of games like Go and Chess. So instead of thinking like a gamer, begin to think like a modern day athlete who trains, reviews the fundamentals, focuses on specific aspects of his or her game, and brings and overall ethic of organizing their approach to being the best. If you can do that, and have fun, then you will take your gaming to a new level, which is important because later in this book we'll discuss the entire realm of competitive gaming. With cash prizes being handed out, accolades being thrown out, and bragging rights among friends at stake, being a better gamer has more riding on it than it used to.

chapter 3

Everything You Need to Know about Buying, Selling, and Trading Games

Buying a game is easy. Go to the store, pick out a game, and give the sales chick or dude your cash. Then, rush home without getting a speeding ticket (the hardest part) and play until you fall asleep on your keyboard or the couch (around 3 a.m.). So why devote an entire chapter to the buying (and selling) of video games? Well, for the discerning hardcore gamer, there is an emerging science to the acquisition of a great game, and more importantly to building a collection of games.

You also can never have enough games. Let's face it; with three or four different platforms active in your house, and a few online subscriptions going, a gaming habit isn't cheap. In this chapter our goal is to spec out all of the known information about buying, selling, and trading games. If you're like me you're on the verge of scraping for change in the sofa to pull together enough cash to buy yet another game. You're also taking many trips to the bargain bin and used sections to pick out old games that you don't get to play much.

Savvy monster game shoppers not only know how to get good deals, but they grab the deals the other guys don't know about. They're also into building collections of titles, while limiting their exposure to bad games. No matter how cheap some games get, they still suck. I'd rather pay $49.99 for Morrowind, than pay $2.99 for Trespasser (sorry Seamus).

Buying New Games

Buying a new game is all about two things: Getting it first or fast, and getting a good deal. These two goals are not necessarily mutually exclusive. There is also the growing trend of special editions to consider, which are "superized" versions of games usually released during the first few months of a product's life-cycle. For some gamers, getting a new game first is just the penultimate version of fun. They are like the people who want to be first in line at the big new summer movie. In Japan, long lines form outside top game dealers for new releases of games like Final Fantasy and Dragon Quest. Getting the game is as big an event as playing it.

Getting It First

Amazon, Ebgames.com, and other sites will let you preorder almost any title. Many smaller Web merchants also take pre-orders and, honestly, some of these guys really specialize in fast access to top titles. Physical stores like Best Buy, Wal-Mart, and EB usually have some pre-order capability as well but I would say that it's riskier to deal with these places because they don't necessarily get things the day a game leaves the publisher. Games typically will ship first from the publisher to a central warehouse and then again from there to the various stores around the country. Depending on the part of the country (or world) you live in, dealing with various mail-order merchants like Chips & Bits, Tronix, and so on, can be a good way to secure the latest releases fast.

The trick to getting something first is two-fold. First, you need to do some research and keep your eye on what the specific ship date is for a piece of software. Most Web and major offline retailers actually put up the ship dates as they track them. This gives you a chance to determine exactly when a title is available and when you're going to have to cough up the cash. If you have a good idea when the game is shipping, you might call your favorite stores and find out when they expect to get their order in.

Pre-ordering is important for Web stores and smaller retailers because they will make sure that the pre-ordered games they have will get to them fast (and thus to you). For example, if ABC Game Retailer only has pre-orders for two copies of Mario Sunshine, they're not going to push their distributor or the publisher to overnight their shipment. If they had 60 pre-orders, on the other hand, somebody will be working overtime to get your copy out.

If you're dealing with a Web merchant you need to decide if you want to pay the extra cost for faster shipping. If you don't, stand in line. Unless you order something two-day air, or are within a two-day ground shipping zone, it is entirely possible many retailers will get the title the same day or sooner than you do. This is why some game addicts have high FedEx bills.

The downside to pre-ordering is that it locks you into a specific merchant, and God forbid they screw-up the ordering or shipping and you get stuck waiting. The earlier you get in on a pre-order the faster you get your title in case demand outstrips supply. You can remove yourself from a list but then you go to the end of the list, or if it's a smaller merchant you're going to earn some ire from them. The other problem is that sometimes sales, store rebates, and coupons don't manifest themselves until after the first batch of pre-orders are fulfilled. All of this means that getting your top priority should be getting it first otherwise pre-ordering and racing to the store the day it comes out is pretty worthless.

Getting a Good Deal

Many companies now offer special deals to early buyers of top games. If you wait until pre-order time, you can hit all the major stores and Web sites to see if any deals are offered. But don't expect price breaks. Most deals you'll find will be in the form of coupons or gift-cards toward your next purchase. You might also find deals on special collector editions that offer bundled soundtracks, figurines, and so on. Over time, I expect special pre-release offers and limited-edition special release versions of software will become increasingly popular. For example with WarCraft III, Ebgames is doing a special rebate offer through its Ebgames.com site for the collector's edition (see Figure 3.1).

Most special releases or pre-release deals come from the big chains like Best Buy, Target, Microplay (Canada), Wal-Mart, GameStop, and Electronics Boutique. These chains like to offer such deals as a way of differentiating themselves from online merchants and other retailers. Often each deal is a little different, so shop around. Try to become increasingly diligent at monitoring the Web sites, and ads of your favorite stores to see who offers the best goodies or other special offers prior to a game's release.

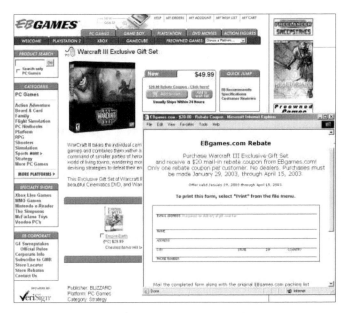

FIGURE 3.1
A rebate Deal through Ebgames for the Collector's Edition of WarCraft III.

Working the Retailers

Every gamer I know has his or her favorite sources for getting a new release. There's no best place to buy. Part of being a monster gamer is knowing how to work the plethora of retailers to serve your needs. Here are some basic guidelines I use:

✔ **Look for aggressive pricing in the mass-market stores.** Mass market electronic, toy, and retail stores usually offer great pricing (especially places like Wal-Mart). Unfortunately, they don't always get things in stock super fast and might not have the best selection of PC games. The Sunday circulars in your local paper are packed with inserts from these guys.

✔ **Check the specialty chains for special offers.** Places like Electronics Boutique and GameStop in North America are located in malls and are usually close to each other so consider visiting both outlets to check prices and look for special deals. These chains are also getting very aggressive at offering deals, special offers, and coupons for games. Be on the lookout. My monster motto here is: Play hard and shop hard.

✔ **Look to the smaller stores for good service.** The individual sole-proprietor stores and small regional chains are good places for support and personalized service. Often these stores are aggressive in getting stuff in stock fast, and they can special order older titles. If you're lucky enough to have a store like this near you, take advantage of it. Don't expect these places to always have the best prices, however.

✔ **For selection, cruise the mail order and online outlets.** Outlets like Chipsbits.com and some of the import stores listed later like NCSX.com and Tronix.com are great shops for monster gamers. These outlets tend to have good pricing, good selections, good service, and fast shipping. Amazon.com is good but I've noticed they tend to run out of stock after initial releases of products and then they tend to take more than 24 hours to ship something. Amazon's pricing on games aren't also the best either. The best thing to do is build a little favorites list of the titles you want and get yourself on all of their mailing lists.

✔ **Don't expect much from the small chains.** Small chain stores like Kaybee Toy & Hobby, FYE, and others carry games. They usually have the worst pricing and selection. I only resort to these stores when I'm looking for an older release that isn't stocked at the other stores and I'm trying to avoid mail order.

Warehouse Stores

If you haven't been to a warehouse club to shop for games you've missed the joy of buying a 'B' list title for $19.99 when its still selling for $30.00 elsewhere. Warehouse clubs like Sams, BJs, and Costco stock both console and PC titles. But don't expect to find any of the major recent releases in stock except on the PC side of things. The prices also aren't always the best, so shop closely.

I find myself shopping for games at warehouse stores when I'm there for something else. Warehouse clubs are like fishing, you drop in a line and hope something bites. Just recently I picked up a very discounted version of Infogrames Transworld Surfing, a decent game for the Xbox which was still selling in a lot of outlets for 2.5 times what I paid for it. The only problem with shopping this way is that you end up with one game and about $200 worth of toilet paper, huge bars of soap, and frozen burritos. If you are just looking for games, I strongly advise you leave your girlfriend or spouse at home. Tell them you are just going down the street to help a neighbor clean out his septic tank or something.

Price Comparison Engines

Another tool to use to find good pricing and availability for various games are a couple of the major price comparison engines that are on the Internet. The four biggest include:

PriceGrabber
www.pricegrabber.com

MySimon
www.mysimon.com

DealTime
www.dealtime.com

Yahoo! Shopping
shopping.yahoo.com

Yahoo shopping only features merchants that are hosted by Yahoo! but that's not significant. PriceGrabber and MySimon seem the most mature though and are useful tools. I would also add that I'd expect Google.com to do something in this area as well. These services tend to be great places to look for good prices on games that have been out a while but be careful to check out the merchants with the lowest prices also. Remember something has to give if you're selling a game cheap, and it's usually the service, or marking up the shipping.

Video Game Store Search Engine

If you want to find out more about smaller stores, other mail-order sources, and local stores in other countries try **www.vgstores.com** (see Figure 3.2) which is a really good and fast growing directory of video game stores from around the world with reviews and other important information about each one.

Using Coupons

Look, I'm no househusband but I don't walk away from good deals, and coupons are a new thing for us monster gamers worth checking out. As a few big chains dominate the retail business of stocking games, the battle for your hard-earned cash becomes fiercer than Cartman's appetite for cheesy poofs. More companies are doing coupons in the major game magazines. This is great because a good money saving offer could finance your entire game magazine budget (which for me approaches figures equal to the national debt).

To really work the system, swing by the magazine rack before you purchase your next game. (But don't get caught with scissors in your hands—at least buy the damn thing if you find a good coupon.) Scan the advertiser's list (usually found within the back five to ten pages of any magazine) for the major retailers. Some are bound to have coupons. For example, in early 2003, I selected several top magazines including *Electronic Gaming Monthly*, *GamePro*, and *PC Gamer*. Table 3.1 shows a list of the deals that I found in these rags.

FIGURE 3.2
Vgstores.com Is a great resource for finding game retailers.

3

TABLE 3.1
Recent rebates found in three major gaming magazines.

- $5 off The Sims Online for PS2
- $10 Gift Voucher if you buy Vexx for the Xbox at Electronics Boutique/Ebgames
- Free Hardware kits if I bought a GameCube or GameBoy at Electronics Boutique/Ebgames
- $20 of Everquest and Logitechs Netplay (keyboard) Controller for PS2
- $10 Best Buy Gift Card if I bought $50 worth of a variety of peripherals including gamepads, steering wheels, and videocards.
- $10 Instantly for Unreal II at Electronics Boutique
- $2 off at Best Buy for America's Army Operation Game and Guide*
- $10 off Nascar Racing 2003 from Electronics Boutique
- $10 off Command and Conquer Generals at Electronic Boutique
- $5(lb) off a game at www.game.uk.com for any Cube game over $39.99(lb)

* It didn't say on the coupon but if you join the actual Army they give you coupon good for a real M-16 rifle!

Some coupons aren't found in the magazines, they're found online via either a site or by signing up for email newsletters. Make sure you sign up for as many of the major sites that have email newsletters. These include Amazon.com, Ebgames.com, Target.com, and GameStop.com. I get them all and they're part of my entire shopping process and can sometimes include special exclusive offers.

Publisher and Developer Stores

Many publishers (and a few developers) offer stores for their products. These stores provide special offers and discounts. They also offer hard to find games and they stock special fan-oriented merchandise like figurines, posters, and shirts for your favorite games or special collector's editions. Table 3.2 lists all the publishers and developers that have online stores and includes information about each one.

 Make sure you utilize the publisher email list systems most publishers have to get the inside scoop on special offers, rebates, and coupons. For example Electronic Arts always sends me a small discount certificate on my birthday (June 25, in case you want to send me a present or some cash), which I usually use to get $5 to $10 off a classic title from the EA store.

Buying Used Games

I used to think buying used games wasn't cool. I still worry about it now. Once a game is re-sold, the publisher and developer don't make any money. If we make it harder for these guys to make money we get fewer games and less choices. On the other hand, here's my rational for buying used games. You can't also expect to pay $49.99 for every game you buy unless you've got (1) a rich uncle; (2) a great job and no other expenses; (3) a really cool girlfriend who likes to support your habit (not likely); (4) or you live on peanut butter (this works for about three month—trust me). To help you get past the guilt you might feel for buying used games, I've put these easy-to-follow guidelines together:

1. **Try to resist buying new releases used.** This is a tough one. You're at EB, you've got $25 to blow and Buffy for the Xbox costs $25 used vs. $44 new. What are you going to do? This is like one of those ethical dilemmas you read about in the Harvard Business Review. You probably buy Buffy and promise yourself you'll buy a new title next time. I try to keep my ratio of new titles to used titles at about 4:1 or better.

2. **Don't buy used games on the PC.** Because many PC Games can easily be copied, publishers already lose a lot of money. Don't add to this hurt; buy

TABLE 3.2
Major publisher and developer stores.

3DO	store.3do.com
Acclaim	www.acclaim.com/store/index.html
Activision	store.activision.com
Atlus Games	www.atlus.com/main.html
Blizzard	www.blizzard.com/market.shtmlwww.sammy-zone.com
Bungie	shop.ecompanystore.com/bungie/bng_shop.asp
Capcom	www.capcom.com/merchandise.xpml
CDV	www.cdv.de/english/shop/result.php3?genre=Fan
Codemasters	www.codemasters.com Clink link that reads "e-shop"
Egames	www.egames.com
Eidos	www.eidosinteractive.com/estore/index.html
Electronic Arts	eastore.ea.com
Epic Games	www.epicgames.com Click link that reads "unreal store"
Fresh Games	www.playfresh.com
Interplay/Titus	www.interplay-store.com
LucasArts	www.lucasarts.com/companystore
MacSoft	www.macplay.com/store
Namco	wamcoarcade.com/namstore/index.asp
Nintendo	store.nintendo.com
Novalogic	www.novalogic.com/store.asp
Sammy Entertainment	www.sammy-zone.com
Sega	www.sega.com/segashop/home_segashop.jhtml
Sony	www.us.playstation.com/purchase
Square	www.squaresoft.com/playonline/merchandise-frameset.html
Take2	www.take2store.com
Tecmo	www.tecmogames.com/store/StoreHome.asp
THQ	www.thq.com/Store/Index.asp
UbiSoft	shopping.ubi.com
Ultima Online	www.uo.com/shop.html

your games new. Besides, price cuts on PC games occur much faster than with console titles so if you're that desperate to get a PC game cheaper, just wait two to three months.

3. **Keep a list of "classic" titles you'd like to add to your collection and buy them used.** I buy used games to round out my title collection. For example, I'm not going to buy a game from two years ago new. Most likely it's discounted to $20 but if I buy it used I'll probably save another $5 to $8. I'm pretty sure the developer at that point isn't going to miss my extra $.75 worth of royalties too much.

4. **Try to buy used games from other players.** The thinking here is that the money goes to someone who most likely is going to use it to buy a new game.

5. **Buy used games for discontinued systems.** I still buy games for my Dreamcast and other older systems. A good game is a good game, and as I get more into the "collecting" of games, used games are a good way (sometimes the only way) to build a collection.

In an ideal world the retailers who sell used games would be required to pay a small royalty to the publishers and developers who make the games we love.

 The worst thing about buying used games is over-paying. If you are a monster gamer you probably read the magazines and Web sites. You should compile a top ten list of games you've never played but still want to. Put a price next to each one of those titles. For example I keep meaning to get a copy of Skies of Arcadia for the Dreamcast which is a great game that I haven't gotten around to playing yet. It's on my list at $20. If I can snag it somewhere someday for $20 I'll pick it up. I also scan online sites like Half.com, Amazon.com Zshops, and ebay for prices on used games as a way of setting a ceiling for used game purchases at local retailers.

Where to Buy Used Games

Used games can be bought online at a few select locations, through person-to-person auctions, and offline at several major retailers such as Electronics Boutique or GameStop in the U.S.

Online

Online sources are usually the first place many people turn to. There are over a half-dozen large sites like eBay and Amazon.com but there are also a number of smaller specialty retailers. Each one has a particular strength and weakness:

Amazon.com

Selling used stuff is profitable and Amazon has been chasing this market lately. In addition, their ZShops program introduces a number of small stores offering merchandise including discounted and used video games. The good thing about Amazon's used system is that it's easy to navigate. To sell your used games on Amazon, click on the "Sell yours here" link on the product page and walk through the signup system.

Half.com

Half.com is a division of ebay where you can list one-off products for a set price. Lots of video games are listed. Listings are offered from both merchants and individuals. Game prices are good and Half.com avoids the entire auction format that drives most of ebay purchases.

ebay.com

There are entire books about buying and selling on ebay so I'm not going to duplicate them here. My suggestions when buying on ebay is to try to bargain hunt for games using the auction format. Since you can get straight prices on Amazon.com and Half.com don't overbid on ebay. Selling on ebay is also fairly easy but before selling a commodity item like a video game you might want to investigate Amazon.com or Half.com. If your item is unique or a special collectors edition, ebay is the way to go.

Offline Options

Offline options for buying and selling games revolve around the major gamestore chains like GameStop, Funcoland, and Electronics Boutique. Most of the chains have small to large sections devoted to used games. Always check the quality of the discs before leaving the store, which they'll let you do, and ask about any frequent buyer discounts. GameStop which publishes Game Informer Magazine recently created a frequent used game buyer program. If you pay $10 to subscribe to the magazine, which itself is decent, you get 10% off all your used game purchases for a year. All the chains trade-in policies that are fairly easy to deal with. You can likely get better pricing online but you have to wait and deal with the task of shipping, collecting the cash, and so on.

Trading Games

There are sites for people who want to trade games but most of them aren't worth recommending. The exception is Game Trading Zone (**www.gametz.com**), which is shown in Figure 3.3. This site has a good interface, a large number of traders,

FIGURE 3.3
Game Trading Zone site (www.gametz.com).

and a good reporting system to catch people who aren't good traders. Trading a game here is easy. You create an account and log in. Once you are registered, you can fill out two sets of lists: items you have you're willing to trade and items you want. A trade matching system helps to match up likely trades with your requests. You are also encouraged to fill out a bio page as part of participating in the community. A full search engine lets you scan the database to search for games people have to trade. A complete set of forums is also on the site to share info and talk about trading, games, or whatever seems interesting.

If you find someone who might be willing to trade with you, the next step is to contact them and see if they agree to a trade. The site gives you email and instant messaging processes to reach someone if they've filled out their forms correctly. The particulars of a trade are up to you. To date, the Game Trading Zone has helped people execute tens of thousands of trades and seems to be growing stronger every day.

Renting Games

I've only rented games a few times because I simply like buying them. However, with so many titles and platforms, renting is becoming a good option. The major chains and local rental stores are getting better at stocking titles (even newer titles).

Want a good laugh? Go to Blockbuster.com and browse the titles available for sale and look at the pricing—$56.99 and up for some titles! To Blockbuster's credit, they were offering a three-for-two deal, so two games for $114 actually gets you three games (an average cost of $37.00 per game, which isn't bad). Unfortunately, they are selling you pre-owned games which you can get for $25 to $30 a title easily elsewhere. Memo to Blockbuster: Just stick to renting and not selling games to us. Shit, I probably just blew my chances of getting Blockbuster to carry this book.

NetFlix, which created the unlimited DVD rental model, has recently given birth to a video game counterpart named Red Octane (**www.redoctane.com**) and to swapgame.com (a U.K. online rental company). Red Octane offers three unlimited rental programs: G2, G3, and G5. G2 lets you rent any two games for as long as you want with free postage to and from Red Octane for $18.95 a month. G3 rents you three games simultaneously for $23.95 a month and G5 gives you five games for $39.95 a month. You can also trade in games for free rentals. For example, one game, if approved for trade-in, will get you two months free off their $18.95 a month rental program. See Red Octane's site for details.

Another new rental option is Games on Demand for you PC, offered through Yahoo! and other sites (see Figure 3.4). These sites pipe PC games through a broadband connection to you offering you single gaming rentals for prices such as

FIGURE 3.4
Gamesmania.com and Yahoo! Games.

$2.95 to $7.95 for three days or $14.95 for unlimited games. Yahoo's package is as follows: ten games for a month for $14.95, five games for $12.95, or three Games for $9.95. You can also pay $4.95 for a single game for 3 days. GamesMania charges $14.95 for an entire month for all its games. Both services offer roughly (if not exactly) the same slew of games. Most of them are crap titles you or I would never play (first release titles aren't among the offerings). That being said, I did find some titles I would play including Civilization III, Deus Ex, Tropico, Commandos 2, and Thief 2. Until these systems add more major titles to their lists, they're not going to be great deals.

Collecting Import Games

Collecting import games requires a bit of knowledge, but guess what? You're in good hands. In the past, you could dive headfirst into the import scene with little problem. Now the anti-piracy tactics of the various console manufacturers really muck things up. Before you buy import games and systems, make sure you know the basics.

Mod Chips

Import games require mod chips. These are special chips you need to install into your console to break the region's copy protection system (see Figure 3.5). Regional protection is what prevents you from playing a cool PS2 game that was released in Japan on your U.S. or European PS2. Placing a mod chip in your localized console is not for the faint of heart. It definitely voids your warranty and it might not even work if you do it wrong. You could also ruin your system. (But then again you could get hit by lightening while you are mowing the lawn.) Although it is not illegal to do this, it is illegal to make copies of software for other people and since many mod chips allow you to play copied games, this does send you down a path toward piracy and crime.

Where does this leave us in the ethical cloud of life? In my opinion it's simple. There are several levels of ethical behavior relating to imports and mod chips:

1. **Buy import hardware to run import games.** This is probably the most ethical process. Lots of players (and developers) do this. They have Japanese consoles to play Japanese titles and U.S. consoles for U.S. releases.

2. **Modify your system to play import games but don't use it to play any pirated titles.** This is the next most ethical approach. Aside from voiding your warranty, at the worst you are robbing local publishers of income they might make from producing the local release of a title.

FIGURE 3.5
A Mod chip for the PS2.

3. **Modify your system to play pirated titles.** What can I say? This is both illegal and certainly unethical.

Mod chip makers are under constant pressure from the console manufacturers and could be shut down if they overstep the law. Retailers offering mod chips come and go depending on the pressure they receive. Furthermore, as consoles begin to connect to the Internet, the chance increases that console manufacturers (or even publishers) will look to see if a mod chip is installed, and if so, they will block the system from utilizing the online service. To combat this, some novel mod chip systems are being developed to switch themselves on or off, although, if you forget, you might get caught one day.

There are several online sources for obtaining mod chips. (These guys will send you your chip in a brown paper wrapper so the postman will think that you're just ordering something from a sex shop. Don't you wish!) Most outlets just sell the chip itself, allowing you to perform the mod yourself. There are others like NCS that will, by appointment, let you send your hardware to them to be modified. Unless you are familiar with installing chips onto boards, don't try the mod at home. If you have a company do the mod for you, the only thing you need to worry about is your warranty. You'll definitely void the warranty on your system. Although some mod chip installers will offer you a warranty, it's one thing to have it offered, it's another to collect on it if you experience problems. Most "warranties" for mod chip installs that I have seen don't take responsibility far any problems outside of the specific mod chip installation so there is a loophole there for people to claim that the "problems" with your machine such as a faulty DVD-ROM drive wasn't their fault. Since the people doing mod chip installs come and go, the best way to find out the reputation of a particular company is to check on various newsgroups.

Getting the Best Mod Chip for Your Machine

You'll find frequent debates as to what is the best mod chip for a particular console. Mod chips need to change when system designs change (which happens every so often with consoles as manufacturers attempt to improve their manufacturing costs and thwart previous mod chip designs). Mod chip makers also change their designs as they attempt to simplify them. To find out the best chip of the moment, you should do a little research when you're ready to acquire one. Newsgroups and a few of the better news sites do track the mod chip arena.

So where does this leave in deciding if you should purchase and play import games? I've compiled a few guidelines to help decide:

✔ GameBoy Advance doesn't have any restrictions on import software.

✔ GameCube users can check out Freeloader from datatel.com, which is a swap disk solution that lets you play imports without making a hardware mod to your system.

✔ Many people still have Dreamcasts and there is still much great software available for this console, much of it released only in Japan. You can purchase a used Dreamcast and have it modified with little financial risk ($100 tops). I think some of the Japanese releases like Ikaruga are worth the effort.

✔ The amount of Xbox software specifically released for the Japanese market is still very low, although this is likely to change.

✔ When it comes to modifying the three current consoles, Xbox, or PS2, the issue boils down to costs and risks. If you can't risk damaging your machine, you really shouldn't play the mod chip roulette game.

✔ If you can afford to replace or repair a machine damaged with a mod, or you can afford to buy a machine specifically for modding, import games might be in your future. You also might consider buying import hardware directly, although the cost may be higher than modding a console. In some cases you can find special versions of hardware release like the limited edition Panzer Dragon Xbox released in Japan.

✔ Don't do a mod chip install yourself unless you're really confident you can do the work necessary. Despite the number of people who say "It's easy," it's not going to be if you've never done anything like it before. To select the best mod chip, go with the mod chip recommended by the installer you choose, and choose an installer that you feel is the most reputable and the most experienced.

✔ If you're going to use Xbox Live! extensively, you'll need a mod chip that can be shut off and undetected by Xbox Live! You might have to still be careful because if you forget to switch it, or the chip fails to switch, or Microsoft figures out some new way to detect mods, you're going to be out of luck.

European Issues for Imports

My dream is that one day the entire Earth will use the same power, display, and other basic consumer electronics standards. Pigs might fly as well. If you currently live in Europe, you'll need to deal with specific issues like power conversion, cable conversion for display output, and the dreaded PAL vs. NTSC issue. To deal with all these issues you really have to want to play games from outside your region. The best place to help you with all of this is the NTSC-UK.com site, which gathers up and distributes import technology and information for European gamers. The FAQ is located at:

www.ntsc-uk.com/MainContent/Import&Tech/ImportFAQ/ImportFAQ.htm

You can also check out a number of other articles on the site at:

www.ntsc-uk.com/MainContent/Import&Tech/index.htm

Swap Tricks and GameShark

If you're not up to speed with the import scene, you probably haven't heard about the swap tricks used to fool machines into booting games by first starting up with one type of U.S. game and then replacing it with an import game. On some systems like the Dreamcast, you still need to modify your hardware to do this, and in some cases these types of mods are risky. The GameShark device (**www.gameshark.com**) also lets you play some import games mostly on the older Dreamcast and PS1 systems. Unfortunately, the swap tricks and GameShark don't work on newer consoles which brings you back to needing a mod chip to circumvent the system's regional protection.

Have Hardware, Need Software

Let's assume you have a machine that can play imported software (mainly from Japan, but also from the U.S. if you're outside of the U.S.). You'll want to buy import games for one of three reasons:

1. To play a game before it gets to your region.
2. To play a game not ever available in your region.
3. To play a version of a game from another region which has features not available in the game released in your region.

The reason you select will obviously impact the price you're willing to pay for an import, the company you choose to get your imported software from, and whether you can wait for the game to be released in your region.

Import Sources

The two major batches of import companies include U.S. based companies and U.K. based companies. The U.S. based companies, especially NCS and Tronix, are probably the biggest, while the U.K. based companies, like Advanced Console Entertainment, specialize in the large U.K. and ancillary European markets. There aren't any major exporters that operate directly from Japan.

You can find dozens of potential import sources on the Web, but about ten or so really stand out. In the interest of full disclosure, I should mention that one of these, Tronix, is owned and operated by a very good friend of mine. My opinion of Tronix (as clouded as it may be) is that they are a top retailer for imports. Another top retailer is NCS. In addition to the stores, you can also frequently find imports for resale on various person-to-person sales and auction sites. Here you'll be buying used titles so shop at your own risk, and closely check the reputation of the seller.

Importer Reviews

Here are some specific reviews of top North American importers that service people worldwide for games imported from Japan. They all offer hardware, software, and accessories. Be sure to check the sites for each one carefully. Skilled buyers surf for the best prices.

National Console Support (NCSX)
www.ncsx.com
Phone: 718-523-5774
NCS is probably the top-of-the-line importer. They have a good site and they stock a wide range of titles and other items imported from Japan. NCS also does some mod chip installations, but you need to email them for information on pricing. Be aware that NCS lists tons of products but not all are in stock.

Tronix Multimedia
www.tronixweb.com

Tronix, like NCS, was one of the first major importers to hit the entire console screen. Owner Joe Cataudella has been in the games retail business and the import scene for many years. Tronix focuses on carrying the premiere titles and fast fulfillment. Tronix also stocks a number of U.S. games and is considered one of the best dual-sourcing stores around.

The Rage
www.therage.com
Phone: 212-208-4668

The Rage is a popular store that offers a good selection of imports as well as good support. It's pricing is a bit higher than others. Some people feel the Rage is also closed for business too much during holidays, although Tronix and others do this also because these importers tend to be small operations. (They need time off to play games their games jut like you!)

Toys and Joys
www.toysnjoys.com
Phone: 866-441-2100

This store is based in Hawaii, which gives them decent access to Japan in terms of coordinating with the local exporters. They also have a number of non-game items and older titles in stock.

Video Game Depot

Video Game Depot is probably best known for its immense inventory of new, used, and vintage games. Their inventory is staggering, with titles listed for NeoGeo, TurboGrafx and Jaguar. But again, not all titles listed will be in stock. Also in spot checking their prices, I found that they run on the high side.

Game Express
www.gexpress.com

A reliable source having less emphasis on imports. Like Video Game Depot, Game Express also has a good selection of many older and some used titles.

 Are there any import sits to avoid? The two that most gamers complain about include Upstate Games and BuyRite Games. If you don't believe me, just type in "BuyRite" or "Upstate Games" into the Google.com search engine and see for yourself.

Other Import Stores

I've mostly covered some of the major importers that are based in North America. Table 3.3 lists others that are around. I caution you to check on newsgroups and other sources to examine the reputations and reliability of these other stores. Also, be wary of new outlets until a few guinea pigs begin to sing their praises.

Collecting Vintage Systems

If you're like me, you might realize it was a mistake to lose track of all your old Intellivision and Atari 2600 cartridges. These games are just not the same when you play them with emulators. Fortunately, you can still acquire these games because there are serious collectors who buy and sell vintage equipment. I'll cover vintage games in Chapter 10, but for now let's look at a few sites which specialize in discontinued systems. I've already discussed some, namely Video Game Depot and Gexpress, because they handle imports as well. In addition to those companies, you'll find some that specialize in vintage systems. You can also check out the used sections at some of the chain stores like Funcoland and GameStop. ebay is also a good place for used vintage products. Specialized dealers, though, are the best places to find old Intellivision and Atari 2600 cartridges. Table 3.4 provides a listing with some comments on top vintage system resellers found on the Web.

You can find even more dealers on the Classic Video Game Nexus page for dealers located specifically at:

home.hiwaay.net:8000/~lkseitz/cvg/nexus/nexus.cgi?Topic=HDealers

Many gamers also trade games, or sell their games using classifieds. There are some useful sites where you can find many of the top classic and retro games. Another

---

TABLE 3.3
Import sites in other countries.

NAME	SITE	LOCATION	PHONE
Another World	www.anotherworld.co.uk	U.K.	01782-279294
Goblin Games & Gadgets	www.goblindirect.com	U.K	01485 570256
Madeira Games	www.madeiragames.com	U.K.	0113 234 0120
Videogame Imports	videogame Imports.com	U.K.	0870 443 0387
Lik Sang	www.lik-sang.com	Hong Kong	852 23862851 (FAX)

TABLE 3.4
Top resellers for vintage/classic video game systems.

NAME	SITE	LOCATION	STOCK COMMENTS	OTHER
Atarifun.com	www.atarifun.com	Texas		Accepts Paypal and checks.
Console Classics	www.consoleclassics.com		Not much Intellivision, mostly Atari systems.	Doesn't accept credit cards just Paypal, checks and bidpay.
The Video Game Source	www.konsolen.de	Germany	Lots of systems and good stock.	English and German Versions of site exist.
Best Electronics	www.best-electronics-ca.com			
	www.4jays.com	Antioch, CA	Lots of stuff including old computer stuff too.	Has physical store you can visit. See site for details.
Atari 2600.com	www.atari2600.com	Chandler, AZ	Tons and tons of stuff including vintage magazines.	Considered one of the best sources online today.
Games of All Types	www.goatstore.com	Milwaukee, WI	Lots of stock and variety.	
VideoGex.com	www.videogex.com	Stockton, CA	Ok stock with a variety of systems served.	Ordering is by phone or email. Need to check availability first.
The Game Trader	thegametrader.com/games	Metairie, La	Large variety of systems served with many games.	Actually a chain of physical stores with six stores spread around Louisiana.

place to look is various thrift and goodwill stores as well as flea markets. Junk shopping in places like this might help you pick up cartridges you can the sell or trade to dealers or other users. Another way to find, trade, sell and buy vintage games is to post your own wanted and available list on the Internet on a homepage. Since many traders troll Google and other search engines for new buyers, this can be a useful way to find new deals. It is also common to post various wanted lists or for sale lists on newsgroups like **rec.games.classic** and **rec.games.video.intellivision**. (For more on the major classic newsgroups, see the classic gaming chapter's section on resources.)

Collecting Arcade Systems

Remember when arcades were everywhere? There was one about three blocks from my school and I used to go there daily to play games. It was a dump (weren't they all). If my mother had seen it, she would have banned me from going there (or she would have burned it down). In New York, every corner store had one or two arcade games. These games got so popular that rumors were flying that we were going to have a quarter shortage. Today arcades are of a different breed; home systems equal or rival arcade systems. But this doesn't deter a number of monster gamers from finding actual arcade systems and putting them in their home. Playing a game like Asteroids on an original cabinet can be really cool. Luckily, with the Internet, you can track down some of these older systems. You can locate dealers for new and used systems as well as dealers for parts. There is an entire suite of sites devoted to fans of true arcade systems.

Inside the Arcade Industry

Arcade systems are sold or leased to operators who then charge for them and hope they get enough plays to cover the costs. Developers are only interested in the sales or lease revenue to dealers and distributors. Once a machine is played out and isn't earning much profit, the distributor picks up the machine and takes it back to the warehouse or deploys it elsewhere. Since games take a lot of punishment, these machines wear out. But guess what? These are the machines that find their way into the hands of collectors and hardcore fans that fix them up. Many of these games are really damaged or don't even work by the time they are sold. This is especially true for older classic arcade titles like Pac Man, Galaxian, and Tempest. This makes arcade game collecting one part deal making and one part hardware repair.

Values can really fluctuate because this is a used market. It's not a good idea to run into an auction or dealer and wave around big wads of cash. The smart monster gamer acts completely calm (think stoic) and disinterested. Then you can work a dealer for a good buy. In the end, a game is going to be worth what you paid for it, and what someone else will pay you for it, and not what the dealer thinks it is worth.

Where to Get Arcade Systems

The three established channels include dealers, various auctions held throughout the country, and directly from other collectors. Each has their pluses and minuses as Table 3.5 shows.

Finding Dealers

Dealers are the easiest to find. Look in the yellow pages under the category "Amusement Devices." Many local operators and distributors also have stickers on their systems saying where they were obtained from with a phone number.

Finding Auctions

Arcade system auctions are held throughout the year and several large auction companies tour parts of the country on a regular basis. The three major auction companies in the U.S. to buy from include:

Auction Game Sales: **www.auctiongamesales.com**
US Amusement Auctions: **www.usamusement.com**
Super Auctions: **www.superauctions.com**

You can also find a number of smaller auctions. The best way to find them is to scan through rec.games.

Outside North America, I'm not aware of any major auctions or distributors. Houses and apartments are small in Europe and Asia making it tough to collect these games. If you live in Australia, check out Leisure & Allied Industries (**www.laigames.com**) or Progress Amusements (**www.progressamusements. iinet.net.au**). Also, the following page on the site of the International Association of Amusement Parks and Attractions (IAAPA) might help too:

www.iaapa.org/facts/f-links2.cfm?group=S&country=Australia

TABLE 3.5.
Sources for arcade systems.

SOURCE	PLUS	MINUS
Dealer	Easy to locate and get to	Potentially the priciest sources.
Auctions	Lots of titles;	Auctions are scheduled events, no guarantee you can get the best price.
Other collectors	Can get working machines	Ripe for being ripped off if you're not careful.

Selling at Auctions

If you start selling at auctions, you'll need to cart your wares to the auction. Most actions charge an assortment of fees and a commission. The commission is usually scaled based on the number of pieces you bring for sale. In general, it's difficult to make a living in the arcade auction business. Most collectors who do sell basically move various restorations or coin-ops they're tired of to generate cash to buy other games.

Shipping Your Merchandise Home

You've just attended an auction, and you've purchased your first cabinet version of Joust. Now the fun begins as you realize you need to get it home! Hope you brought a truck or you made some other arrangements. Most auctions require you to remove your purchases within a few hours after the auction ends. Cabinets are not easy to move. In some cases auctions will provide shipping options but don't count on it. Most serious collectors rent or bring a truck with them to the auction.

Many collectors use Forward Air (**www.forwardair.com**). Despite their name, they use trucks only. They are fairly inexpensive and very reliable. However, you need to bring your goods to their distribution points (usually in big cities near a metropolitan airport) and pick it up from one. To work with this shipper (and many others), you need to wrap and "palletize" the load. Palletizing is putting your shipment on a standard wooden pallet. Forward Air isn't the only option for shipping a game across country. There are some fairly inexpensive services that go door-to-door. You can find them by visiting the Arcade Shipping Database created by William J Piniarski (**www.paraseek.com/arcade**). This is a one-stop shop for reviews of services and links to the places you can get to help you crate your coin-ops. You'll also find tips on packing your systems to avoid the least amount of scratches and other problems.

Getting Information on Repairing and Restoring Systems

As I said earlier, after you find a system to buy (and get it home in one piece), you'll need to get the system up and running. To do this, you'll need resources for repairing and restoring your systems. You can look for people who can actually do the repairs, but true collectors will want to repair and restore their own stuff. Repairing and restoring machines used to be a real pain but the Internet has helped the cause with postings, how-tos, and other useful documentation. I will caution you, however, that not all of the information available is useful (or well written). A good way to start is go to Google and type in "Arcade Restoration."

Here are also some sites I've selected (the best ones, of course), to help you get started:

Bob Roberts Site
personal.msy.bellsouth.net/b/o/bob147
Considered to be the premiere arcade restoration site. This site will lead you to Bob's parts operation and his many articles on restoring arcade systems.

Arcade Restoration
www.arcaderestoration.com
A great comprehensive site with lots of material including Bob Robert's stuff. Lots of photos and how-tos. Probably the best place to go to get your feet wet.

SPIES Archive
ftp://ftp.stormaster.com/pub/Spies/arcade/index.html
The Internet archive for board pinouts, test equipment docs, faqs, and more. Not a great place to start per se, but a resource you will find a need to visit at some point.

Appolo's Arcade
www.appolo.com
Ton's of information including links to manuals, paint color matching for cabinets, tutorials, and more.

The Basement Arcade
www.basementarcade.com
A very strong set of links to other relevant sites makes this an important resource.

Aside from Bob Roberts and Arcade Shop (listed later), there are a few other major vendors where you can find parts for restoring projects. The first is Happ Controls (**www.happcontrols.com**), which makes a number of products for arcade systems. Arcade Controls.com (**www.arcadecontrols.com/arcade.htm**) has a number of links to vendors and other sources for building and restoring controls. There are also a host of artists who have recreated cabinet art you can use to restore cabinets. The "repros" as they're called by collectors are usually done by interested individuals. Table 3.6 lists a few resources for getting or finding quality classic game repros that have been created.

Multi-Game Restorations
Since a number of the main boards for classic games run a number of games many collectors build multi-game systems that let them play any number of titles housed

TABLE 3.6
Cabinet repro resources.

Arcade Shop	www.arcadeshop.com	Sells much more than graphics but has an extensive supply of graphics as well.
Dragons Lair	www.dragons-lair-project.com/dave	Lots of side panels art.
Fabulous Fantasies	www.fabfan.com/bezel	Several of the major classics are offered.
Wizzes Workshop	www.wizzesworkshop.com	Several overlays for Tapper, Asteroids and Marble Madness are offered.

within the same cabinet. People do this by creating cabinets that can house various instances of MAME or other boards that can support multiple titles. This certainly saves space and is a useful pursuit for many people.

A good site to examine this outlet of arcade restoration and development is:

www.mameworld.net/pc2jamma

More Tips for Arcade System Collectors

I spent valuable time talking with Al Warner, who is one of the better known video game collectors. Al has a site called Al's Arcade (**www.alsarcade.com**). Al got started collecting games purely by accident. He attended a local computer show and stumbled across an auction next door. That day he bought his first game. He came back the next time and bought ten more. Talk about hooked! Al passes along these pearls of wisdom for would-be or current collectors:

✔ Check out Manjiro Works located at **www.manjiro.com**. This is a great site of arcade information from Japan and elsewhere. There is a link to subscribe to their newsletter, which is highly recommended.

✔ Collect for the fun of it. Don't expect collecting to be a money-making hobby. Collecting takes effort, and you should buy games you will play over and over. Don't invest in games you'll stop playing after you master them. It's better to spend $100 at an arcade and master a game there, finish it, and then move on.

✔ Don't deal with games that are broke or are going to break. Games don't last forever but look for games that still have life in them. If you really get into collecting, you might need to learn to restore and repair them.

✔ People invest in cabinets to play games with very unique control setups. Games like Star Wars, which featured a specific flight yoke or Robotron with its two joysticks are vintage titles collectors favor because they are fun to play in the arcade cabinet form.

✔ Cycle your games around. Al actually moves his games around with a truck to his friend's houses, to make space for all of his games. (Don't you wish you could be Al's friend?) If you don't have friends with big garages, consider renting some storage space.

✔ Be wary of games that people are really anxious to get rid of. This is why lots of things don't work. Pretend you are buying a used car: kick the tires, negotiate on pricing, and be ready to walk away if the deal isn't good.

✔ Be careful when restoring a game. The first thing you should do is deal with all power issues: check the voltage, ensure it's proper, and make sure current is even.

✔ Don't expect to get the best deals with dealers. Dealers carry overhead and who wants to pay that unless you have to? This doesn't mean dealers are inherently bad, just inherently different.

✔ Watch for swapped out parts. You might buy an old game and send in the board somewhere to get it fixed, only to discover that a few of your parts were swapped out. Posting on various newsgroups and talking to other pros will help you avoid dealing with people that take advantage of others.

✔ Pricing is often regional. Prices in New England and the West Coast are higher than what you'll see at auctions in the South or other parts of the country. Serious collectors will want to consider going to auctions in regions where prices are lower.

But Wait, There's More ...

I bet you never thought someone could write over twenty pages of information about buying, selling, and trading video games. In all honesty I wasn't sure myself. As I said at the start, even experienced gamers can benefit from some help now and then in acquiring their games. The monster gamer needs to think about all the options, look for all sorts of ways to experience as many games as possible, spend the least amount of money, and to think about growing an maintaining a collection of games, new and old, local and international. I've given you all the knowledge to do just that so let's stop now and enjoy what's left of the day playing our latest acquisitions!

chapter 4

CREATING A MONSTER GAMING PC

If you want to create a monster gaming PC, you've come to the right place. You'll learn in this chapter that there are two approaches you can take for getting a rig that kicks ass and makes your friends envious. You can custom build one yourself, or you can order a killer machine from several leading manufacturers who target the game buying elite. In either case, and certainly if you're going to custom build your own rig, you'll need a crash course in what makes a better gaming system and a better PC. After all, you don't want to settle for the typical crap everyone else buys. This requires understanding various nuances of how PCs are built as well as how to keep up with the latest hardware developments and critical software configurations that will separate your machine from just another ordinary power-user machine.

In this chapter I'll help you put your own killer machine together as well as order one from one of the leading companies. If you're dead set on building your own rig, this chapter will get you started and the resources in the next chapter will take you even further into the world of features like cable mods, case mods, and overclocking. Just in case you're new and you haven't cheated by reading Chapter 5, special modifications such as extra fan holes, neon light effects, and LCD panels are called *mods*. But don't confuse these kinds of mods with software mods, which are redesigns of major games. Overclocking is a type of mod where you actually crank up the speed of some components beyond their natural state to squeeze extra performance out of them. These techniques will be discussed in more detail in Chapter 5.

What Makes a Great Gaming PC?

Processor speed? Well, that's just one part of the equation, although graphics speed and resolution are damn critical. A good gaming rig is one that offers the best state-of-the-art graphics you can afford but also doesn't skimp on features like hard drive speed, sound quality, storage space, ports for controllers, networking capability, and more. If you think it's good enough to just drop in the latest graphics card in your machine and say, "Cool, I'm done," you're dead wrong. My top list of great PC gaming features (in order of importance) include:

✔ **Graphics and Displays**: The speed at which the new generations of graphics and display technology debuts is now faster than that of newer generation processors. Because games are so visual, having a fast graphics processor has become even more important than having a fast main processor.

✔ **Sound and Speakers**: Jazzing up audio quality is probably the biggest upgrade many monster gamers have made to their rigs in recent years. Advances in home theater technologies, and better audio and music in games, not to mention digital audio with .MP3s and Internet radio, are really driving audio quality for the best rigs.

✔ **Memory and Motherboards**: Memory is like sex. More always seems better. For monster gamers, having as much memory (or sex) as possible is a good idea because many gamers still want to check out their email, edit a document, and maybe even download a few files while they game. And as we all know, multitasking eats memory.

✔ **Processors**: We finally get to processors. It's number four on the list if you're counting. I remember the days when 386-33mhz was state of the art. Today, machines hitting 2, 3, and 4Ghz is commonplace. Dual processor systems (64-bits and more) are popping up everywhere. Users are power hungry. At the top of the food chain are monster gamers who are geniuses at finding ways to suck up all this power and use it for something fun. But processor speed isn't worth scrap if the rest of your machine can't keep up and deliver the goods. Don't get me wrong; processors are still super important, and given the choice I'll take the fastest I can get. But speeding up your processor should be lower on your list of priorities as you build your monster gaming rig.

✔ **Storage and Removable Media**: The only thing growing faster than the world's insatiable appetite for speed and better graphics may be its need for more storage. Right now my iPod has more room than the machine I had two years ago. Thirty Gigs seemed enough before I went and installed 25 games on it, ripped 200 CDs, and stuck 1,000 high-res digital photos on my hard drive. The bottom line is that you can never have too much storage. No monster gamer I know wants to swap out one game to make room for another. That sucks.

✔ **Ports and Peripherals**: Is it me or are new input/output port types sprouting up faster than international players on NBA teams? In the past several years we've added USB, USB2, FireWire (IEEE 1394a), and the next generation of FireWire also known as FireWire 800 or IEEE 1394b . Sound cards now provide ports for 5.1 surround sound. Add to this list s-Video going in, RCA video, cable, and more. And speaking of USB, show me a mainstream system that gives you more than two ports? In terms of peripherals we've got yokes, wheels, wireless mice, gloves, and weird devices (see Figure 4.1) that we're supposed to use to play RTS games with. This is enough to drive anyone mad.

✔ **Operating Systems and Configurations**: There are more flavors of Windows than there are ice cream. Meanwhile, Linux is being used to run servers, and some people actually do enjoy running Mac OS X, which does kick ass even if it's not known as the gaming platform of choice. In building a monster rig you need to consider less which overall OS you use (I mean if it's not Windows then how do you expect to play games?) and more about which flavor you use and how you configure it to wring the most performance out of it. You also should understand how to setup a multiboot machine so you can make Windows co-exist with a Linux install. This will help you do other stuff when you're not gaming or writing some crappy memo with Word. I'll cover configuration topics like this in Chapter 5.

✔ **Case Design**: Today's craziest rigs are custom built hot rods (I call them Monster PCs) with tons of modified cases that keep them cool while making them look really hot. When you're a monster gamer you care about what's under-the-hood first, but you'll also want your PC to be the coolest one on the

FIGURE 4.1
It's a bird, it's a plane, it looks like a mouse but it's not—It's Microsoft's
Sidewinder Strategic Commander, a specialized control for RTS freaks.

block. My advice is that your monster rig should run good under the hood and
look good in the hood.

✔ **Don't Forget the Little Things**: One of my favorite scenes in Pulp Fiction is
when Travolta explains what living in France is like to Samuel L. Jackson's character and he says "It's the little things ... like mayonnaise on french fries, and
calling a Big Mac, 'Lé Big Mac'." When it comes to building or buying a PC,
the little things that often make a big difference include how easy it is to add
memory, pull the damn case off the machine (or get it back on), or where the
ports, front panel doors, or fan(s) are located.

Breaking It all Down

One of the things that suck about writing a book reminds me of the process of
buying a new car. The second you drive the damn car off the lot you lose way
too much of your hard earned cash. In writing, as soon as I finish a chapter I get
worried that something technical that I've written about will be dated and lose
its value. To give you a better deal, I'll try to integrate the present with the future
and drop some good advice your way that you can use as far into the future as
I can take you. The fact is that if you begin to understand the components, and

you understand the basic trends contributing to the making of good components, you'll be able to determine what's likely to be considered state-of-the-art and not just some passing fad. In short, I want to save you from spending your money on something that looks really cool right now only to discover a few months down the road that you really blew it buying some trendy junk.

I'll also try to deal with price issues. I'd love to just recommend the expensive, top-of-the-line gear but if you're like me (my girlfriend has me on a tight budget), you've got to watch your cash at times. As I cover different components, I'll point out when you can get away with buying the cheaper stuff. You don't have to be a rocket scientist to figure out that prices are always dropping on even the high-end gear so a little bit of patience really pays off: Today's break-the-bank products will be tomorrow's affordable ones. For example a GeForce 4 TI chip recently just got demoted from SOA because of the release of the Radeon 9700 and the GeForce FX cards. Its price will drop considerably making it a great deal for the value-oriented monster gamer.

4

GAMING HARDWARE SITES

I spent a lot of time on this chapter and Chapter 5 so you could get caught up in a hurry on the basic tech talk as it relates to gaming hardware. With the time it takes to learn this stuff, you could learn one or more foreign languages. However, for my sanity and the sake of a few trees, I can't cover everything. If you want to learn more, the place to turn is several major Web sites that focus on the nuts, bolts, MHz, and minutia of computer hardware. What follows is a list of the best of those sites. Spend a few days on each of these sites and you'll be the most knowledgeable hardware guy on the block. Just be sure to charge your neighbors when they come asking questions about what to buy for their next PC.

Tom's Hardware (www.tomshardware.com):
One of the originals and still one of the best.

SharkyExtreme (www.sharkyextreme.com):
A little more hipper and game oriented than many of the others but not necessarily as deep all the time.

Anandtech (www.anandtech.com):
A good site with wide coverage.

Arstechnica (www.arstechnica.com):
A bit more of a newsy site; not as much the hardcore hardware review site as the others are.

Other sites not listed here include **MonsterHardware.com, Procooling.com, Gamersdepot.com,** and **www.hardcoreware.net**. New ones pop up all the time so be on the lookout for new ones.

Whenever possible I'll avoid discussing specific brands and models since they will likely change quite a bit; however, some brands like NVIDIA for graphics and Creative for sound cards are market leaders and they tend to stick around. The same thing goes for major components like Pentium class processors, ASUS motherboards, and so on. So, I'll be specific where it makes common sense. Okay, enough basic crap. Let's dig into the gear.

Video Cards

In the late 90's chipset companies popped up like mushrooms in a manure pile. If all of these companies were still around, I'd need an entire chapter just to cut through the options. Lucky for you I can now only count four major companies that are fighting it out for graphics supremacy: NVIDIA, ATI, Matrox, and S3. (S3 is now a division of Via, a huge motherboard, CPU, and chipset company based in Taiwan.) NVIDIA and ATI sit at the top of the food chain but the other two companies are strong contenders. ATI produces its own boards as well as licenses their chipsets to companies who produce their own boards. NVIDIA primarily just licenses its chips. Matrox only makes its own boards and S3 only licenses its chips. Among the various board brands there are a bunch of other companies such as Creative, LeadTek, and others.

At one point I thought NVIDIA was going to win the chipset battle but then ATI brought out the Radeon 9700 board (based on its R300 chipset) and showed the world that it was still a contender. As I write this book, rumors are flying that S3, once a stalwart in the graphics market who fell hard, may be back as well with a new chip. Matrox itself was out of contention but its newest line, while still not top flight, provides some special features that may make it popular for some gamers. But even with these resurgent players, NVIDIA has created such an awesome organization that it's going to be the company to beat for some time.

Graphics card technology seems to rev every six months, although this cycle shows signs of slowing down. The life span of today's cards run about one year or more. After that, you'll likely be foaming at the mouth to drop a new card in your machine. The card vendors also need to sync up with the latest releases of Microsoft's DirectX technology, which itself has typically revved on a yearly basis. By sync up I mean they need to provide drivers that support all of the features available to programmers via the DirectX API. Unfortunately, this doesn't always happen. For example, when the Radeon came out its feature set was more inline with the capabilities of DirectX9 than any of NVIDIA's chips until the GeForce FX debuted.

So what does this mean to you? How do you figure out what part to stick in your machine? Here are some tips to consider depending on your particular needs:

✔ **Single-Monitor Gaming**: Unless you read some amazing headline saying so-and-so just jumped ahead of the leaders ATI and NVIDIA on one of the big hardware tech sites (more on these in a bit), consider choosing a card made with chips from these two companies. If you're still asking me to tell you which chipset to choose forget it because I'd be hard pressed to give you an answer. Here's the reason: NVIDIA recently released its NV30 chip that has become the chip used in the GeForce FX card. The first tests with GeForce FX show it's ahead of ATI's 9700 but not by much. To challenge this, ATI is readying its R350 chip, and NVIDIA is readying yet another new technology as well. You get the idea.

✔ **Multi-Monitor Gaming**: If multi-monitor gaming is your thing you should be aware that both ATI and NVIDIA make good multi-monitor cards but the champ in this department so far is Matrox. Their Parhelia cards, which can support three monitors (the company calls this *surround gaming*), are really hard to beat. I'll cover multi-monitor specifics a little later.

✔ **Replacement Cards**: If you need to pick up a replacement card or a card for a system you're building yourself, I suggest you go with a card that gets good quality ratings and offers the most amount of RAM you can afford. Try to buy it from a reseller who you trust. That way you'll be able to return it if something's wrong.

Among the two major chipset companies there are a number of boards you can choose from but not all boards are created equal. Differences can be found in the amount and speed of on-card RAM, the types of ports offered, and pricing. There used to be more differentiation in speeds but NVIDIA stopped allowing its board manufacturers to overclock their chips. ATI as of this writing still allows overclocking so boards based on its chipset might vary some.

If you're looking at new card companies I suggest you check out their Web sites and see if they offer good online support and software downloads. Also take notice of the overall quality of their site. Newbie component companies pop-up out of nowhere with killer prices but occasionally the quality of their support, drivers, and other materials can really suck. You don't need headaches like this when you're installing a new board, or dealing with some compatibility glitch down-the-line. I like to stick with component brands I know have some semblance of quality service.

Video Tech for the Future

Being a monster gamer you should always be looking out for what's coming next. I already mentioned that NVIDIA recently released its first NV30-based board, the GeForce FX. The NV30 chipset is super-amazing but it doesn't totally blow away ATI's R300. So what's next? After the NV30, NVIDIA is expected to release the NV35 in about six months. The NV35 will be a refined NV30 which means it'll probably be faster and sport some revised design features to improve other parts of its structure, all in the name of improving throughput and capability. The next big release from NVIDIA will be the NV40 which will debut sometime in late 2004, if not later.

Don't expect ATI in the meantime to sit on its butt. They are jamming to get out their next chipset, the R400, by 2004. This will likely be followed by the R500. Prior to the release of the R400 we're likely to see a R350, which will be a refined R300 chipset meant to keep pace with NVIDIA's offerings. The NV40 and R400 are expected to coincide with whatever the spec represented by DirectX 10 will be. My take on it is that DirectX 10 will mostly provide enhancements to a standardized shader language (based on C for Graphics or Cg as it's known).

If the growth rate for new features continues every six months, the technology should double in power very soon. By "power" I mean both speed and rendering quality. Today's top cards put out frame-rates at over 60 FPS and resolutions of 1600x1200 depending on the application. The next-generation gear will push 100 FPS, provide even higher resolutions, and pack in more features that enhance display quality, such as full screen anti-aliasing and more. It doesn't get any better than this monster fans.

Monitor Mania

The current SOA for monitors is not so stable because of the rapid migration to flat-panel technology and the resulting price wars. We can divide the monitor world into the last gasp of CRTs and the newer flat panel LCD monitors. CRTs are still alive and kicking, mainly because they are so cheap. LCDs are much more expensive, and in some cases their diagonal screen size is still not matched by LCDs. CRTs also still beat the pants off of LCDs when it comes to issues such as "motion blur." But let's face it, LCDs are the future and I'm not just telling you this because I own gobs of stock in LCD companies.

Makers like Sony are phasing out their CRTs about as fast as they can run for the hills. Inside of five years it's safe to assume every major gamer will be utilizing

LCDs, although a growing number love using wall projectors. In some cases, monster gamers might be using some hybrid HDTV/LCD displays. (I'll cover HDTV in Chapter 6 and I'll tell you everything you need to know about projectors a little later in this chapter.) The newer LCDs are really taking on the motion blur problem. But if you play lots of games with super high refresh needs (such as first-person-shooters), you better look before you buy. The refresh rate and the blurring might really drive you crazy.

So, the big question is, should you go CRT or LCD? My advice is that if you want a great deal and you're not that excited about LCDs yet , go with the CRT. In this camp, Samsung and NEC-Mitsubishi make great monitors. ViewSonic has also introduced new monitors for gamers that utilizes its UltraBrite technology which improves the color quality of the imagery displayed.

ViewSonic has also reportedly shown a concept 18" monitor that provides "depth" to its imagery. This technology gives you the impression that you are wearing some form of shutter-based 3D glasses. It's still in development and there are some refresh issues, but if there is a potential for a "futurized" monitor beyond CRT or LCD this would be it. 3D holographic chess boards like the ones shown in Star Wars in 1977 are being worked on but don't go searching the aisles of CompUSA anytime soon for one. The drones who work in these stores would probably lock you up in the back.

If you're ready to plunge into an LCD display, on the other hand, there are a few options to consider so let's investigate them next.

LCD Displays: Analog vs. Digital Input

LCD displays have two types of input. Analog is akin to the inputs used for CRT displays. LCDs, however, are digital devices and thus they can be hooked up digital-to-digital provided they provide the required port (called a DCI port). (Your video card will also need such a port for this to work.) Digital-to-digital is the way to go. This will become the standard in a few more years. If you're planning on upgrading your monitor before you upgrade your video card, be on the lookout for this issue and make sure you can hook it up straight to a digital display. Most video cards now ship with two ports: a DCI port and a regular analog VGA port. In the future expect vendors to slowly start dropping support in some or all of their cards for traditional analog VGA ports.

Buying the Right LCD Display

There are many LCD manufacturers right now pushing out a lot of different makes and models. So how do you get the right display for your needs? In general LCD panels from Samsung, Hitachi, and ViewSonic are considered excellent but there are some smaller manufacturers like Solarism that are catching on. Regardless of the brand you buy, the feature most important to gamers, aside from overall image quality, is what is known as *response time*.

Response time represents the speed (in milliseconds) that the screen refreshes based on a new signal. To refresh 60 times a second (which is a great barometer of speed), an LCD would need a response time of 16.66ms (1000ms/60 seconds). If you find monitors having less than 16ms response time, they will likely be suitable for gaming. My advice is that you should write this number down on a card right now, stick it in you wallet (or purse), and when you go shopping pull it out and check the gear you're looking at. Once you get in the store you'll be dazzled by all of the fancy displays and features so you'll likely forget what you are supposed to be looking for! There are screens on the market which are getting as low as 10ms.

 Response time is not calculated in a standard fashion so be careful about what you read as response time. A response time that's off by 5ms could be the difference between 12ms and 17ms, which would pop you under the "magical" 60 frames-per-second number.

In addition to response time, you should look closely at picture quality, but you don't need to be good at math to figure this one out. Here you'll want to look at features such as the black level of the monitor, its perceived sharpness and contrast, and how well it displays color. Color is still an issue for many LCD monitors. Although the latest designs are much better at displaying color, you'll still find a wide range of capabilities among makers on saturation and brightness of color, as well as the differentiation between subtle shades of colors. Many of these features can actually be measured and are presented in major reviews.

Another thing to look at is something known as *bad pixels*. Unlike a CRT which beams electrons at a tube, a LCD has a specific pixel for each pixel the screen will display. That pixel is individually controlled. A defect in a screen can cause some of the pixels to look bad. Screens are tested to some extent for this but it is accepted in the industry that bad pixels happen. If the bad pixel is particularly bad, and it's in the center of the screen, you don't want the display. If the bad pixel is at the very edge you may not even notice it. Before you buy a display make sure your retailer has a good return policy for bad pixels. You don't want a few bad pixels to tun into a bad hair day for you.

Aside from basic picture quality, some people are surprised to discover that LCD displays are really only designed for a fixed resolution. For example, a 1024×768 display can only go this high. It can go lower, but it actually stretches the screen and re-scales it from the lower resolution to the higher resolution. If you're going to run it a lot at a lower resolution than its top resolution (Web designers have to do this a lot to test their pages), you might be concerned about how it scales imagery.

When it comes to extras be wary when reading reviews on LCDs. Most reviewers are likely to not be thinking precisely of gamers. Such reviewers tend to like monitors that throw in lots of extras such as speakers, USB ports, and other garbage you don't need. Besides this junk just drives up the cost. (If you have extra cash laying around for such junk send it my way. I still want to pick up a few games I can't afford just yet.) I don't give a damn how good the speakers are; they're not as good as the separate systems I'll recommend. Tom's Hardware (**www.tomshardware.com**) is one site that actually specs out a score for gaming specific use for gear and hopefully other major sources like *PC Magazine* will do this in the future. Our needs are different from some office weenie who is playing Minesweeper while his boss thinks he's working.

MULTI-MONITOR GAMING

I promised you earlier I'd cover multi-monitor gaming—one of the cooler things to define a monster gaming PC setup. When it comes to multi-monitor gaming you can go with two-monitor setups or three monitor setups. Three monitor setups are currently only being pushed by Matrox under the brand name "Surround Gaming." It's pretty wild when you see it in action. Unfortunately, only the Parhelia line of cards supports it, and it doesn't work for every game. Although the Parhelia boards are really cool, they're not super-boards like the ones NVIDIA or ATI are pumping out.

To run more than one monitor, your graphics card has to support this feature by including the multiple ports or port splitting cables. Most cards today implement multi-monitor support because they offer both a DCI port and a traditional VGA analog port. You can hook up one of each depending on your available monitors. Of course, the VGA analog port will not offer the same image quality as a DCI port. As DCI becomes the standard, you can expect to see double DCI plugs for multi-monitor pleasure. Perhaps we'll even see cards that support three DCI plugs (probably through two ports—one with a splitter cable like the Parhelia cards offer).

Once you have the right card you'll need to configure your system for it and you'll need games that support it. The best list of games that support two or three monitors can be found on Matrox's Web at **www.matrox.com/mga/3d_gaming/surrgame.cfm**.

You can read a killer article on multi-monitor gaming at: **www.tech-report.com/reviews/2002q4/multimon/index.x?pg=1**. Keep in mind that not all games support multi-monitors and if you need the mouse to stay on one screen you can get in trouble. Mouse Jail, available at **www.dr-hoiby.com/MouseJail/index.html**, can help with that. It is a utility that confines the mouse movement to the primary monitor so you won't have any problems. (I just wish the Mouse Jail people could come up with a utility program to better confine unruly relatives. This could really be handy during the holiday season.)

Sound and Speakers

Before we discuss soundcards and speakers, we need to decode some of the jargon surrounding audio. There is so much of it these days that it's enough to drive even a tech head like me nuts. Still this stuff is important because it will make you a more savvy buyer and user of any of the audio gear available for your gaming or other needs.

✔ **5.1, 6.1, 7.1 Audio**: No these aren't scores for Olympic snowboarding. They refer to speaker setups—the most famous being Dolby 5.1 audio. The ".1" in all of these refers to a subwoofer element. The first number refers to the number of speakers that surround you to douse you in a 360 degree orgy of sonic goodness. For a long time, 5.1 speaker setups (3 front, 2 back, and a subwoofer) was the standard. This wasn't good enough for some sound junkie so he or she decided to add a sixth speaker. Then, some nerdy engineer figured out a way to add a seventh speaker. Figure 4.2 gives you a graphical representation of all of these setups. At the time of this writing not every game supports 6.1 audio, and none to my knowledge supports 7.1 audio, although some savvy systems can still make use of these advance speaker setups. The Audigy 2 card from Creative supports 6.1 as do some games like GTA3. DirectX9 includes native support in DirectSound for 6.1 audio systems.

One thing to note about 6.1 vs. 7.1 is that the sound pouring out of the additional speakers in the rear is the same. So technically, 7.1 and 6.1 are the same except 7.1 is louder. This is sort of like that scene in Spinal Tap where Christopher Guess is showing how his speakers can go "one louder." With the extra rear speakers, 7.1 audio can fill a larger room more adeptly.

✔ **Dolby Digital**: Ray Dolby was a pioneering audio engineer. His company Dolby Labs created Dolby Surround, Dolby Pro Logic, and Dolby Digital 5.1. Dolby 5.1 is the original 5.1 encoding scheme also known as AC-3 for the name of the codec that is used to encode Dolby 5.1. Dolby 5.1 is the standard

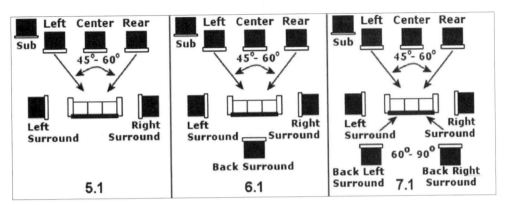

FIGURE 4.2
The speaker layouts for 5.1, 6.1, and 7.1 audio.

for DVD audio. No other audio track can be encoded on a DVD per the rules until there is a 5.1 track. Dolby Digital EX is an enhanced version of Dolby 5.1 that adds some speakers to the back. It's sort of like 6.1/7.1 but not perfectly pure. Audio is recorded in 5.1 and then engineers figure out how to shift some sounds to the back setup without breaking the 5.1 encoding.

✔ **DTS**: This stands for *Digital Theater System* and first came on the scene in 1993 with Speilberg's Jurrassic Park. You see it (or hear it!) in theaters a lot but it's seeping into homes too. However, no DVD will be solely DTS due to the DVD standards so DTS has only slowly been adopted into homes. DTS allows for a higher standard of encoding than Dolby, thus it creates better sound. This shouldn't be an issue for games but those of you running DVDs on your system might care a bit. DTS EX is a system that has a specific 6th channel but to date it's not exactly out there in droves. Many DTS systems that are advertising 6.1 audio use a method similar to Dolby EX where the technology is layered onto the older standard to fool you into thinking it's 6.1.

✔ **EAX**: This is a standard developed by Creative that covers how environmental audio (read 3D audio) works in games. EAX did compete against another standard from a company called Aureal known as A3D but they're gone now. EAX now only competes against inherent 3D sound technology in Direct-Sound but many games go beyond that to support EAX. Three versions of EAX have been released with Creative offering the EAX technology to other soundcard companies to promote the standard. The newest version of EAX, which is dubbed EAX Advanced HD, is used now exclusively with Creative's Audigy Series. The most advanced feature is that it can separate each sound to create an effect as if sounds come from their own environment. Now things can sound like they're coming from the hall to the left, or the padded room on the right. Only a few games support EAX Advanced HD but by end of 2003 it should be pretty much everywhere.

Sound Cards

When it comes to sound cards most gamers have only heard of Creative. These guys have been in the soundcard business longer than some of us have had a PC or even been alive. They dominate the market to the extent that you might wonder if they had any viable competitors. There are a few, although Creative usually provides the best deal.

The market for sound cards is separated into three tiers: motherboard audio, "gamers/multimedia" soundcards, and true audiophile cards. The first tier has been around since Intel and others started including some level of audio capability into their core-logic chipsets. For years, motherboard audio really sucked but it was better than the alternative—listening to your girlfriend scream at you about doing housework while you were playing your favorite arcade-style game. Today, things are better. NVIDIA's nForce2 chipset really raised the bar for motherboard-based audio. Some think that the sound quality can now compete somewhat with Creative's cards. The next generation of nForce Soundstorm Audio (Soundstorm is NVIDIA's brand name for the audio technology in the nForce chipset) could put motherboard audio directly on par with card based systems.

The "gamers/multimedia" sound cards represent the second tier—a step up from motherboard sound. Creative has dominated this space for years, most recently with their Live! series of cards and now with their Audigy/Audigy2 line. This tier is really focused on mass market pricing (under $250). The goal here is not to push the boundaries of sound technology. The big difference between this tier and the next higher one is really quality and features. Creative's Audigy2 line is packed with features, but the audiophile level quality of sound isn't perfect—most hard-core musical types would never use these cards. Joining Creative in this market is Terratec, a high-end company which is making forays into the lower-end card market. Philips has also made some cards for this market which are sold under the "Edge" brand. They aren't bad and they often get good marks for sound quality.

The highest tier of cards represents true audiophile cards from manufacturers such as German-based Terratec and M-Audio. These cards are manufactured for home-recording enthusiasts—those high end guys that make way too much money at their day job. This technology offers the purest sound and best sampling capability but you can't always expect to find the support drivers that work with games. Cards like this often introduce technology that eventually shows up in the lower-tier cards. That's good news for monster gamers on a real budget.

I lied earlier because there is actually a fourth tier—a series of "external sound-boards" made by Yamaha sold under the Cavit brand. These are external systems that hook up to your system via USB. They're actually very cool and the sound quality is excellent. Unfortunately, they don't offer all of the latest and greatest game hooks that you might want. But they do provide good solutions for people in unique situations such as laptop users wanting a great hookup or people who want a system that is also a killer amplifier.

Which Card Should You Get?

So now you expect me to make a recommendation? Well, that's pretty easy. For high-end gaming, go with the Audigy 2 and forget about everything else. Using this card is like being stuck on a desert island with your favorite centerfold. It's a comprise but a damn good one! If you have an AMD-based system you might flirt with a nForce capable board. You get fantastic audio included in the price and maybe it'll be enough. If you crave the penultimate non-game audio experience, look at the offerings from M-Audio or Terratec. If you want an in-between solution, Terratec's gaming-specific solutions are considered excellent products with perhaps a better technology for sampling quality. The Yamaha Cavit systems are sleek, and they have a unique set of features and Mac compatibility that might make them work for you.

Speakers

I grew up with the Walkman. It's a wonder I can hear a damn thing. The aural decay due to the age of the Walkman is going to hit the world like an epidemic some day. If you can still fish a few quarters out of your sofa you should invest in hearing aid companies. So when it comes to speakers, I'm one of those guys who likes it loud, with the base pumping. I like to really piss off the neighbors. And if I don't hear any distortion I'm happy. On the other side of the fence are those pesky audiophile guys. I swear if these clowns aren't the most stuck up group of gearheads going I don't know who is. To true audiophiles, speakers may be the most important part of any sound system and there are a multitude of speakers and styles of speakers you can select from. For our purposes, we now want to focus on PC-powered speakers. But keep in mind that I'm not here to tell you what speakers to buy if you're going to hook your PC up through a fancy stereo system.

When selecting standalone PC speakers you should focus on speakers that conform to the setup of your room and are supported by your soundcard. If you go to a big computer store or electronics chain that sells these speakers, such as BestBuy or CompUSA in the U.S., you'll realize that they don't stock every option, and half the time their testing feature doesn't work for every speaker they carry. This really pisses me off. So now you're stuck with one of two choices: Flag down the latest reviews you can or settle on companies you've got some basic good faith in. (Or there is a third option. You can send me $9.95 and I'll tell you what to do. Just kidding!) Some of companies I suggest you check out include Yamaha, Bose, Altec, Boston Acoustics, and Cambridge Soundworks/Creative. One company that has racked up many kudos, though, is Klipsch which makes the ProMedia line of multimedia speakers. These are killer speakers and the reviews they get tell the story. They are also THX certified (as are all the speaker sets I've listed in Table 4.1). Just be aware that Klipsch speakers are at the high-end ($250 to $300 or more). Moonsoon, another high-end maker, also garners great reviews.

If you stick to the major brands, and double-check reviews on specific models, you'll find a set of PC-powered speakers that'll work well for your system. The important thing to realize is that when you troll for reviews on even the better known speakers opinions will vary widely. Speaker reviews bring out the anal retentive in a lot of people so don't necessarily believe the first person you read.

When shopping at stores for speakers bring along a portable MP3 or CD player and hook it into the speakers to test their quality. If you have to, take your girlfriend with you so that she can chat it up with the dorky sales guy so that he won't harass you as you do your rigorous sound "taste" test. Make sure you bring your own

TABLE 4.1
THX certified multimedia speakers.

Altec Lansing ADA 885 4.1 System
Creative MegaWorks® THX® 5.1 550 speaker system
Cambridge SoundWorks® MegaWorks® THX® 5.1 550 speaker system
Cambridge SoundWorks® MegaWorks® THX® 2.1 250D speaker system
Klipsch ProMedia 2.1 System
Klipsch ProMedia 4.1 System
Klipsch ProMedia 5.1 System
Logitech Z-560 4.1 System

WHAT DOES THX CERTIFICATION MEAN?

THX is a quality control certification process that was started by George Lucas. (If I have to explain who he is stop reading now!) Lucas wanted to be sure that movie theatres had good sound. Movie theaters had really crappy sound systems and Lucas wanted to change that so he formed THX to help certify the quality of sound for theatres. THX isn't an "algorithm" like Dolby. Instead, it deals with issues like the positioning of the speakers in theaters, sound proofing, audio range, and so on. As the THX brand came to stand for overall sound quality, this technology began to expand into home theater and multimedia.

If a speaker system doesn't have the coveted THX certification you can't always assume that the quality won't be good. Tons of great systems like the Monsoon system I mentioned aren't THX certified. And only until the Audigy 2 card was released did a sound card pass a THX certification. THX simply guarantees that a certification group thinks a specific product meets their arbitrary standards for quality, which they don't specifically release their criteria for. In addition, they only certify equipment which applies for (and pays for) certification. So if a company makes a product that could pass THX certification, but then doesn't apply you would never know.

The fact that THX is moving into the multimedia speaker and soundcard market means that there is an independent (if secretive) standard for quality being established. If that standard begins to shift lots of buyers to THX certified equipment, it could raise the bar for everyone. And if we vote with our ears that THX is maintaining a great standard, the entire process works its magic.

---

music. The Engelbert Humperdink-like crap they use as stock CDs may not be quite your thing. Run away (fast) from those lame-ass "special demo" CDs that have been mastered to show off the speakers. What I've done is actually downloaded to my iPOD (only the best baby!) a few MP3 files of various game effects and soundtracks to test the speakers with. If you go to one of these superstores you can easily find me. I'll be the guy camped out with a pile of CDs.

Headphones

When it comes to headphones, the best place on the Web for advice is HeadRoom (**www.headphone.com**). They sell most of the major brands and accessories at decent prices. According to HeadRoom, only a few major headphones qualify for their recommendation. They currently recommend phones that have strong impact and bass and are "tolerant of the harshness often found in the digitally synthesized sounds of the gaming environment." They also recommend "reasonably good coherence (phase response) so as to provide accurate spatial cues..." Taking all this into account, the site suggests the following headphones for gamers:

✔ **Beyer 250-80**: Solid phones

✔ **Sennheiser HD580**: These get mentioned a lot by gamers and are probably the favorite but, they are on the pricier side of the scale. Other Sennheiser models are mentioned too.

✔ **AKG K401**: Higher priced alternatives to Sennheisers

✔ **Grado SR60 and Grado SR80**: Both are recommended as great less expensive alternatives to Sennheiser phones

HeadRoom also recommends utilizing a headphone amp in-conjunction with most of these headphones to help pump things up a bunch. Their favorites are the AirHead and the Total AirHead headphone amps—each of these runs just over $100. If you are really felling rich, you can pick up one of HeadRoom's Home headphone amps, which will set you back over $500. If this will put you in the doghouse, no problem according to Headroom because they suggest "the Grado SR60 or the Koss PortaPro" as strong inexpensive options.

The problem with all of these headphones is one thing—no integrated microphone. These aren't headsets. If you need a headset for some games, Plantronics (**www.plantronics.com**) is a good company that makes a wide-range of headsets for gaming. We'll talk more about headsets and voice communications software in Chapter 7.

The World of CPUs

We've now paid homage to the multimedia components by emphasizing them over the brains of your rig—the CPU. That's not to say your CPU isn't important, but we are talking about games here and not lame-ass spreadsheet crunchers designed for Dilbert cubes. Let's face it; a machine with dual Pentium 4s without a killer 3D graphics card is about as useful to a gamer as a calculator when you are taking a Wood Shop class. When it comes to CPUs, there are really two major options. The first is Intel's Pentium line and the second is AMD's Athlon brand. Within each of these titan CPU families, you'll find more family members than you'll find at the Bradford Family. Coupled with a few specialist CPUs from Via and Transmeta, there are a number of choices and items to cover when it comes to deciding on a CPU. And let's not forget that the CPU architecture you choose will drive other crucial decisions like which motherboard and memory to use.

Intel Pentiums

"It's all about the Pentiums Baby!" or so goes the spoof of that awful P. Diddy song from Weird Al who reminds us how incredibly valuable a single CPU chip can be. Intel is built on the premise of Moore's Law, which states that the transistors on a chip can double every 18 months. This has led to a doubling of CPU power every 18 months or a halving of prices for an existing CPU every 18 months. This mission statement from Intel Co-founder Gordon Moore is sort of the underlying principal of the entire computer and software industry and Intel wears it like a badge of honor.

The Intel Brick Road

The latest version of the Pentium chip is the Pentium IV running at 3.06Ghz. This is known as the Northwood Chip and is expected to be succeeded in 2003 by the Prescott version of the Pentium IV. Prescott could reach speeds of 3.2 to 3.4 GHz. Prescott will be followed in late 2003 or 2004 by Tejas, which is expected to be the final Pentium IV chip and will reach clock speeds in excess of 4GHz. After Tejas rumor has it that we'll see Nehalem, which will be a total redesign expected to take Intel chips to awesome speeds of 6Ghz or more. Don't expect to see this chip until 2005 or 2006 at the earliest. All of these chips are not to be confused with Intel's Itanium line of 64-bit chips. Those chips are designed for servers and are completely incompatible with traditional 32-bit x86 architecture. Applications have to be completely recompiled for these chips and thus you won't be playing games on them anytime soon.

HyperThreading

When it comes to the latest and greatest Intel processors you're going to start reading a bunch about HyperThreading. *HyperThreading* is where the CPU fools the OS into thinking it's really two processors. This enables the CPU to simultaneously process more instructions much as two processors would. However, don't think this means the processor will be as fast as a dual processor. Applications need to be written to take advantage of HyperThreading. Fortunately, many state-of-the-art games by design already are programmed in a manner where they can benefit from HyperThreading and Intel is sure to provide support (and cash) to help programmers enhance their apps to take advantage of this features. Programmers are likely to support this feature because they really like cash. The result is that certain games might be able to run a bit faster or smoother because of HyperThreading. However, don't expect any program to require HyperThreading. My research (digging through the trash bin behind the Intel corporate office) tells me that mostly 3D graphics action titles, simulations, and so on will take advantage of HyperThreading.

In the Land of AMD

Many monster gamers have a soft spot for AMD. We like challenges and AMD has a big one as it fights with Intel. We also know that competition brings out the best efforts and AMD's Athlon processors have given Intel a little scare.

The AMD Roadmap

AMD's Athlon chips are set for a big overhaul in 2003 as the company transitions from its core Athlon XP line, the latest of which is the Athlon 3000 XP, to its Athlon 64 product line (codename Clawhammer). With a name like Clawhammer, they must be out for blood. AMD is also releasing Opteron, which is a server-oriented chip version of its 64-bit CPU (known previously as Sledgehammer). Initial test versions of these chips running in 2002 were under 2GHz, but because of the better design, they are much more powerful than what the clock speed indicates. By the time full production ramps up in 2003 and the chip has been refined in 2004 and beyond, you can expect the speed of Althon 64 to really crank up to the 2.5 to 3GHz range.

Intel vs. AMD

We've now discussed the basics of each processor so let's see who we should select as our dance partner for the big ball. At one point in the early slug match of this game, AMD was really sticking it to Intel. They were pumping out great chips, pushing prices down, and making gamers seriously drunk with excitement. AMD really courted the game community and we enjoyed the attention. Intel, however, didn't just turn the other cheek. With the its recent round of Pentium 4s, it boosted clock speeds fast and furious to the point that they easily hit 3GHz in early 2003. AMD meanwhile has fallen behind a bit from their earlier market position. They have had to work hard to educate users that even though their CPUs have a slower clock speed, they still come close to matching the throughput of higher-clocked Pentium IV chips. That's why AMD started branding its Athlon CPUs as Athlon 2600 XP and Athlon 2700 XP. (The number refers to a benchmark AMD runs to how comparable the chip is in throughput regardless of clockspeed. Unfortunately, Intel doesn't do this.) So the 2700 runs at 2.7Ghz even if the quoted clock speed is actually less. (In the case of the 2700 it is about 2.25Ghz.) Is this confusing or what? Despite this marketing slip, AMD's Athlon 2800 chip and future incarnations of Athlon are solid chips and their pricing is still aggressive enough to make some real value.

AMD will get another shot at Intel as the Opteron/Althon 64 (aka the Hammer/Clawhammer chips) debut. Again the clock speeds will be lower than other Intel chips but the throughput will be much closer or better so AMD will have to show everyone all over again what sort of price/performance it has over the current champs at the top-end of Intel's line. My guess is that Athlon 64 chips (assuming AMD can ramp their clock speed up), will really put them back into the game. If not, I'm not gonna send in my bid for the CEO job.

All this being said, I think that the chips prior to Athlon 64 are going to be hard to choose on a pure power basis over the equivalent Intel chips. Once Athlon 64 is released, AMD should show some serious life and it seems possible that Athlon 64s will have the edge for monster gamers. Other issues such as the speed of supporting chipsets, bus speeds, memory, and so on may become the true differentiation point. Don't factor out price as well.

Motherboards, Memory, and Chipsets

The key ingredients to getting a system's components to work in unison like a well-oiled machine are a killer motherboard, supported by a strong core-logic chipset, fast memory, and a fast bus. The bus represents the rate at which the computer can shift data from memory to the CPU or other elements of the system. If you have a fast car you can drive it through Montana at an average speed of a buck-twenty easy. (Just make sure you have some bribes for the cops when they pull you over.) Run that same car in LA and grandmas with walkers can get downtown faster on a Monday morning. Computers operate like this: A slow bus will gum up a fast CPU in no time and slower memory will drag down the true speed of the processor. So the key issue with memory and motherboards is making sure the freeway is free-and-clear.

There are essentially two main motherboards available. One group supports Pentium processors and the other group supports AMD processors. (There are some other derivatives, which I'll mention, but let's focus on the main two.) Depending on the CPU you select, you will choose a motherboard that supports that CPU. All of the big time motherboard manufacturers make boards for both—you needn't worry about that issue. Within each CPU type, you will need to decide on a supporting chipset that deals with all the core-logic for the system, which is all the other stuff like input/output, memory management, USB, parallel ports, and so on. Several manufacturers make chipsets for both Intel and AMD based systems and each one has various competitive features. Your CPU and chipset will determine the specific models of motherboards you can consider. In most cases, most major manufacturers have offerings for various combinations.

Choosing a Chipset

Chipsets are made by a number of companies including Intel and AMD. Companies like VIA, ATI, NVIDIA, and SiS also make chipsets that are commonly used. On the AMD side, VIA is the market leader, although NVIDIA is a growing force with their nForce chipset. Although they currently only support AMD, don't be surprised if they eventually move over to the Intel side of the fence. One feature I really like with the nForce chipset is that its integrated sound capabilities are pretty significant, which for motherboard-based audio is quite an accomplishment. On the Intel side, Intel's own chipsets, SiS, and VIA all compete with each other.

Before you can zero in on a chipset you need to determine what memory you intend to use. (I'll cover this in the next section.) To make use of the best memory options, you need a chipset that can fully enable its usage. When we were all using SDRAM you couldn't just pop in DDRam and expect it to work. You'd have to get a chipset/motherboard combo that supported it. So while your CPU type limits the range of chipset brands you can consider, choosing a chipset before figuring out the RAM that will pair up with it is like putting the cart before the horse.

If your memory choice is too exotic, such as the latest super-fast DDRam, your options for chipsets will be very limited. My advice is to come up with a list of memory options and then look at the benchmarks that have been posted on the major tech sites. These benchmarks often appear before the actual release of new motherboard/chipsets so you can easily determine who's producing the best stuff at any given time. But make sure that the testing methodology used doesn't favor one over the other too much.

Aside from price issues, another differentiating factor could be a few features like onboard sound, integrated graphics (which 99% of the time we could care less about), or USB/USB2 support.

Once you've selected a CPU, chipset, and memory you can look for a motherboard. In many cases the same combination of CPU and memory will equally narrow your motherboard choices. Configurations like size, quality, the BIOS supported, and others will need to be considered. When building your own machine your biggest concern should be with its overall quality and design. From the myriad of reviews I've read about motherboards, there are a number of companies who get good strong marks but the overall favorite seems to be ASUS. They are continually held up as the standard by which all others are judged.

Memory

Today's rigs are designed to support three main types of memory architectures. That's the easy part to figure out as you'll see. Unfortunately, manufactures and other techoweenies use some very confusing language to market and describe the various memory technology. These people seem to take a perverse pleasure in trying to mislead users about the speed of some memory modules. To top it off, not all memory (even memory of the same types) is perfectly alike; some manufacturers are considered better than others (at least until new guys come along to dethrone the champs).

The three main types of RAM architecture are:

✔ **SDRAM** (Synchronous Dynamic Random Access Memory): Wow, that's a mouthful. This RAM is the most widely used. It also goes by the name of PC100 RAM or PC133 RAM, which indicates the speed it runs at. A short while ago 133RAM was state of the art. Now it's just old news.

✔ **RDRAM** (RAMBUS Dynamic Random Access Memory): This is a patented type of RAM developed by Rambus Corporation and is supported by Intel much to some people's disagreement because of its cost. It's a completely incompatible scheme from SDRAM but is considered extremely fast. Due to the nature of the process involved in making this RAM, it's much pricier than SDRAM. It runs at much higher clock speeds but each cycle moves less overall memory data. The higher clock speed makes up the throughput, though, and this RAM is thus considered superior to SDRAM

✔ **DDR SDRAM** (Double-Datarate Random Access Memory): This is a variation of SDRAM that was supported by a number of other companies including VIA and AMD, the companies who pull a lot of weight in board and system design. It was developed in response to the need for faster RAM, which didn't force a company into the patent-laden royalty world of RDRAM. It's less expensive than RDRAM and it's also quite fast. Cheap and fast is good! You can find DDR RAM (it's shortened name) running at 233, 266, and 333MHz. The "DDR" technology effectively "doubles" the speed of this RAM because it can transfer twice the information during a regular cycle. If the RAM transfer speed is 133Mhz and you transfer twice during that time, your actual rate is about 266Mhz. Two for the price of one is always a good deal and you don't need one of these stupid supermarket cards to take advantage of this deal!

✔ **DDR II SDRAM**: This is the next generation of DDR RAM and promises even higher clock speeds and throughputs. It's expected in 2003 or 2004. It will be backwards compatible with DDR RAM in the sense that DDR RAM modules can be placed in sockets that also accept DDR II RAM. However, this doesn't mean you'll want to mix and match RAM chips. What it means is that you can entertain buying a DDR II RAM-compliant motherboard, and then replace you DDR RAM with DDR II RAM when you can afford to. Expect batches of DDR II RAM to eventually run at 533 MHz and hit throughput of 5.4Gb/s (Gigabits).

✔ **DDR III SDRAM**: This is the RAM that is expected to succeed the DDR II RAM in 2005.

So What's PC1066RAM, PC2100 RAM, and PC2700 RAM?

Bill Hicks the late great comedian once said, "If anyone in my audience tonight is in marketing I want you to kill yourselves." He then joked that the marketers in the audience were laughing and saying, "Oh that's an awesome joke, Bill's going for that anti-marketing market, that's a big market!" Hicks made this joke in anticipation of market labeling practices like PC1066RAM and PC2700 RAM.

Memory manufacturers have been using numbers to showcase the clock speed of their RAM (66, 100, 133) but now they've decided to use a different scheme: They are using numbers to refer to a memory modules' total throughput in Mb/sec (Megabits not bytes). Why did they do this? Because Rambus markets their memory on clock speed and Rambus memory runs at a much higher clock speed, although not necessarily at the same throughput. This is a bit of marketing "gobbligook" that we all have to adjust too. Aside from Rambus, who isn't doing this per-se, I'm assuming that most marketers will use the throughput number in marketing memory— although I bet Bill Hicks would think I was a fool and communist for saying that.

What about Latency?

As if all the marketing talk wasn't enough to confuse you about throughput, you also need to deal with latency when you buy memory. Latency, or as it's technically known *CAS Latency* (CAS stands for Column address strobe) is the measure of the ratio between column access time and clock cycle time. The lower the number the better. For a while, the CAS Latency was 3 (sometimes noted in shorthand as CL3) but now most high performance RAM is CL2 or better. Latency is a big deal in any technical situation so when overclocking RAM the most often first step is to force it to hit a lower latency number. Many well built CL3 rated memory modules can actually run at CL2 levels.

Picking the Right Memory Horse

Got all the basics of memory memorized? Now you're going to ask which memory you should use? Well, here's the bottom line: The faster the better but be realistic because even the top-of-the-line memory might not improve things by more than 5% to 10%. The price-performance gain of memory is a bit more skewed than processors because, as a rule of thumb, the faster it is the more wickedly expensive it gets. At the same time, various brands of memory are of a much higher quality and thus their actual throughput is better. Also, because memory can be overclocked, the better brands are better at being overclocked.

So if every ounce of speed is important to you, by all means buy the the top-of-the-line memory you can get. And when it comes to brand name memory Corsair (**www.corsairmemory.com**) is the company to deal with. Their Xtreme Memory Speed is the brand of choice for overclockers and monster PC makers. Other major brands such as Crucial, Kingston, VIA, and Micron are also really good. Try to stay away from the no-name brands. If there isn't a name on your memory modules, it's probably not worth sticking them in your machine.

Storage and Removable Storage

Games are like teenagers—they never seem to stop growing no matter what you feed them. Games now take up 200MB or more of space. And let's not even talk about the number of MP3 files I know you all have on your machines. So when it comes to hard drives, insanely bigger is not only better but a *must*. However, we also need speed.

The standard spec for most drives that gamers want is at least 80 to 100GB running at 7200 RPM. Caching capability is also a requirement. Some users and high-end game PC makers even build raid-arrays for their systems. A raid array consists of two or more harddrives of the same size and specs that are used in unison to deliver data faster to a system. They're not twice as fast but they are faster than a single drive. Raids are used in high-end servers but have found their way into some very high-end desktops. The big thing holding back most drives in terms of speed, other than the drive itself, is the speed of transfer due to the traditional cabling interfaces usd to connect the drive. Thankfully, the industry is heading toward a solution called Serial ATA that you'll want to be on the lookout for.

Serial ATA Drives

Serial ATA is like the "check in the mail" thing that you keep expecting to come at any time. Because it requires both changes at the motherboard level and different cabling scheme, it's adoption has been slowed down a little. The cabling, after all, is one of the important features of the Serial ATA technology; gone is the thick ribbon like cables (which advance system builders turn into specialized rounded cables). Taking its place is a thin cable that, while fast, is much more conducive to airflow in your system. Drives based on Serial ATA should be emerging by the time this book hits the shelves but it will take a good year or two before they become the defacto standard. The other important aspect of Serial ATA is that it has a much greater and quicker capacity to enable higher speeds of transfer.

Removable Storage

Do gamers need to care about removable storage? Um, yeah. If you expect to load a game you buy, make a custom MP3 CD, or a critical backup of your Windows system, you'll need some sort of read/write removable storage. For many years, the choices were floppies, Zip drives, CD-R/RWs, and tape backup devices. Today, however, the options have grown. Technologies such as DVD-RW are in widespread use. They allow us to not only burn CDs but also DVD videos.

 You need to realize that DVD+RW drives don't always create DVDs that work in all DVD drives. Over time, this should improve but unfortunately many of the cheaper and older players will have difficulty reading "user burned" DVDs. So if Grandma is getting a DVD so she can watch video of the kids you send on DVD, make sure the system she buys is compatible. Otherwise, you're going to need to pack up the station wagon (well, SUV) and pay her a visit.

What about floppies and Zip drives? I still use them. Floppies are handy to move a config file or "sneaker net" something to someone who doesn't have access to a network. I also recommend Zip drives because they are wicked cheap now. (Iomega recently released a Zip 750mb drive, which is a good buy.) I also love the little disk-on-key drives because they're great for saving games so that they can be moved between the office and home without gumming up (or getting caught using) office email. You can get disk-on-key USB drives from iomega.com, apple.com, and other places. A 16MB version is only $30. Another great storage extra is an MP3 player like the iPod because it is really a portable harddrive. Iomega and other companies also offer standalone Firewire hard drives, which are fast and easy.

So what lies ahead after DVD-RW? Eventually the laser technologies used to read and write CDs and DVDs will evolve from red lasers to vaunted blue laser technology. When this happens, we should begin to see new forms of optical media. All in time for game developers to find new ways to store gigantic games and take over the world.

Ports and Peripherals

A PC is a dumb box as far as the outside world is concerned. But when you connect that box to things that you can interact with, your box wakes up. That's where the myriad of ports come in. Some of these ports have been with us for a long, long time. Hell, parallel ports as a technology is older than many of you reading this book. Before the advent of USB we used to have to plug our joysticks into something called a *gameport* which we had to buy separately or hope it came with our soundcard. Ports are stubborn things in the world of hardware; they don't like to be upgraded. Companies that make ports are like the U.N; they love to argue over new ideas for eons it seems. Thankfully, we're finally getting some new ports that really improve things.

For any new PC you buy or upgrade, here are the ports you should consider to extend your machine:

✔ **USB 1 and USB 2**: USB 1 is the first iteration of Universal Serial Bus, a fast serial transfer method for PCs. These ports are now used for keyboards, mice, joysticks, wheels, and more. Most PCs include just two of these and they are usually located on the back. Any gamer in the world wants and needs more USB ports. Thus, we have to turn to USB hubs that expand the ports for us, not to mention putting them in a position where we can more rapidly plug stuff in and out. Many newer PCs, and certainly a lot of do it yourself PCs are integrating four or more USB ports into their machine placing one or more at the front of the machine where it's easy to plug in a gamepad or digital camera. The next iteration of USB is USB 2 and it increases the throughput of USB quite a bit. You should look for USB 2 to be pretty much standard by 2004.

✔ **Ethernet**: Today most Ethernet setups run at 100 Mb/second. It's also very cheap to integrate at the motherboard level. This saves you a PCI.

✔ **Firewire**: Also known as IEEE 1392, this is a super-fast alternative to USB and USB 2 that a lot of consumer electronics use. If you plan on getting a digital video camera, iPod, or some other major devices, this is a must have. Most PCs don't integrate Firewire into their systems or motherboards. You may have to give up a PCI slot for it but you can get an expansion card for less than $50. Soundblaster Audigy 2 cards include an integrated Firewire port so if you grab one of those you get Firewire to boot.

Other than these items, you'll need a parallel port for a while since not every printer is USB-specific yet. and don't forget when it comes to video cards look for it to have DCI outputs for digital LCD displays. Also, if possible NTSC out/svideo out as well since you might actually want to pop it on a TV or output it to videotape every now and then.

Gamepads, Wheels, Joysticks, Keyboards, and Mice

Until we get mind control readers we need something to tell our games what to do. No monster gaming system is complete without a top-of-the-line mouse for first-person-shooter games. You probably also need a gamepad or joystick of some sort and let's not forget your flight sim and driving game wackos. If you're a real gadget guy, you can spend hundreds to get the most accurate feel and response. Come on, admit it; you'd easily plunk down $400 or more to shave several seconds off your best laptime in Nascar Racing. Table 4.2 provides a summary of the major game input devices.

 No matter what device you purchase and use, make sure you also download the latest drivers for everything, and of course get USB devices. For mice, you'll also want the best surface. Many monster gamers swear by Func Industries mouse pads, which you can find at **www.func.net**.

Operating Systems

I've saved operating systems for the end because there isn't much of a choice to discuss. Windows is the gaming platform of choice for PC users. However we do want to pay homage to Linux and Mac OS X. Let's first pay our respects to two awesome operating systems that may yet play a role in your life as a gamer. First is Linux. As a server OS, Linux is the darling of admins everywhere. I'm a part-time admin myself and I run a Cobalt Linux appliance. I've had to reboot the thing twice in two years. All on the same day, and only because the patches I was applying required it. Contrast this with my Windows 2000 servers, which require me to reboot once a week as part of my basic maintenance.

Linux just keeps growing. It's like the Energizer Bunny. Many online gaming services use Linux clusters for the backend on their systems, and Linux even has some games unique to it as well. Some killer games, such as Quake, have even been ported to Linux. A company known as Transgaming (**www.transgaming.com**) is building technologies that make it easy to port PC games over to Linux. Because Linux makes provides such good server support, some multiplayer games actually release Linux programs for server purposes. One example is Linux Quake Server. If you want to run a great server for a game, or maybe even host a fan site or

TABLE 4.2
Gaming controllers for the perfect PC.

INPUT TYPE	COMMENTS
Keyboard	Microsoft's keyboards are really good and if you can learn to use their Natural Keyboard Pro you'll have a hard time going back to a regular keyboard. Microsoft is just rolling out Bluetooth compatible wireless keyboards. An alternative is Logitech, which makes a complete array of keyboards including several good cordless ones.
Gamepads	The best makers for PCs are Microsoft with its Sidewinder Series, Gravis (which is what I use), and Logitech. Logitech and Microsoft have cordless controllers but look for Bluetooth cordless devices at some point in the future.
Joysticks	The issue here is whether you want force-feedback or not. Force-feedback is fun but it can be distracting and it raises the price. Both Microsoft and Logitech make excellent controllers for both.
Steering Wheels	*Wired* Magazine did a great review of steering wheels and picked the Mad Catz Andretti brand as the best on the low-end, and Logitech the best for those wanting to spend a bit more. However, a lot of people prefer Thrustmaster's NASCAR line of wheels and Microsoft also makes a good wheel, although it usually doesn't get ranked as high Thrustmaster. For top-of-the-line treatment, rob a bank and get the Thomas Super Wheel with peddles which run $380 to $1,055. They are available at www.thomas-superwheel.com.
Mice	You have to go optical here and I'm a huge fan of Microsoft's optical mice. They're great devices and USB and cordless models are available. Bluetooth will likely offer one someday. Logitech also makes great mice and has a new model with a great base charging station for those of you wanting to go cordless. First-person-shooter fans would shoot me if I didn't mention the Boomslang mouse from Razerzone. This was a high-end mouse engineered for FPS games. Unfortunately the company hit the skids, although they're still managing to sell a few left over from their once higher-flying days at www.razerzone.com. Some people weren't fans but those who have one and love it are feverish in their support.
Flight Sticks	When it comes to Flight Sticks most people go with the Thrustmaster series. Thrustmaster has been making quality Flight Sticks for a long time winning numerous awards. CH Products is another venerable maker and offers some flight yoke-styled devices as well as sticks.

(CONTINUED)

TABLE 4.2 (CONTINUED)
Gaming controllers for the perfect PC.

Strategy Controllers	For the RTS fans out there, Microsoft offers its Game Commander product. I've not used it but it looks interesting since it provides fast capability to control units and other features of major RTS games. Another specialized controller for this market is Thrustmaster's Tactical Board, which is almost a mini-keyboard you can control with one hand and offers numerous presets and options. Both can also be used for other types of games.

---

community, do consider Linux. When it comes to selecting a Linux distribution, most end-users favor Mandrake's distribution while Red Hat is considered the most industrious.

As for the Mac OS, it's not a bad gaming platform. In fact Mac OS X is an awesome OS. If only more games were available. Still, with the help of Mac friendly game publishers like Aspyr (**www.asypr.com**), many of the top titles are becoming available for the Mac. The Mac actually has a small, but vibrant, indie-games community. It's certainly not the primary choice for any monster gamer but if you're a Mac user reading this book then owning a Mac doesn't preclude you from being a monster gamer, it just means you've got a few less games, on a very cool OS.

Now on to Windows. As much as we like to poke Microsoft in the ribs, they really are into games and they're trying really hard to give us a killer gaming experience. As an OS, Windows has its faults, but like a good spouse, you're married to Windows for better or for worse. On the plus side, Windows XP is a good upgrade of Windows and we're getting better and better versions of DirectX almost yearly enabling new features and effects for a new generation of Windows games. If you're still running an older flavor of Windows, however, you should upgrade, although, many people like me, prefer to hold out with Windows 2000 for as long as we can.

The next version of Windows is code-named Longhorn and it's going to make a huge difference to users. (I hope I don't sound like a Microsoft commercial!) Without getting into the details of what's expected to make Longhorn so cool, the big improvement is that the entire file-system acts like a database meaning it will be much faster, and much easier to sort, organize, and find files on your system. It will hopefully also be a bit faster, handle larger and larger drives, and more. Longhorn is expected sometime in 2004.

The Little Things

As I said in the beginning of this chapter, when evaluating parts for your own system, or a pre-built machine, don't skimp on the little things that can also make a big difference. These include:

✔ **Airflow and Cooling Design**: We'll talk a lot about heat in the next chapter but it is increasingly one of the primary concerns of high-end kick-ass PCs. Look for machines with good cooling design. Also look for motherboards that support multiple fans and smart airflow design.

✔ **Easy to Replace Components**: The overall design of a system should make it easy to remove casings, unscrew components, and add new cards. Many sites show you the inside of their machines and will boast about how easy it is. If you don't see this kind of stuff, ask, or check reviews to see how easy it is to stuff an extra hard drive or new soundcard. This includes removable hard drive cages, tooless thumbscrews (how many times have you stripped screws trying to under casings before PC makers got this problem?), and smart inner wiring.

✔ **Locking Panels**: Does the front panel (if it has one) allow you to lock it to secure it during LAN parties?

✔ **Strong Power Supply**: Good machines today need lots of power. Old 300W power supplies don't cut it like they used to. Make sure the rig has a good 400W power supply.

Cases

Don't settle for just another white box. Gamers want machines that show some style. All the big game PC makers are offering some cool custom cabinets and many have multiple colors. However, you also want to make sure the case you select has lots of space and assembly areas for drives and breakout boxes as well as multiple fan capabilities. If you're going to build your own PC, check out the sources I'll provide for cool cases in Chapter 5.

Buying a Pre-Built PC

When it comes to buying a game PC from a manufacturer there are three major game-specific companies, two major PC makers playing in the market, and a few of up-and-comers. The three major game-specific guys are Falcon Northwest, Voodoo Computers, and Alienware. The two major PC makers are Dell and Gateway who are increasingly targeting gamers with specific offerings. The up-and-comers include CyberPowerPC, IBuyPower, and Vicious PC.

Falcon Northwest
www.falcon-nw.com

Falcon is probably the elder statesmen of the monster gaming PC vendors. Its systems have won rave reviews from much of the technical press. Falcon puts lots of attention into the details of their rigs. A great example of this ethic is their reasoning for not putting custom fan covers on their machines:

> "Laser cut logos on the grills of air-intake fans are getting a lot of press these days. Why not? They look sexy and PC makers can boost their ego by making their fan grill into their company logo. The truth is few company logos were designed with good airflow in mind. That snazzy grill will limit airflow and cause turbulence over the fan blades behind it, which increases noise. The standard thin wire grill is the standard for a reason: it'll keep you from cutting your fingers and provides maximum airflow, which is the whole point of the fan in the first place."

Falcon offers two distinct lines of PCs: the Talon line is its budget minded line while the Mach V is its top-of-the-line fighter jet. To help compete with the snazzier cases of other vendors, Falcon recently introduced its Exotix line of custom case paint jobs. For $400 (maybe less someday!), Falcon will do a custom metallic paint job on your case that will really make it standout. Figure 4.3 provides an example of just such a case. Also note that Falcon is the only one of the top tier makers offering both Pentium and AMD Athlon systems.

Alienware
www.alienware.com

Like Falcon, Alienware is known for making great systems. But it also stands out for its slick marketing with their custom colors. Alienware also makes a laptop system for gamers and recently introduced a compact media center PC that is designed for people who want to put a PC in their living room to surf the Web, play games, capture video (like a TiVo), and play MP3 files. Alienware's main line of high-end gaming PCs are known as the Area 51 brand but it has a few lower-end lines to play to more price-conscious shoppers. Their machines and customer service get good reviews and while they started out small they arguably are the biggest company in the specialized game PC business.

Voodoo
www.voodoopc.com

Alongside Alienware and Falcon Northwest, Voodoo is the third of a trio of top-tier gaming PC makers. Voodoo makes three main classes of computers. It's F Class

FIGURE 4.3
Falcons custom painted casings.

is the top-of-line brand followed by its E-Class and then it's lower-end C Class. It's M Class is a series of gamer-focused laptops similar to Alienware's offerings.

Like Falcon Voodoo will customize the paint job on your system but also does the keybaord, and monitor although this is more of a color-scheme offer vs. the more extensive custom paint jobs Falcon offers.

Which One Is for You?

In many ways you can't go wrong with either Falcon, Alienware, or Voodoo Computers. All routinely get rave reviews and all have their own fans. Most of the reviews I've seen over the years for all these systems (and some of the up-and-comers) usually don't declare a hands-down winner. My advice is to visit each company's Web site, configure the machine you want (or can afford), and see which one has the best components and prices. In terms of specialized PCs from any of these vendors, the compact Media PC from Alienware is a very interesting design. It's what is being called a Windows Media PC for the living room. Alienware's laptops are also interesting for people who want to game-on-the-go, although there are mainstream laptop alternatives to consider as well.

Moving to the tier below you will want to consider Dell or Gateway. Both companies make great machines, and their pricing will be a differentiation point from the custom jobs like Falcon. However, as great as these machines are, they're not special pieces of hardware. But if you're on a budget and want a great deal, it's worth pricing and evaluating these players. As the biggest guys on the block, they get such an economy of scale on parts that they can help save you money.

And finally we come to the up-and-comers. Remember today's promising rookie is potentially tomorrow's franchise player. Among the up and comers, Vicious seems to be making a run at the super sleek high-quality construction end that Alienware, Voodoo, and Falcon occupy. Reviews of their systems have been solid. Cyberpower PC is a good company for those of us who want lots of choices for components and really low pricing. The quality of their machines is good. Their tech support is a bit mid-level but I do my own tech support anyway. If price is your biggest issue, I totally recommend giving them a look. iBuyPower has gotten decent reviews but so far they seem to be settling in somewhere between the upper-tier and CyberPower's low-cost approach.

Popping Pills

Honestly, after going through all this I'm popping back a few aspirin. It's mind-boggling how much there is to know. If you're a major gear-head you probably already realize many minutia I left out like how HyperThreading is in old Pentiums but they never turned it on until the first 3GHz Pentium IV. You could write an entire book on this stuff. I'll save that for the next guy.

Still we've covered everything possible you really need to know except how to build it all yourself into a killer gaming pimp-rig. That's the next chapter. So if you feel like I do after learning all this stuff, take two aspirin and read Chapter 5 in the morning.

chapter **5**

BUILDING, MODDING, AND ENHANCING YOUR OWN GAME HARDWARE

I'd be a fool if I thought that I could show you step-by-step how to completely build and mod your own PC from start to finish in this chapter. Instead, this chapter will serve as a "do-it-yourself roadmap to modding." Often the hardest thing about doing something yourself is finding the right stuff and getting the right start. When it comes to the black art of building a PC and then doing various mods to soup it up so it's the pimp-daddiest rig at all the LAN parties, the hard part is knowing where to start. In Chapter 4 I covered the big tech decisions. In this chapter we'll focus on finding ways to assemble all of the components we discussed in Chapter 4. We'll also look at how you can upgrade an existing machine. Then for the daring among us, we'll explore a series of mods to our machines to make them really scream and standout.

What Sorts of Mods Can You Make?

We first should discuss the types of mods that can be performed on a machine. Mods fall into several categories, each with a few subcategories.

Overclocking Mods

Overclocking is the practice of forcing various components into modes where they run faster either by resetting jumpers on the equipment or changing BIOS configurations. Your basic components including CPUs, memory, and graphics cards all ship with a standard speed (i.e., MHz, GHz, and so on). The manufacturers usually dial the speed back a bit to give the component some headroom. At higher speeds the component might fail and manufacturers don't want lots of angry people calling them saying their CPU just died. Monster PC owners for years have figured out how to juice up the clockspeed on these components to wring extra performance out of their system at no added cost.

A Warning About Overclocking

This is the first of many warnings about overclocking: *When you overclock something you're basically playing a game of Russian Roulette.* The component could fail which at best means you dial-it-back again and lament the fact you can't overclock it. A less optimistic scenario would be that you could burn it out. At worst you could fry your machine and really screw things up. I don't care how many people say overclocking is safe. That's like the guy who jumps of a bridge ahead of you and says it's safe. Sure it's safe because he didn't crack his head open on the rock just to the left of him that both of you still don't know is there!

Although we'll discuss overclocking in this chapter, and I'll even show you where to go to learn more about it; please understand that overclocking is becoming less of a good idea. Why? As newer components debut they become denser, faster, but also hotter, and even more sensitive to overclocking. The result is that the risk-reward ratio for overclocking is just not as good as it used to be.

Case Mods

These mods involve changing your PC case design to incorporate see-through panels, neon lights, extra fans for cooling, LCD panels for extra displays, and other cool effects. You can even add a coffee maker, or other crazy stuff (see Figure 5.1). What people are doing with case mods today can best be described as a form of art. Some of the wilder designs are pretty impressive.

Cable Mods

Cable mods represent a good example of the state of modern day PC modding. To improve the airflow of their systems at one point, modders devised a way of slicing the IDE ribbon cables used to transfer data from the hard drive to the system. This allowed their cables to be wrapped into a round cable. This was

.:to assemble--The Caffeine Machine:

Caffeine Machine

Final hardware configuration:

- Abit VP6 motherboard with dual 1.0GHz Pentium 3 processors
- 1 GB of PC133 SDRAM
- GeForce 256
- 1x20GB Maxtor boot drive plus 2x40GB Maxtor storage drives in RAID 1, all hot-swappable
- CD-ROM, Sound, & Network

FIGURE 5.1
Nick Pelis wanted coffee with his machine, probably so that he could stay awake longer during marathon sessions of Battlefield 1942 (as seen on Pimprig.com).

often a laborious process involving Xacto knives, a cutting board, and electrical tape. Today, you can actually buy pre-built drive cables. They are much more expensive than doing it yourself but it's nice to know that there are now "off-the-shelf" components for modders. It's also worth noting that as serial ATA begins to take hold in the future, cable mods may become somewhat obsolete.

OS Tweaks

In addition to hardware, you can also perform OS mods. At the end of this chapter we'll discuss how to tweak Windows XP (and maybe a few older flavors) so it runs fast, looks great, and stays that way. Another key OS tweak is multi-booting, which allows you to have multiple operating systems on a single machine. This is very useful for those of you who want Linux and Windows capability off the same box. Some gamers might even stick an old copy of DOS/Windows on a machine to play old games that no longer run under Windows XP.

Knowledge Reigns Supreme

To build your own PC you'll need to really educate yourself. If you've never done this before it's not terribly difficult to do but you can't do it without some basic knowledge, and you can't build a killer-rig without some specialized knowledge of the basic components. I covered many of the components in Chapter 4. What we haven't covered is the knowledge needed on how to assemble all those various components into a self-built PC. There are several places you can go to acquire the knowledge you'll need and I'll try to be as specific about them as possible:

✔ **Books:** Excellent books are available on building and repairing PCs. Unfortunately, not all of these books are up to date. They are also not necessarily focused on helping you wring the last ounce of performance from your machine or perform cool mods.. The sister book to this one, *Monster PCs*, is focused on some of the latest and greatest performance issues, and is especially focused on modding. Table 5.1 lists several top titles you might want to get.

✔ **Web sites:** Although you can find a ton of PC sites, the problem with many of them is that the information provided is not clearly written. Thus, you should be careful to thoroughly read many sites, and don't just follow the first tutorial you see. Look for multiple recommendations and definitely turn to books and magazines to support what you find on the Web.

✔ **Magazines:** There are a few magazines worth reading including *Maximum PC* and *PC Upgrade*. Many of the big game magazines also run tech columns that can be useful. These columns are usually a bit on the short side but they often provide high quality professional photos that can help shed better light on a particular building, upgrading, or modding topic.

TABLE 5.1
Three good books to have as you build and mod your PC.

BOOK	AUTHOR(S)	COMMENTS
Upgrading and Repairing PCs (14th Edition) ISBN 0789727455	Scott Mueller	When you've had 14 editions printed it means your book is really good. This is the major book on the basic topic of PC architecture. It's not a modders guide but it provides a very fundamental look at core PC building and upgrading.
PC Hardware in a Nutshell ISBN 0596003536	Robert Bruce Thompson & Barbara Fritchman Thompson	While Mueller's book is considered a bible, this book is considered a smaller, more opinionated compliment to that title.
The Extreme Gamer's PC ISBN 0072226374	Loyd Case	This is not the first book I'd buy on building a gaming PC. I'd get the other two first and supplement them with the latest from the Web and the resources I've mentioned, as well as this book.

✔ **LAN Parties:** LAN parties are great places to find people who've built and modded their PCs. If you haven't been to one go and you'll learn a lot. Look for people who are willing to share their experience. Just don't pepper them with questions while they're trying to lay the smack down on someone in the finals of a Quake III tournament.

✔ **Newsgroups and Forums:** If I had a penny for each time I read some moronic or totally biased comment about tech advice on a newsgroup or Web forum, I'd be living next door to Bill Gates. The problem is that the signal-to-noise ratio is really high. That being said I often find myself trolling newsgroups using Google's search engine (groups.google.com) and various Web-based forums for help. Here are some tips that can help you separate the wheat from the chaff:

1. **Don't stop until you find the Golden Goose.**
   Keep searching until you find a post where the person really knows what he or she is talking about. Look for a post that is complete, makes sense, and even provides links or other corroboration.

2. **Don't listen to abject opinion.**
   I hate these kinds of posts and unfortunately the Web is full of them. I do however, love posts where the user provides good context for their opinion, such as "You can overclock Corsair memory, because it's so well built as compared to others that I have tried."

3. **Use the "complete" thread capability on Google.**
   By clicking the complete thread link on any Google newsgroup search result, you can read the entire thread of conversation. Often you'll find that information makes more sense when you get the complete context.

4. **Search smart.**
   Take the fifteen minutes required to read Google's documentation and learn to write search strings that can help you find good posts (or good sites for that matter). A killer search string looks something like:

   "case mod" lights -fan

   The advanced searching feature offers additional components you can use as well and I highly recommend them.

Building Your Own PC

There are many people today who tinker with PCs in their garages, dens, and bedrooms. Many of these people are monster gamers, although the community of PC modders includes many enthusiasts who do it just for the fun of creating cool

PCs. At this point I'm making two assumptions: You've read Chapter 4 and you have a clue about the basics of building PCs. To get you on the road, I'll present the tools, techniques, and knowledge that can help you build PCs.

Tools You'll Need

Having a good toolkit is important for anyone building or modding a PC. But don't think you can visit the garage and just grab tools that are lying around. You'll need some specialized tools including:

- ✔ **Safety Glasses:** Contrary to popular belief, a pair of Raybans aren't safety glasses. Don't try to look cool. Just get a pair of goggles or wraparound glasses.

- ✔ **Cordless Drill:** Get a corded one if you want but cordless is better.

- ✔ **Dremel Multipro:** The Dremel Multipro tool is the one tool that you really need to be a serious modder. A tool like this will set you back a little less than $100.

- ✔ **Metal Cutting Jigsaw:** A jigsaw may also be needed for some jobs. Most good jigsaws are rated for metal up to 3/8" at a 90-degree angle. Be sure your jigsaw includes metal cutting blades. A good one will go for $100 to $200.

- ✔ **Metal Cutting Snippers:** This is a low cost alternative to a jigsaw but isn't always as effective.

- ✔ **Screwdriver Set:** Get a good screwdriver set from Dewalt or Black & Decker that has interchangeable heads, including socket heads you can use on some screws that might end up with their heads stripped.

- ✔ **File:** Your Dremel should help you sand down case holes and such but an extra file or some 200-grit sandpaper can be useful.

- ✔ **Electrical Wire Cutters and Pliers:** A good pair of small snippers are good for cutting electrical wires or those strong plastic cable ties many systems use.

- ✔ **Soldering Iron:** This tool isn't required for most mods, but it may be necessary for some mods. Only buy it if you come across a mod that requires it.

- ✔ **Xacto Knife:** A good razor blade knife is essential for some mods like rolling your own I/O cables.

- ✔ **Needle Nose Pliers:** You'll need a pair of these pliers for those times when your fingernails aren't long enough or strong enough.

- ✔ **Rulers and Squares:** Don't get just a yardstick from the local lumberyard. Go and get a really nice metal ruler with centimeters and inches. Get a T-square and also some triangles so you can properly measure twice.

✔ **Lubricant:** Ask your local hardware store for some metal cutting lubricant to use on your drill and any saws that you may be using.

✔ **Sharpie:** Aside from a pencil or two, grab a Sharpie pen. They are great pens and make nice thick lines that you can follow with your Dremel or saw.

✔ **Plastic Ties:** Once you untie everything, you'll eventually need to tie it all back up.

✔ **Masking Tape:** I hope I don't need to explain this one for you!

The Build Order for Creating Your Own PC

When building any PC, there is a process you should follow. Let's explore the steps involved before we move on to PC mods:

1. Assemble your components and tools and organize your workspace.

A good PC is the result of a patient builder having the right space and tools. Getting a good clean work area is critical. Make sure you have good lighting and even consider using a pen light, and one of those simple positional flood lamps. It's also good practice to have everything you're going to put in your PC available before you begin building.

2. Inspect and populate the motherboard.

Start with a thorough inspection of your motherboard to make sure it's in good shape and nothing is broken or messed up. Look for cracks, broken pins, or components that aren't well seated. Populating the motherboard includes putting in the CPU and memory, and setting various jumpers or other cabling. Make sure you read the instructions (good or bad) that came with the motherboard. These instructions usually explain various jumper settings you might need to make in conjunction with any components you populate the motherboard with. Take your time here as this is one of the more crucial steps in building your own PC.

3. Install hard drives and removable storage.

When I'm installing a hard drive and other storage in a case it's easier if you can move the case around on its side and risk dropping the odd tool or screw. This is why I install the hard drive and other components for the drive bay before I install the motherboard on a new PC. Installing these items is pretty straightforward, you will want to line up the drives in the bays you've selected and then screw them into place. Make sure that you've selected the correct jumper or dipswitch settings to indicate if the drive will be the master drive for the system or the slave drive. This setting should be found in the documentation for your drives. The setting might even be stickered right on the drive. Most drives ship pre-configured as master drives.

4. Get the motherboard into the case.

Once your motherboard is ready for action you'll want to get it into the case, which is often easier said then done. You'll want to examine not only how the motherboard mounts to the case but also how the various power, fan, LED, and other cables connect to it. You must line up the holes in the case to the holes on the motherboard. ATX standard cases should have a number of holes that have the letter A (among others) next to them. These should properly correspond to the holes on your motherboard. Various "standoff" connectors are used that are usually made of plastic or brass, both of which are used to help ground the board. You'll first put these into place in the case, and then snap the motherboard over them. Most plastic standoffs are complete once you snap the motherboard onto them while the brass ones have a head to screw on to secure the board.

5. Install expansion cards including video and sound.

Once you get the drives and motherboard set up, you'll want to put in your various expansion cards. You'll likely start with your AGP capable graphics card. Each card will fit in a slot and sometimes it takes a few tries to get it in the slot properly. Take your time here and gently ratchet up the pressure until it goes in cleanly. You might also inspect the card before doing so. Newer graphics cards require sufficient cooling. Consider two things when dealing with these cards. First, if your system has a mounted fan (or you're adding one), make sure you get the power cabling for the fan to its proper destination. Second, place any other cards in the box as far away from the video card as possible depending on your setup in an effort to improve airflow.

6. Hook up power.

You may have already hooked up the internal power cabling. Some of you may have also decided to test the power to the motherboard once it was installed and populated—a good idea. However, now that you've got most of your PC enabled, it's time to truly test the power. Start by rechecking all of your connections including all power supplies, fan, drive cabling, expansion cards, and chips. Connect a monitor and let the power flow. Hopefully, all goes well!

If your motherboard beeps a bunch, no you don't have mail, you've got problems. Every BIOS is different so you need to refer to the manual that came with your motherboard. You can also check the BIOS manufacturer's Web page to decode the beeping structure. You can also check out **www.bioscentral.com**, which has a big databank of BIOS codes and helpful forums. Beeps can indicate poorly installed memory, bad BIOS ROMS, and other problems. If you don't hear any beeps but your display is blank, you've got a power problem. Some beeps are normal and if your display works that should help indicate you're booting up normally.

7. Boot and configure the BIOS.

Since you don't have an OS on the hard drive (unless you put in a boot floppy), your system won't boot up. In fact you'll probably need to configure the BIOS now anyway. At this point you'll want to refer to your BIOS manual. These manuals aren't very detailed so a trip to a Web site or two may be needed. As part of setting the BIOS, you'll need the hard drive specs for your system's drives. Most drives include this information on a sticker on the drive itself or at least in the manual. If you're SOL, do a search on the manufacturer's site and you should be able to find what you need.

Two potential resources for people with higher-order BIOS issues are The BIOS Companion book available in ebook format at **www.electrocution.com/biosc.htm** and Wims Bios site located at **www.wimsbios.com**. This site is considered to be one of the best BIOS help and resource sites on the Web.

8. Format the drives and install your OS(s).

It's now time to actually make your new rig do something. This means formatting the hard drive and installing the basic OS, which in this case will probably be Windows XP Home or Pro. If you're going to set up a multi-boot system, you'll want to read up on this first so you can install your operating systems in the best order. To format your drive, you should get a DOS utility. You don't necessarily need to perform a low-level format of your drive. You shouldn't need to do that but if you do, you should always use the software that comes from the manufacturer. Doing an incorrect low-level format can seriously harm the drive.

A regular format is accomplished with basic DOS fdisk and format programs. You may also want to check out Partition Magic—a program from PowerQuest (**www.powerquest.com**). This program performs a much more robust format for creating hard drive partitions.

9. Optimize the OS and create a backup image.

Once your OS is running, you'll want to start surfing the Web and installing all sorts of games and other programs. Wait! The best thing you can do at this juncture is to tweak the OS as much as possible and then create a backup image. This will make it much easier to do clean installs in the future after you've "gunked" it up so much through constant use and tons of software installations.

Tweaking the OS involves going to windowsupdate.microsoft.com and installing any patches and other fixes this site recommends. Then you might uninstall any

Windows components you don't necessarily want, set you screen settings, sound settings, and so on. You can also install a few basic utilities like additional sound software for your Soundblaster Audigy card and updated drivers for your graphics cards. I'd then do one super quick disk optimization. Finally, you'll want to use an imaging program that creates a special style of backup of your hard drive. Norton Ghost is a favorite for this process.

10. Run benchmark tests.

Once your system is set up, the final thing to do is run some benchmarks and see what sort of throughput you're getting. 3Dmark is a good benchmark program for graphics and there are some other benchmarking programs and diagnostic utilities I'll mention a bit later. Assuming you're satisfied with the results, you're ready to start installing and playing some games.

Modding Your PC

In this section, I'm going to cover some of the more basic big picture issues you need to think about when building your own monster gaming PC. I'll introduce each of the major modding techniques and explain, as best I can, what the mods are, how they're accomplished, and then I'll list a few good Web sites that provide tutorials where you can learn more. To get started, I'll present two sets of resources you'll find helpful: great PC modding fan sites (Table 5.2) and the biggest retailers of mod equipment and kits (Table 5.3).

I can't chase down every review of these resellers so I definitely suggest you check out **www.resellerratings.com**, **www.bizrate.com**, and **www.Pricegrabber.com** as good sources of information on store service and reviews. Anandtech (**www.anandtech.com/ratings**) and Tom's Hardware (**www.tomshardware.com**) also provide a ratings service.

High Charged PC Issues

We've covered the basics on how to build a vanilla PC. But when it comes to building a high-powered modern-day system there are some bigger issues we need to cover. Otherwise you could be up a creek without a paddle. The three big issues that come into play when creating your own turbo charged pimped out gaming rig include heat, airflow, and noise. They're all closely related as you'll learn next.

Heat

Newer components such as the latest graphics chips and the fastest CPUs create lots of heat. If components overheat, your system will begin to falter or worse—

TABLE 5.2
Major PC modding, overclocking, and tweaking sites.

Site Name	URL	Site Name	URL
[H]ardOCP	www.hardocp.com	Modders.Net	www.modders.net
Club Overclocker	www.cluboverclocker.com	Moddin.Net	www.moddin.net
		OC Addiction	www.ocaddiction.com
Gideon Tech	www.gideontech.com	Overclockers Online	www.overclockersonline.com
Got Apex	www.gotapex.com	PimpRig	www.pimprig.com
Gruntville	www.gruntville.com	Tweak3D	www.tweak3d.com
Mod Fathers	www.themodfathers.com	Twisted Mods	www.twistedmods.com
Mod the Box	www.modthebox.com	The Virtual Hideout	www.virtual-hideout.net

TABLE 5.3
Major PC mod supply stores.

Store Name	URL	Comments
PC Mods.com	www.pcmods.com	Provides easy to shop interface, top components, and good information. This site gets good reviews.
Directron	www.directron.com	Features large selection of products, however, reviews are a bit mixed on their service. Lots of on-site content worth reading too.
Case-mod.com	www.case-mod.com	Provides good selection and gets decent reviews.
Voyuer Mods	www.voyeurmods.com	This site is a little harder to navigate than others. The selection is decent. The store gets high marks from reseller ratings.
Crazy PC	www.crazypc.com	Features lots of stuff for sale and good reviews.
OverClock UK	www.over-clock.co.uk	One of the highest rated UK stores with a great site and good selection.
Kustom PCs	www.kustompcs.co.uk	Another good UK site with good selection and reviews.
Xoxide	www.xoxide.com	Great site, good selection, but gets faulted in reviews a bit for showing stuff in-stock that isn't, so beware.

components could fail and become defective. To combat heat, PC developers utilize fans and airflow to bring in cooler air and pump out hotter air. Most PCs we've all used provide only a single fan mounted at the back of the case. Today's bigger rigs include heatsinks, multiple fans, and even water cooling systems.

Airflow

Airflow is a design and power issue. From a design standpoint, good airflow can be enhanced through the use of rounded cables, positioning of components, vents, and the use of one or more fans.

Noise

The more heat you create in your system, the more fans you'll need to combat it. Unfortunately, the more fans you have, the more noise you'll create. To combat this, modders try to use the quietest fans and noise reduction matting. They also utilize a system that doesn't require all of the fans to be running all of the time. I run my PC 24x7. After many weeks of running it I had to shut it down the other day to do some electrical work in my home office. When I shut the machine off I realized how much quieter the room became. I could actually hear myself think for once. This convinced me that fans really suck.

Getting the Right Balance

The goal with handling heat, airflow, and noise is to contain these factors without compromising your power goals. The best way to do this is twofold. First, evaluate how much power you need. The less computing power you need, the less heat you'll generate and the fewer fans you'll need. Secondly, resign yourself to building a state of the art heat control system, which I'll describe later.

Case Mods

Case mods are the most widely performed PC mods. Aside from a few cable mods, fan mods, and tweaks, the majority of your time will be spent modding your case so that your system can look cool and project your wacky personality.

Adding Windows

This mod involves adding one or more windows to the side of your case. You can get windowing kits from various suppliers. Some come pre-cut in the shape you want (squares, circles, ovals, and so on). Others require you to cut the material yourself. You can even buy some pre-cut panels, but you'll need to find panels compatible with various standard cases.

You can cut your own windows with a Dremel tool. The basic procedure is to cut the hole you need after tracing the outline of it on your case. Once you've cut the hole, you place molding along the edge and attach the window on the inside of the case. Good kits will come with much of the material pre-cut. Some kits include etching materials as well. Windows usually attach with heavy-duty stick tape but you can you can also use stronger bonding glues.

While most window mods involve side view panels, you can also purchase kits for top view windows. For these kits, you'll need to decide if you need one with or without a fan opening. Some modders go for the entire glass house look. You can buy clear PC cases from Clearpc.ca and Xoxide, which sells the Xclear case at **www.xoxide.com/clearacatxca.html**. Be warned, however, because TechTV reviewed both cases and they take some work although they are fun to build. The cases run from $100 to $200.

Window Etchings and Stickers

Three types of window etchings are used by PC modders. The most common are stickers or appliques. These are decals (custom or pre-made) that you apply to a plain old case window. Installation is simple in concept but not as simple in practice. You can find a good overview of the process at **www.gideontech.com/guides/etch**. Basically you order a custom or pre-made etching from a good supplier such as PC Mods and then you place and squeegee the etching on the back of the case. The good thing about this process is that you can remove it and clean the window later if you want to change it.

Higher-end etchings involve laser etching the window itself. This is permanent but it produces a higher-quality effect. Some venders offer pre-made ones and others will do custom jobs. You'll want to do this to the acrylic window before you install it. The final type of etching involves sandblasting the window itself. This was done early on in the mod movement.

Case Badges

Case badges are sort of like stickers for geeks. They're small domed stickers you can apply to your PC to display a message. These badges started when companies like Intel would pay companies to put an "Intel Inside" sticker, decal, or badge on their PCs to build brand awareness. In the PC modding scene badges are used for much more than "Intel Inside." There are entire sets of badges for game lovers (CounterStrike and Half-Life logo), badges for cards like NVIDIA or processors like Athlon, and non-branded items like a Jolly Roger or funny parodies like "Evil Inside." You can even buy kits to make your own "stinkin" badges (**www.razgavor.com/ezdome.htm**) or find places on the Web to order custom badges for your CPU, keyboard, or monitor based on your submitted artwork (**www.securisysagency.com/case_badges_custom.html**). Table 5.4 provides you with a few places to find badges that will appeal to monster gamers.

TABLE 5.4
Places to get some "stinkin" badges.

Store Name	URL
Directron	www.directron.com/gamebadges.html
Crazy PC	www.crazypc.com/products/casemods/casebadges.htm
ThinkGeek	www.thinkgeek.com/cubegoodies/stickers/5b43
CaseArts	www.casearts.com/game1.html
PC Decals	www.pcdecals.com
Kool PC Mods(backlit badges)	www.koolpcmods.com/lightbadge.htm
Kool PC Mods(aluminum badges)	www.koolpcmods.com/aluminumbadge.htm
Kool PC Mods(custom aluminum badges)	www.koolpcmods.com/custom.htm

Another cool decal/sticker thing you can find are port identification labels. A few sites that sell those include Name That Computer (**www.namethatcomputer. com/portID.htm**) and Securisys Agency (**www.securisysagency.com/cable_ port_labels.html**).

Case Lighting

Case lighting involves several types of effects and kits. The most common lighting used is *electroluminescent lighting* or *cold-cathode ray lighting*. These give off little noise or heat like neon does. Electroluminescent lighting is available from **www.PCMods.com**. It is very bendable and modders will buy six foot chunks or larger of it and use it on the inside of their case in some way. You can also get tape version as well making it easy to mount. Various colors (red, green, blue, and so on) are available.

Cold-cathode ray lighting is brighter but not as flexible as electroluminescent. It also has a larger power demand. Various colors are available and some companies have started selling tubes that mix several colors together (see **www.pcrange.biz/ index.php?page=p_tricck&id=1**).

You can also get lighted fans and tiny LED lighting mods that you can squeeze into other areas of your case such as by the floppy drive for interesting effects. Some lighting kits even include a sonic hookup that makes the light pulsate based on audio coming from your PC.

Most kits are fairly easy to install. In the case of CCR tubes, you'll need to mount some brackets in a spot, which requires drilling some holes. Good kits should include templates to help. The big thing to remember is that the power has to be inverted (through a power inverter) to make the lights work. In some cases that's a fairly important and bigger piece of the kit. Inverters can also get warm or at least warmer then the light itself so many people recommend mounting it near an exhaust fan and as far from sensitive components as possible. Inverters can also generate noise. When reading reviews take note of the noise factor.

Another key issue with the inverters is the risk of shock. Good lighting kits work to minimize the shock risk by better shielding the inverters. Be sure to ground yourself and read the manual to avoid getting a shock.

 For lighting that uses adhesive to stick to the case, one cool tip is to first heat the adhesive with a hairdryer. That makes the gum gooier and gives it a better chance to bind to the case.

When it comes to lighting, most people go for EL tape mods. Tweakmonster.com is considered to be one of the best sources for EL tape. Not only is its REV3 Light-strip product well reviewed but their site has some good tutorials and docs to help you. Check out **www.tweakmonster.com/articles/lightstripmods/index.htm** and **www.tweakmonster.com/lightstrips/index.htm** for more information.

Painting the Case

Who wants a boring case? While you can get all sorts of fancy cases, some people opt to get a case, sandblast it down, and then paint it themselves. This can be a really cool mod to separate you from the pack. It can also be a lot of work. If you're not dedicated to doing it well, it's not going to look that good. PC-Workshop.Net has some good painting tutorials worth checking out. You're going to need a lot of stuff to do it right including a sander and several grades of paper, polish, primer, terrycloth, and other supplies.

The basic process involves lots of sanding, priming, and then more sanding and priming, and eventually polishing. (Are you tired yet?) Some people only paint the outside, but others will paint the entire case and even give it two tones. Some places like Directron will even take submitted artwork and custom airbrush it onto your case (**shop.store.yahoo.com/directron/artwork.html**). Their pricing seems a bit low so I'm not sure how great their work is. One vender that has done some incredible custom case painting is Computers Divine (**www.computersdivine.com**). Custom jobs start at $100.

LCD/VFD Panels

Another cool mod is to add a LCD display panel to your PC. This panel can then be programmed and used for lots of things like displaying the internal temperature of your rig. Some modders are into displaying other system stats, showing what

SHOUTcast station they are tuned into, and how many frags they have racked up. This is a area where you can really let your creativity run wild. There are two types of displays you can use: LCD and VFD. For each type, you can find ones that can be mounted externally to a system, monitor, or keyboard and ones that are mounted in drive bays.

The two most popular manufacturers are Matrix Orbital (**www.matrixorbital.com**), which you can order from directly as well as find in several of the major modding resellers on the Web and Powertip, a manufacturer from Taiwan that makes some large screen VFDs and LCD displays. Two other good sources are CrystalFontz (**www.crystalfontz.com**), which sells direct and Korean-based Virtual Lab System (**www.vlsys.co.kr/en**), which sells very easy to install LED systems through a variety of Web retailers. Seetro (**www.seetron.com**) is a source of serial based LCD displays.

The LCD Online Store is a great source for hundreds of different LCD parts. The problem is that the store wasn't designed for people who don't have a clue of which specific model they're looking for. Once you've figured out what you want though, check out **www.azo-store.com**. Other good stores are Mod Warehouse.com (based in Europe) and EIO.com (**www.eio.com/lcdprodt.htm**).

Most LCDs are sold separately from their connection kits. You'll thus need a packaged product or a separately purchased connection kit. You can also buy kits that don't require soldering. Otherwise, be prepared to work harder as you hook up the cabling required to make it work. If you haven't done this type of work before, I'd recommend getting a pre-wired kit from a vender like Mod Warehouse.

Most LCDs hook up directly to the parallel port of your PC. You can also find hardware and software to drive your LCD display through a serial or USB port. In any of these cases, you'll need to snake the cable back through your machine and then outside of it to connect it to your parallel port. (Thankfully we don't need this thing anymore with USB printers.). You can also mount it externally.

For software to run your LCD, there is much to choose from. Some manufacturers will offer their own (such as CrystalFontz) or will include a licensed copy of third-party software. The best independent packages for Windows are described in Table 5.5.

Many LCD displays are used to report back various motherboard supplied information. To do that, though, you need a motherboard-monitoring program. The mother-of-all-motherboard-monitoring software is Motherboard Monitor, which can be found at

TABLE 5.5.
The major LCD software packages used to run LCD display panels.

PROGRAM	SOURCE	COMMENTS
LCDriver	Lcdriver.pointofnoreturn.org	The low-level driver which can be programmed in a variety of languages. You can create your own custom solutions.
LCDC	www.lcdc.cc	Shareware package that is considered one of the best.
PowerLCD	www.powerlcd.com	Very fancy but only works with a few of the higher end displays.
LCD Max	www.lcdmax.de/index_en.htm	Package from Germany.
LCD Center	www.borderfield.com	Provides lots of features and works with LCDriver.

(mbm.livewiredev.com). It's very extensive and works with a number of programs to display information either in your system tray or on other external displays.

Airflow Design

Earlier I mentioned that heat and airflow are critical issues with advanced PCs. Fortunately, a number of common mods exist to improve airflow and cooling in PCs. These include routing of cables to increase airflow, adding extra fans, using water cooling, and more. As an advanced PC builder, you should be familiar with the following products, and mods:

Fan Mods

Basic fan mods include adding additional fans to your system, increasing their size and speed for increased airflow, and placing them directly on various components, or positioning them in other areas than the back, such as the front, top (blowhole), or sides. Since fans also create noise there are fans and mods for fans that involve quieting them down. Some systems even use fancy external or software based controllers that adjust fan speeds based on internal temperature readings. On the cosmetic level, some people add fancy grill plates to their fan exhaust hole, as well as LEDs for a lighted effect.

Types of Fans for Purchase

If *The Graduate* was filmed today I think McGuire would have said, "Are you Listening? ...fans..." In today's souped-up PCs, fans are everywhere. Fans come in many sizes ranging from 40mm to 120mm. They also come with different RPM settings and noise levels. The most common are 80mm fans. At this size you will find the most variety of features such as lighted fans, and so on.

Before you buy fans for your system you should decide on how important various attributes will be to your cooling plan. You also need to know what sort of features your motherboard offers. Fans with adjustable speeds and which report back speeds and other settings must be used with a motherboard that supports such features. Check the hardware monitoring and "fan sensor" capabilities of your motherboard to see how many fans it will support.

There are several major brands of fans that are popular. Panaflo from Panasonic is one of the top brands as are ones from Vantec, which has several lines. SunBeam Tech makes a number of lit fans. Another popular brand is Titan, which makes aluminum-framed fans. You can find all of these and a few other brands at most of the major mod shops on the Web.

Installing fans can be as easy as screwing them in near open fan ports on your case. Unfortunately, many modders install fans in places not previously open on their cases such as the top. If so, you'll need to cut open holes, use some edge mounting to take care of sharp edges, and custom mount your devices. You can buy a fan mounting kit from **www.pcmods.com** for $7.99 (cheap!) including molding, templates, and screws. If you're mounting a fan on the front of your case you might need a fan duct to build a wind tunnel like effect. These are inexpensive and pretty easy to install. Supplying power to your fan is usually pretty easy but some fans that are popular in the market need adapters. These fan tails help you easily add power connectors to popular models from Panaflo, Rheobus, and Baybus. Multiple fan setups might also benefit from controllers.

Fan Controllers

Fan controllers are components that fit in your drive-bays and allow you to control fan speeds for all of the fans in your case. Most controllers support four fans but there are some that look like controls to a fancy car stereo that can do more. Some nice ones even offer USB and Firewire ports you can hook up.

 You can see a good sample tutorial of wiring your own bus at **www.caseetc.com/ cgi-bin/caseetc/rheostat.html**.

The best-selling knob-based controllers are made by SunBeam Technologies (**www.sunbeamtech.com**) and can be found at most of the major mod shops on the Web. Vantec (**www.vantecusa.com**) makes a higher-end line of fan controllers called Nexus. Vantec offers two types of controllers: a 4-knob based line and a single knob with LCD temperature display and front end USB/FireWire ports. A third option comes from Thermaltake (**www.thermaltake.com**), which makes a line of fan controllers called Hardcano. This line includes fan control capabilities and a specialized fan for your hard drive. Zalman Tech (**www.zalman.co.kr/usa/product/zm-mfc1.htm**) offers another great controller—the MFC-1, which offers six hookups.

Other Cooling Options

Fans or forced air aren't the only cooling options available to monster PC builders but they're by far the most common. Other cooling options that you may need to utilize include heatsinks and water-based cooling. Heatsinks are devices that attach directly to chips to pull the heat out of them and dissipate the heat. Many heatsinks also include fans to help with the dissipation. It's not uncommon to see these fans on PCs you buy and on other components like videocards and RAM chips. Coolermaster is one of the most respected brands in heatsinks. Thermaflow from Vantec (**www.vantecusa.com**) and Thermaltake (**www.thermaltake.com**) are also considered good brands.

Heatsink-guide.com is a site devoted to heatsink info. They also produced a good 101 guide for Anandtech.com (**www.anandtech.com/showdoc.html?i=1115**).

Heatsinks are installed by gluing the heatsink to the chipface using a thermal compound. Many heatsinks include a compound but the most often used is Antec's Artic Silver Thermal Adhesive, which sells for about $8.

Water based cooling involves using water sent through pumps to absorb the heat and then carry it out of the CPU via an exposed radiator that has a fan which blows the heat off the radiator. The big advantage of water-based cooling is that it's much quieter than fans and much more efficient. A system that works well could reduce the need for four loud fans to a single quieter fan.

The downside to water-based cooling is that it's a much funkier setup than adding a few more fans to a rig. It involves plastic tubing, water, and more. It's just not a run-of-the-mill setup and if it ever springs a leak you're toast. Water cooling systems are also more complex to install, require outside power in many cases, and more upkeep (draining and cleaning the system, and so on). To find out more about how a typical water cooling system is installed and operates, see some of the tutorials listed in Table 5.6.

Cables and Airflow

Other than cooling by fan, heatsinks, and water, the only other major way to ensure a cool system is to improve the airflow in the system. The chief culprits in this case

TABLE 5.6
Water cooling system overviews, tutorials, and resources.

WaterCooling 101
www.wc101.com

Procooling
www.procooling.com

Extreme Cooling
www.extremecooling.org

Mod The Box Review of Ahanix Iceberg 1 Water Cooling Kit
www.modthebox.com/review93_1.html

Tutorial on Overclockers Club
www.overclockersclub.com/iceberg1watercoolingkitreview.php

Tutorial on Gruntville
www.gruntville.com/howtos/peltier/index.php

are cables, be they power cables, IDE cables, SCSI cables, and so on. To combat this issue, modders are building rounded cables and using cable ties to reduce and cram cables into the smallest size and get them as much out of the way as possible.

There are a few key products to be aware of to help improve airflow. The first are wraps and ties. Wraps are plastic accessories you can use to bunch cables together and pull them to one side or the other to open up a wide path of space in your case to increase airflow. You can find these at most modding shops. Ties are just simple plastic ties you can use to bind them to parts of the case to pull the cables around.

For rounded cables you can either make your own (**www.digital-explosion.co.uk/index.php?articleID=26**) by meticulously cutting and wrapping your own IDE cables or order them from a mod supplier. Be careful with rounded cables, however. Go for high quality cables that are 18 inches in length because they will produce the best spec for data transfer according to the standards IDE cables are developed around. To read more about the pluses and minuses of rounded cables, read the article located at **www.dansdata.com/rcables.htm**. The good news is that we'll eventually have serial ATA to use and we can get rid of ribbon based hard drive cables.

Overclocking

Overclocking is the art (and science) of pumping up the internal speed of various system components to achieve faster overall system performance. Most computer parts and chips ship to run at a specific speed. An example would be a CPU that runs at 1GHz. This speed is actually never actually the highest speed the chip or component can run. Manufacturers set the speed lower to ensure that the yield of the production run of chips hits a certain level to create a good return on their manufacturing investment. If they test a batch of chips and find that 5% to 10% of them fail at 1.2GHz but they all run fine at 1GHz, the entire batch, regardless of the individual capability, will be sold running at 1GHz. This means that if you can figure out how to configure the component to run at the higher speed your specific chip or component may actually hold up fine and you get a free boost in power.

The downside of overclocking is that you could lose at this game of electrical engineering roulette. You could fry the component, or worse other components. A couple other notes on overclocking risks. First, just because a component works at first, even for a few months, you still might have shortened its life-cycle. Overclocking has also not brought with it the returns made by earlier efforts. As components become faster and smaller, the risk-reward ratio of overclocking seems to be dropping. Cooling will also be an issue. If you punch up the power, you'll likely be increasing the heat and need for component cooling.

I've compiled some good resources to help you decide for yourself (see Table 5.7). Overclocking is a substantial enough topic I could not do it perfect justice here. The first places to explore are the big tech sites like Tom's Hardware, SharkyExtreme, and Anandtech.com.

More on PowerStrip and Graphics Card Overclocking

I wanted to add a few more notes on PowerStrip because after overclocking your CPU, you might be interested in overclocking your graphics card. PowerStrip is a well-known utility that can really help you twwak your card. However, you should first start by looking at what your card's basic drivers offer. Next, there are many independent tweak tools for various cards you can find on the Web that will help you potentially overclock your specific card.

A couple of other notes concerning graphics card overclocking is that it is highly recommended you overclock in very fine increments as well as provide extra cooling as you increase the clock speed of your card. Furthermore, you might also consider underclocking or dialing back a card which can increase quality of rendering if not necessarily speed.

Tweaking Your System's Software

In addition to mods and hardware overclocks, you can tweak the system software itself. I covered very simple BIOS tweaks by referencing a good article on Arstechnica but you can also spend a day or more on the Web reading more sites

TABLE 5.7
Overclocking resources.

RESOURCE	HOW TO FIND	COMMENTS

Overclocking FAQs and Basics	www.hyperformance-pc.com
	www.modthebox.com/overclock.html
	www.modthebox.com/overclockpt2.html
	www.sharkyextreme.com/hardware/
	  guides/cpu_oc_guide
	www.extremetech.com/article2/
	  0,3973,391524,00.asp
	www.tweak3d.net/articles/octips
		These pages will give you a good 101 intro to overclocking CPUs.

Overclocking Help and Sites	www.extremeoverclocking.com www.tweak3d.net www.sysopt.com/ocdatabase.html www.hardocp.com www.arstechnica.com	Major sites with good articles and up-to-date overclocking info on the latest hardware.

Overclocking Athlon and Pentium IV specifics	www.tomshardware.com/cpu/19990826
	  (Athlon)
	www.sharkyextreme.com/guides/hwGuides/
	  article.php/10709_1380951__6(Pentium IV)
		Good articles on specifics of overclocking the two main processors of the moment by two of the best hardware sites.

Graphics Card Overclocking help and utilities	oc3dmark.octeams.com/tips.html
	  Good overall tips
	www.entechtaiwan.com/ps.htm
	  PowerStrip
	www.guru3d.com
	  Lots of resources and tips
		PowerStrip is software used to potentially overclock your graphics card. Offers lots of non-overclocking features also. Available for $29.95 or in a free shareware version as well. Supports Radeon 9700.

Overclocking Memory	www.overclockers.com/tips1039 www.radiativenz.com/guides/memoryguide	A good set of 101 sites on memory and the issues of overclocking it.
Tweaking the Bios	arstechnica.com/guide/building/bios/ bios-1.html	One of the things I've done in this chapter is give a bit of short shrift to working with your systems BIOS to wreak performance out of your hardware. This article can help you with that.
UseNet Groups	alt.comp.hardware.overclocking alt.comp.hardware.overclocking.amd	The Usenet is still a great resource for a topic like overclocking.
The Book of Overclocking	Published by No Starch Press ISBN: 188641176X	This book has gotten excellent reviews and covers from top-to-bottom all of the basics and many specifics about overclocking most newer CPUs. (Athlon 64 isn't covered.) Doesn't heavily cover BIOS tweaks or funkier cooling ideas like water cooling, etc.

and commentary on BIOS tweaks. You might also want to look into updating your BIOS depending on how old your motherboard is. This can open up new possibilities for your system.

Other than the low-level BIOS, the most important piece of software to tweak is the OS itself, which will likely be Windows 2000 or Windows XP. There are three major tweaks here. The first is multibooting, which lets you run more than one OS on your machine (e.g., Linux and Windows XP). Then there are OS specific tweaks, which can be divided into two categories: ones that result in performance gains and ones that let you mod the entire look and feel of your system. Let me quickly run through a few programs and resources you should know about:

Multibooting
Multibooting is one of the more difficult things you can do because it involves a lot of planning and some specialized software. I don't recommend doing anything concerning multibooting with your machine until you've completely backed everything up. Consider setting it up on a virgin drive if you can. Since there are many aspects to multibooting and I'm pressed for space, I'll list a few good resources and tools to help you get started:

Richard's Multiboot Menagerie
www.techtv.com/screensavers/answerstips/story/0,24330,3399433,00.html
A simple but good article on how someone built a 57 OS multi-boot computer.

System Commander 7
www.v-com.com/product/sc7__ind.html
Good product for building a multi-boot system.

Extended Operating System Loader
www.xosl.org
The Extended Operating System Loader is a well-liked open-source tool for creating a multi-boot system.

Partition Magic
www.powerquest.com/partitionmagic
Partition Magic is the leading independent patitioning software for PCs. It has multi-boot capability and is a great package.

Boot It!
www.terabyteunlimited.com
Boot It! is a well liked multi-boot setup and management tool. It's free for 30 days and costs only $29.95 to register.

Microsoft's XP Multi-boot Doc
www.microsoft.com/windowsxp/pro/using/howto/gettingstarted/multiboot.asp

This site provides basic info on multi-booting with XP but just because it's from Microsoft's perspective doesn't mean this is the only way to do it.

Object Desktop and Windows Blinds
www.stardock.com

Visit Stardock and get the best utility for customizing the look and feel of Windows. It can do some pretty amazing things. Check the site for more info.

WinCustomize
www.wincustomize.com

This is the best site on the Web to download skins and skinning programs for your Windows desktop. It includes links to all the popular customizing programs like LiteStep, Cursor XP, and more. Once you've got your hardware looking the way you want, come here and get Windows looking the way you want.

Tweak Managers
www.magictweak.com
www.tweakmanager.com
www.tweaki.com

Between these three shareware/commercial packages, you should be able to tweak the bejesus out of Windows.

TaskInfo2003
www.iarsn.com

This is a great task improved manager for your system. It can help you identify processes and programs running that you want to stop or otherwise locate and exterminate.

Measuring Performance

Once you've bought, built and/or tweaked your system to the max, one thing you'll want to do is run a variety of diagnostics on it to see just how powerful your rig is. This is the realm of benchmark software. And while benchmarking can measure a snapshot of core performance that doesn't mean that you will get that power showing through on every game. Still benchmarks are fun things to do, and they give you ideas on what to tweak next and what sort of results you've gotten from various mods, overclocks, or new components. I've listed the key products in Table 5.8.

TABLE 5.8
Want to know how fast your PC is? Check out these top PC benchmarking software packages.

PRODUCT	URL	COMMENTS
3D Mark	www.futuremark.com	The graphics benchmarking utility. People also use major games like Quake, Doom, and Unreal.
PC MarkSys Mark	www.futuremark.com	Other benchmarking programs from the makers of 3D Mark.
PC Magazine Benchmarks	www.winbench.com	Free downloads and order forms for utilities used by PC Magazines testing labs.

Console Mods and Extensions

Hardware mods are essentially the domain of the PC but there are still a few things worth discussing about consoles. (If you're interested in Mod chips and you haven't read Chapter 3, go back and read it.)

Xbox Mods

The Xbox is essentially a PC jammed into a console and thus it's getting a lot of attention for mods. The problem with many of these mods is that they require a "mod chipped" Xbox, which for many reasons means that we're out of luck. The Xbox mod and hacking community is very big as these types of communities go. People are replacing components (e.g., adding a bigger hard drive) and doing all sorts of funky stuff. The best list of mods I've seen for the Xbox is at **www.xbox-scene.com/tutorials.php**. I'm not going to warn you again how most of these mods will destroy your warranty! I'll present some of the more useful and easier mods to perform and I'll include Web links where appropriate.

Playing Halo and Other Xbox Games Online without Xbox Live

Technically, this is more of a hack than a mod but I hadn't presented this nugget yet and I kept meaning to. Microsoft didn't develop Halo as an online game but they did make it network capable. Other games are network capable also. With a bit of software, cables, and a PC or Mac, you can setup these games to play online. Complete instructions and software can be found at

✔ Using GameSpy and Xbox Tunnel to play Halo and other games online: **gamespyarcade.com/support/tunnel_xbox.shtml**

✔ Xbox Connect is another program to help you play online: **www.xbconnect.com**

✔ Aquaduct is for those of you with Macs: **www.postpose.com/aquaduct**

Most games that offers network multiplayer capability through the Ethernet port of the Xbox can work with tunneling programs.

Changing the Name of Your Xbox

When you play multiplayer games like Halo, your Xbox usually has a unique name. This name can be seen on top of your Xbox picture. This name comes from a file stored on your Xbox named *nickname.xbn*. The name stored in this file is initially derived from the name of various saved games you have on your system. By now it likely has some dumb name you never intended to use like ASSLICK. So before you go online to play HALO you probably want to change it. There is no direct method for changing the name but there is a back door. Several games give you the opportunity to change the name if you know where to look. Some of these games include Dead or Alive (DOA), Moto GP, and Cel Damage. Here are some techniques for how you can change the name using these games:

✔ In MotoGP the name of the last driver you create will become the name of your Xbox.

✔ In DOA3, you need to get a high-score in the game's survival mode. The Xbox name will then be one of the choices you can replace with the new name.

✔ If you save a game in Cel Damage, the name you supply becomes your new name.

Using USB Peripherals on the Xbox
www.gamegizmo.com/products.php?sysID=10&catID=4&pID=1250
The Xbox controllers are actually USB controllers but the interface to them has been changed so that you can't exactly use USB peripherals or use Xbox peripherals on your PC. However, there are now some cables that allow you to use USB peripherals on your Xbox.

Use Xbox Controllers on Your PC
Lik-Sang acquired the SmartJoy line of cables allowing them to offer a cable converter that lets you use an Xbox controller on your PC. You can get this converter from their site at **www.lik-sang.com**. The cables only cost a few bucks but you can find a do it your self mod on the Web among other places at **www.blagged-hardware.net/index.php?index=41&pg=1**.

Using PS2 Controllers on Your Xbox
www.extreme-mods.com/products/xbox-joybox.htm
The Xbox Joybox available at Extreme Mods makes it so you can use PS2 Controllers on your Xbox. instead of buying three extra sets for both machines you can buy one complete set of controllers for the PS2 and use them for both machines.

Installing Linux on Your Xbox
www.xboxhacker.net/forums/index.php?act=ST&f=12&t=10520

If someone creates any device having power equivalent to an old GameTime watch, you'll find someone else who wants to get Linux on it. Got a new toaster? Someone is trying to put Linux on it. The same is true for the Xbox except people are making some serious headway. I don't recommend you do this to your Xbox (modded or unmodded) but if you think it is worth doing and you won't blame me when you screw it up, check out xbox-linux.sourceforge.net and pick up a copy of 007 Agent Under Fire before they fix the bug:

Xbox Skins
www.extreme-mods.com/products/xbox-skins.htm

Extreme Mods carries a line of decals you can use to specifically skin your Xbox with different colors. Now you can make it stand out a bit from the crowd when you're playing multiplayer Halo.

PS2 Mods

The PS2 offers little in the way of mods compared to the Xbox. This is primarily due to its proprietary hardware design, however, with the Linux kit and Qcast the PS2 has some interesting additions worth checking out.

Using the PS2 to Listen to MP3s and Other Digital Media Files
www.qcast.com

Somewhere, somehow this has to be a product of the year type thing. With Qcast and a PS2 equipped with a broadband adapter, you can stream media files (DivX, Ogg Vorbis, MP3, JPEGs) from your Linux, Windows, or Mac OS machine to your TV through your PlayStation. The software costs $49.95 and includes special server software for your PC and a client-side CD for the PS2. ArsTechnica has a great review and background story on the product, which I recommend reading (**www.arstechnica.com/reviews/003/qcast/qcast-1.html**). Aside from having a problem with some higher-resolution MPEG files, the product is getting rave reviews. Qcast turns your PS2 into a recognizable node on your home network. You can use Wi-Fi networking if you can't snake a regular Ethernet cable between your PS2 and your PC. The software also supports multiple PS2s, although you'll need extra copies of the client. Here's hoping they push out a Xbox version soon.

PS2 Linux Kit
www.us.playstation.com/hardware/more/scph-97047.asp

If you want to develop your own programs and games on the PS2, you need to check out the PS2 Linux Kit. I'll cover it a bit more in Chapter 11.

Add a Fan to Your PS2
www.extreme-mods.com/products/ps2-usbfan.htm
As if the world needed another device with a fan, you can buy this USB port fan extension to keep your PS2 cooler potentially extending its life.

Skin Your PS2 and Controllers
skinefx.com/catalog
www.gameconsoleskins.com
www.extreme-mods.com/products/ps2-skins.htm
Three companies sell decal skins for the PS2.

GameCube and GBA
Nintendo's hardware is the last of the bunch in terms of extensions and mods. The Gamecube doesn't offer many mods but it does have Freeloader, which enables you to play most imports without a mod chip and people have been doing backlight mods on GBAs. The GBA has a few very cool accessories, though, that you should check out.

Adding a Backlight to the GameBoy Advance
www.tritonlabs.com
The recent release of the GBA SP sort of dampens the mod scene for the GBA platform. Prior to the announcement of the SP many people were clamoring for a backlit screen. After a bunch of engineering efforts, a kit called the Afterburner kit appeared to let you create a backlit screen. Unfortunately, the work required to do so was not insignificant. If you don't want to do it yourself, check out **www.portablemonopoly.net** which will do it for you. Be warned however they are small and slow.

Watching TV on Your GBA
www.lik-sang.com
Available from places like Liksang.com, the Pelican GBA TV Tuner is somewhat of a bulky device that successfully turns your GBA into a portable TV. Keep in mind that it doesn't work on the SP.

Playing GBA Games on Your TV
www.lik-sang.com
There are two ways to hook your GBA games up to play on a TV. The first is Nintendo's own GameCube adapter. This is a $50 device that attaches to the GameCube and lets you play GBA games through your TV. Of course, this costs

a lot just to play GBA games on your TV. A less expensive option (less than $40) is the TV de Advance product which you can find at shops like LikSang.com This option requires a bit of work taking your GBA apart. A good tutorial for the product is found at **http://207.44.176.77/~admin28/gbaemu/faq/tvdeadvance/ tvdeinst2.html**.

Playing GBA Games In Da Tub
www.madcatz.com/MadCatz/product_details.jsp?product_id=2301
I'm in the tub with my GameBoy Advance using Mad Catz GBA Duck. I hope they find a way to make this thing work for the SP. It is really cool and I can't imagine why it took me an entire book to figure out someone had made something I wanted a while ago.

Downloading Carts to Your PC and Building Your Own GBA Games
www.gbadev.org
www.flash2advance.com
Using cabling and a Flash card reader/writer available at many import and mod shops, entire communities of people are making their own games which you can find on the Web. (I've listed one of the bigger sites.) Unfortunately, the existence of the capability to do this also means you can use the same cabling systems to copy existing GBA games, which you shouldn't do. You can also use flashers and software to make backups of GBA saved games (fine by me) and could be useful for people who want to swap saved games on the Internet.

Freeloader
www.dateldirect.com
Freeloader is a swap disc system to play imports on unmodified Gamecubes. No mod chip needed. Simply install freeloader, wait for the prompt, and then swap it out with the import disk of your choice. It doesn't necessarily work for every last import. Check the Web site to find out which games it supports.

Gamecube Cooling Fan
www.extreme-mods.com/products/gc-coolingfan.htm
Like its PS2 counterpart, there are also third-party fans for your cube.

Gamecube Skins
www.extreme-mods.com/products/gc-skins.htm

Monster Gamers Are True Modders

I wish I could write more about modding but by now I think you have a lot of good information to help you get deeper into the modding scene and trick out your PC and consoles. As a monster gamer you expect the most be it from a game, yourself, or your hardware. Whether it's hardware mods, or mods of our favorite games, the entire notion of tricking something out, or turning up the power, and creating something new was born out of the gaming scene. The two just go hand-in-hand.

SETTING UP A KILLER AUDIO/VISUAL SYSTEM

This chapter, in fact this entire book, owes some of its birth to the day I got my Xbox. It came as a gift from a contact involved with Microsoft's Xbox marketing. I had provided some consulting help to these folks and they wanted to do something nice for me. They didn't have to do that but I certainly wasn't going to look a gift Xbox in the mouth. I took the Xbox home and set it up so I could play HALO, and play hooky from work. I plugged the thing into my Sony big screen TV but the entire image was distorted and messed up. This made me nuts. Since it was a gift, I couldn't take it back to the store. My mind raced ahead to how I would need to ship it back and bother the nice people who sent it to me. Instead, I looked on the Web to see if there was a solution to my problem. I searched Google—nothing. I checked out some Google Groups and then I found what I needed. It turns out that the Xbox and certain Sony Projection PCs don't get along. The missing component is the HDTV hookup pack. So I ran downstairs and grabbed a small Panasonic TV and I was up and running in no time. I got to play HALO for a twelve-hour marathon, and the next day with bags under my eyes I ran to the local store and grabbed a HDTV pack. Later I'm playing Halo in 60 inch glory in my living room. The Flood was defeated, and the world was saved in more ways than one. The only problem was that work was pilling up at the office and my small staff was beginning to send out a search party to locate me.

My first lesson from this experience was that this game stuff is really complicated, and not everyone knows all the tricks they need to get by. I thought, there is a book in this. So I called my publisher and the idea behind *Monster Gaming* was born. Now instead of playing games all day I get to sit and write about them. What was I thinking?

My second lesson relates more to the actual topic of this chapter: audio and video systems can be a real pain in the ass. In writing this chapter, I figured I would do a bit of research, such as visiting the local bookstore and grabbing as many home audio/visual magazines as I could. In case you haven't noticed, magazines on this topic are plentiful. I figured I'd leaf through them at home and find the latest info, some good tips, and so on. Magazines are usually a great source of knowledge for me. My lesson came quick—no monster gamer can expect to learn anything from audio/visual magazines when it comes to gaming. I would have learned more by randomly asking bums on the street what the best projection screen is for games, or how to select the best HDTV set. I leafed through over 3,000 pages of this crap over the past few months and my conclusion is that the people reading and writing this stuff have never owned a computer or played a video game.

Console Time!

If you are a console person and you felt a little neglected after reading the previous two chapters, don't worry. In this chapter I'm going to focus more on consoles, although this chapter won't be entirely devoid of PC stuff. When gaming moves into the living room, we're moving much more onto console turf.

Of the three consoles, it's time for the Xbox to shine somewhat because it is the only one to include hardware support for HDTV. If you hook up the right equipment with the right games and configure your system properly, you'll experience the future of gaming in its earliest glory with your Xbox. As my friend Ross Rubin said to me at E3 several years ago, "I think we're looking at the last generation of NTSC-based consoles." Well, Hallelujah Ross, we're almost there. In the meantime we need to try and get the most out of what we have already. We need to enjoy other ways to take the experience of gaming off the typical TV and audio hookup and turn it into something that great games like Splinter Cell, Windwalker, and Halo deserve.

Mastering the Basics of Video

I covered some of the basics of audio in Chapter 4. If you haven't read that chapter, go back and bone up on the audio stuff. I also reviewed some of the basics of video—monitors, video cards, and LCD displays. In this chapter we're going to take the next step and deal with three key aspects of video:

1. **Next-Generation Displays:** CRT-based low-res television sets have been around since the dawn of computer games. With the onset of DVD and newer technologies like plasma and LCD screens, the TV in the living room is changing big time.

2. **Video Projectors:** When I started writing this book I asked gamers on Avault.com to tell me about how they were taking their gaming experience to the next-level. One surprising discovery was just how many people were skipping big screen TVs and moving to projection units. One guy even wrote me to say he would lie in bed and aim the projection unit at the ceiling and play until he feel asleep. Is this cool or what? I don't think my girlfriend would let me try that one, however. Although we once rented a projector and I used it to project Winamp visualizations onto the ceiling of our bedroom with some cool music going. That was a big hit.

3. **HDTV Technology:** This is the new standard for TV that's headed to North America soon, and I would suspect the rest of the world eventually will catch on. If you haven't seen HDTV, go to a big electronics store and take a look. HDTV unlocks the power hidden in consoles to produce much higher-resolution pictures. For years, some of us have been hooking consoles up to VGA monitors to generate crisper and better pictures. With HDTV we'll be able to avoid having to do that.

Video Basics and HDTV

The four types of video modes in use today are NTSC, PAL, SECAM, and HDTV. NTSC is used in the U.S. today but will be replaced by the HDTV standard. PAL is used in Europe and SECAM is used in France. HDTV will replace low end NTSC in the U.S. by 2006, which means we'll probably see higher-resolution displays everywhere by 2007.

There are two types of basic signals used in video today: *interlace scan* and *progressive scan*. Interlace scan requires a TV to first draw the odd lines in a picture from top to bottom. This is done quickly (in a 60th of a second). Then, the even lines are drawn in the next 1/60th of a second (hence 30 FPS for NTSC video). Progressive scan is much better because it draws the entire picture from top to bottom in one feel swoop. The picture is much clearer and crisper. You can now find a number of DVD players and other consumer devices that provide progressive scan output.

HDTV offers three major formats of picture. First is a resolution mode with 480 scan lines(which measures roughly 640x480 or low resolution VGA). The second is a resolution mode with 720 lines that is done in a progressive scan format known as 720p. This format has a resolution of 1280x720. The final mode is 1080I, a 1080 lines of resolution mode interlaced which runs 1922x1080. The aspect ratio of HDTV is 16:9 just like the movies, hence HDTV's letterbox shape.

The Best TV to Get for Gaming

The problem with selecting a TV is that there are many technologies competing for TV dollars. Because HDTV is starting to replace TV in the U.S., this is a crappy time to buy the wrong TV. Include the need to get the best game images and PC imagery in your living room and the selection process just becomes more difficult. I wish I could cut through all of the confusion about specific models and manufacturers but the consumer electronics industry is just too weird for me to completely decipher. Instead, I'll run through the basics and hopefully steer you in the right direction.

The three major technologies for TVs you can select from include CRTs, LCDs, and Plasma. CRTs are familiar turf. The only issue is the price you're willing to pay and what sort of picture quality you need. The bigger debate today is Plasma vs. LCD. Plasma is less expensive and has good capability for moving images. LCD is gaining on Plasma, however, because it requires less power and it isn't as susceptible to "burn in" as LCD is. LCD is an expensive technology in higher screen sizes although the refresh rate at the larger sizes is still a work in progress. Remember for games, you really want a 16ms or less refresh rate. A recent *PC Magazine* article suggested that LCD is about to break the 30-inch barrier. This will put it in much heavier competition with Plasma displays in the years 2004 to 2005. Eventually, LCD displays will likely win a huge chunk of the overall market.

If you want a big flat screen TV, plasma is probably your best bet now. You can easily find 40" and 60" plasma displays. For big screen LCDs, you'll need to consider LCD projection screens. In smaller sizes below 24" you can find some great LCD displays. LCD displays are best for using in living rooms that also incorporate PCs for entertainment.

Projecting Your Games

Video projectors are a fast moving business as the prices come down and more people use them for applications other than boring business presentations. Many manufacturers are producing them and various options are available. The key to selecting one is to understand the basics. The main attributes of a projector, aside from price and the core tech it uses is how bright it can get, its resolution, contrast and the types of hookups it can accept.

Projectors use three major types of display technology to drive their systems. (CRT is a fourth type but it's very bulky and wicked expensive.) The three major types used are LCD, which is the market leader. Then there are two variations of DLP (Digital Light Processing) technologies used: single chip and three chip versions. DLP technology involves tiny chips called *Digital Mirror Devices* (DMD) that have microscopic mirrors, one for each pixel, that project out the image. Three chips are better than a single chip because a separate chip is used for each R,G,B color. This approach is much more expensive. According to ProjectorPeople.com, projectors using three chip DLP run from $20,000 to $30,000. If you consider the conventional wisdom that they'll fall in price by 50% every 18 months, you'll need to wait for three to four years before these things become a little more affordable. The biggest problem for single chip DLP is that the brightness is just not quite there yet for the single chip solution. These machines max out at 2,000 lumens and, if you plan on using one during the day in a space with lots of ambient light, you'll need something that is 2,500+. However, for rooms that will be better protected against ambient light (say a bedroom or living room, in the evening, with the shades pulled), you can get by with 1,000 or more lumens.

Projector brightness is measured in ANSI lumens. DLP and LCD projectors will each feature various capabilities for brightness. Most ultra portable projectors (single-chip DLP ones) have a range of 800 to 2,000 lumens. The amount of light you need depends on how much ambient light there you have and the size of the image you will want to make. The higher the lumens the more visible the projector will be in brighter lighting conditions and the bigger the image that can be supported. The brightest projectors run 2,500 to 7,000+ lumens but will be much less portable (10lbs to 30lbs).

Resolution for most projectors runs in three major ranges: 800x600, 1024x768, and 1280x1024. 1024x768 is a really good resolution and the prices are dropping enough to make this the current sweet-spot. Brightness uniformity is also an issue.

You'll want to evaluate projectors in reviews, see them with your own eye, and talk to others about how even the lighting is in the image, especially around the edges. According to experts, the brightness uniformity should be 85% or better.

Connections are also important since not all projectors will feature connections for typical home-video equipment or consoles. You definitely want S-Video and composite inputs. Some projectors also have DCI input. This will give you the best picture if you have a compatible DCI graphics card for your computer.

The contrast ratio is also an area to look at. This describes the ratio between white and black, and the larger the ratio the better the capability of the projector to differentiate between shades of colors. There are two types of contrast ratios used. The first is Full On/Off and the second is ANSI contrast ratio. They are different so don't compare one ratio reading using Full On/Off with one using ANSI. The Full On/Off will be a larger number even for the same projector.

Fan noise is also an issue with projectors. I hate white noise so the less fan noise, the better. This may be less of an issue when you've got Dolby 5.1 rocking through your living room or headphones though.

When buying a projector you may want to keep HDTV and Interlace in mind for several reasons. First, you might actually want to use your projector to watch TV someday or even HDTV broadcasts. Second, the Xbox can output some titles in HDTV mode so you could take advantage of a system that offers the higher resolutions. Earlier I said that a 1024x768 projector would be fine for gaming, but if you plan on doing a lot of TV watching with it consider the pricing of lamps and the overall resolution (higher is better).

Projectors don't project interlaced video, they convert traditional interlace signals using a line doubler method that changes the interlace signal into a progressive scan format. It does this by waiting for the full image (the first and 2nd 30ths of an image) to come in and then it projects them to the screen. Some machines reportedly do this better than others, so when shopping for a projector you might ask about this.

Lamps

All projectors use lamps. Lamps provide the light that pushes the image onto your wall. Lamp life typically runs between 1,000 to 2,000 hours. This is also known as the lamp's "half-life," meaning that at this point the lamp is expected to be half-as-bright as it was when you got it. Even at the halfway point you might actually still find the image suitable, although it will continue to degrade. Given how long people play games one should consider how easy it will be to replace lamps. Lamp replacement usually runs $299 to $450. Buying an extra lamp at the time you purchase a projector might not be such a bad idea.

If you consider the average cost of a good projector to be $2,500, then your first 1,000 to 2,000 hours will cost you $1 to $2.50 an hour to play. If you average 25 hours per week, you're looking at about 200 to 400 days of playing time before you need a new lamp. Most of you will likely burn through a lamp a year playing games on a projector if you play games at a clip of 100 hours per month.

Getting Your Projector

Enough with the projector babble. What should you get, and where should you get it? As for what to get, single-chip DLP models or LCD models are your best bet right now. Projector People has a great top ten list for top-ten sellers on their site at **www.projectorpeople.com/hometheater/top-ten-projectors.asp**. I also recommend watching that list to see what is popular with home users.

While it does pay to shop around, Projector People (which I used as a source for this chapter because their Web site is so good) is a great outfit with a large selection and incredible knowledge. Their prices are pretty good too. I checked on C|NET's shopping tool (**shopper.cnet.com**) and their top-selling home-theatre projector was just 10% more than the rock bottom place I found with C|NET.

What's Next?

Display technology has advanced much slower then other computer technology such as processors, sound, and storage. Fortunately, there are some big things on the horizon. A few companies are working on holographic screens. This isn't like Star Wars per se. It's more like a picture projected onto a piece of floating glass in mid air. It's a very neat effect. Another major display technology in development is called *Organic Light Emitting Diodes* (OLED). This technology enables the actual screens to project light so a separate source of light isn't needed. OLED is used now with some PDAs and cellphones but eventually it could make it to screens. The cool thing about OLED screens is that the surface they work on might actually be incredibly flexible enough so that you could have a giant screen that rolls up and fits in small case (imagine a 50-inch portable display).

Then there is The Cave, which was developed at the University of Illinois, Chicago's Electronic Visualization Laboratory (**www.evl.uic.edu**). This is a fairly well designed fully immersive VR display environment and can also be found in a commercial version from Fakespace Systems (**www.fakespacesystems.com**). Don't even ask the price!

A Quick Snippet on Audio

In Chapter 4 I discussed audio in detail so there isn't a huge need to cover it here, hence the majority of this chapter is focused on video issues. The big thing about living room audio vs. PC audio is that there is a good chance you'll be hooking your system up to a regular amplifier and stereo system, perhaps one that is part of your total home theater system. None of that changes the definition of Dolby Surround Sound, 5.1, 6.1, or 7.1 audio. So where does that leave us for extra info? First, there are powered-speaker setups for consoles specifically. Many of the makers mentioned in Chapter 4 have setups that work or that are adaptable to consoles.

Monster Cable's Monster Gamer Division also has some speakers for consoles they specifically push. Other than that, assume you want a good stereo system with lots of extra hookups in the speaker and ideally ones that can accept optical audio as well which you can output using some cables, and so on. Beyond that, the key issue for audio is the positioning of speakers. Hot Hardware has a great article on that which you can view at **www.hothardware.com/hh_files/CCAM/ speakersetup(1).shtml**.

The Living Room PC

People have been putting PCs in their living room for years but until recently this wasn't a big practice and the PC makers themselves hadn't really offered much to bring the PC into the living room. Gateway's Destination PC was perhaps the first machine to break into the living room scene. In 2002 through 2003 things began to change as Microsoft created Windows XP Media Edition and PC makers like Gateway, HP, and Alienware began creating entirely new forms of the PC running Media Edition that were dedicated to the living room. I think these new machines hit the mark and as plasma and LCD screens grow in usage, we'll begin to see living room displays that do the PC justice.

Other than getting a better display, the living room PC incorporates two other features. First are enhanced media capabilities—the other is a remote. In terms of enhanced media capabilities, I think the best example is Alienware's Navigator Extreme product (**www.alienware.com/mce_main_sff_purchase.aspx**), which is available in two models: the Pro and Extreme. This product comes in a very stylish consumer electronics style design and packs an Intel Pentium 4 processor and a

NVIDIA GeForce4 Ti 4600 in a box that also features a fancy remote. It has front ports for a keyboard, mouse, Firewire, and USB devices. It also features built-in Ethernet and headphone jacks. The system features DVD read/write and can record TV shows like a TiVo. It provides a hell of a lot of computing power, with PVR (personal video recorder) capabilities, Dolby Sound, and remote control. To read more about the specific capabilities of Windows Media Center Edition, visit **www.microsoft.com/windowsxp/mediacenter**.

If you want a wireless keyboard and mouse to go with your living room PC (always a good idea), check out Logitech (**www.logitech.com**) which makes excellent wireless devices. Logitech sells these devices under its Cordless Elite Duo and Cordless Navigator Duo brands. Microsoft's offers some devices also (**www.microsoft.com/hardware**) but be careful about getting Bluetooth capable systems, which may not be compatible with your system unless you add a Bluetooth card. This card could set you back another $70. For your own remote control device, check out ATI's Remote Wonder product found online at **www.ati.com/products/pc/remotewonder**.

Recording Your Games

Recording your game sessions can be useful for a number of reasons. Recording games to help your friends learn how to beat a game is fun and useful. You can also record games to document high-scores. (A screenshot can be faked so what good is that!) If you run a fan site, having some movies of games is good for traffic, and even just a frame-grab off a console is good for screenshots. Recording games is easy if you just hook things up properly through your VCR. The harder part is if you want to grab live game-play to your computer, off a taped session, or grab a quality screenshot. That will take some extra equipment.

When it comes to taping games the mistake most players make is that they send a signal out from their TV to the VCR and then hit record. Don't do this! You should go to your VCR first, then connect to your TV set. The quality of your tapes will depend on the type of VCR and connection you use. An S-Video cable out will do the best job and most modern day VCRs support S-Video. In terms of VCRs, some VCRphiles heavily recommend Panasonic's top-of-the-line 4-Head HiFi VCRs. These sell for $100 or less and, from what my research tells me (no I didn't ask the bums on the corner!), they have excellent recording quality. You could also try Super VHS for better quality, but not many people have those devices and thus your ability to pass your records around gets more limited.

To get the potential best quality, consider using recordable DVD systems. Keep in mind these devices aren't cheap yet. The cool thing about recordable DVDs is that you can record component video output from your console or PC. I'll cover more on component video output later in this chapter.

Capturing to Your Computer

Capturing to tape is one thing. Capturing to your computer is another ball game. Video capture falls into three camps: low end, high end, and videophile land. I'm not interested in videophile land where you can spend endless hours talking about what's the best cards, or talk about equipment only used by the highest of high-end "videoheads." I just want to capture decent video or screenshots for my fan site, or for other needs. In terms of the low-end, I recommend a few devices. Dazzle (**www.dazzle.com**) and Pinnacle Systems (**www.pinnaclesys.com**) make low-end (less than $75) devices that capture video through a USB port. Both devices offer S-Video and composite video capture making it easy to directly pipe in video from your consoles. Higher-end ATI and Nvidia boards also may offer capturing capabilities. On the higher-end, Canopus (**www.canopus.com**) makes some excellent capture cards that get great reviews.

Capturing from Your Computer

The quality of video output from a computer will suffer as it is converted from the higher resolutions of VGA to the lower resolution of PAL or NTSC video. There are a couple of options you can consider. First, get a video card that will output a composite signal. Many higher-end cards have this as an option either in their core offering or a sister offering like ATI's All-in-Wonder product. Another option is to get what is known as a *downscaler*. A downscaler will take a VGA signal and output it to NTSC video. High-quality downscalers will create a crisper and better image by integrating circuitry to improve the resulting image. Key Digital (see the next section) makes a huge line of downscalers that you might want to consider if you're really going to create a killer tape for reproduction.

Hooking Up Your Consoles to a VGA Monitor

Lets detour from the living room for a second and discuss another critical audio/ visual item concerning consoles specifically. For many people another big option for consoles is to hook them up to VGA monitors. The dot pitch, and superior screens means that you can get a great picture playing a console on a VGA monitor if you have the right equipment. People have been hooking up consoles to monitors for years but it was perhaps the Sega Dreamcast which had a first-party VGA box peripheral that turned many people into converts. The beauty of the Dreamcast on a VGA monitor was really something. As such, a slew of users is using various converters and other hookups to enable a whole new generation of consoles to work on VGA monitors.

Walk before You Run

Before we get into the nitty-gritty of hooking up a console to a VGA monitor, we need to discuss some basics of display technology and cables. (Ugh, more of this!@!?? When will it end!) Console display technology involves several types of output. The first is composite video, which we've discussed already. The second is S-Video, which is a superior to composite. Finally, we have component RGB, which is the best of all. The problem with component RGB is that there are several forms of it.

All component video cables carry the key RGB signals on separate wires, with syncing and audio information on others as well (except for some systems of component video which use the Green line to embed itself, also known as, Sync on Green). You might also see component video described as (Y Pb Pr). The first form of RGB cable most people are familiar with is VGA itself. This is an RGB cable but it is housed in a single cable. More familiar to people with Xboxes and other devices in North America is a cable that eventually splits into several RCA-type cables that connect to the back of your TV or other display device.

In countries outside North America a different adapter is used called an *SCART adapter*, which features 21 pins (hence another term RGB21). The problem here is that there are two forms of SCART, European and Japanese. While the interface is the same, the pin-outs are completely different. Why should this matter? Well depending on the solution you use to upscale your video to VGA, you'll need a Japanese RGB/Japanese SCART cable.

There is also a third style of component cabling called the *D-Terminal cable* that is used exclusively by the GameCube. Did you expect Nintendo to do something standard? Come on now.

If you intend to use any device that will accept component video, be it a new TV set or a converter box, you'll want to get the right component cable. In most cases that means getting the right cable direct from the vendor or from a third party. However, in the case of VGA upscaling, one of the most oft-recommended boxes is a Japanese unit from an outfit called Micomsoft. If you're gong to use this device you'll need a cable that outputs in Japanese SCART format, which I will tell you now is not easily found. Many people resort to buying a European SCART cable and rewiring it to the right pinouts. To find correct pin out information visit **www.gamesx.com/avpinouts/rgb21pinj.htm**.

Running VGA Converters and Line Doublers

Now that you're up to speed a bit on video signal and cabling issues lets talk about the specifics of VGA cabling options. There are two types of converters-those that turn input into VGA video, which are known as *upscalers*, and those that convert VGA output into NTSC or PAL video, which are known as *downscalers*.

Upscalers are sometimes called line doublers but that's a bit of a misnomer. The issue here is that the lines really aren't being doubled—you're just "deinterlacing" the signal, which is why you hear the term *deinterlacing* used as well. The term *doubler* comes from doubling the number of lines delivered to the screen at a single moment and *not* in doubling the amount of lines up from 480 to 960. Doubler devices essentially take 480i and turn it into 480p.

There are some doublers that actually can scale an image up to 960, which is useful on very large (100") screens to keep them from have a "scanline" looking image. Doublers also increase the signal frequency from 15.75Khz to 31.5Khz to help reduce flicker in the image by painting the screen more often. If you get a doubler that increases the number of lines, it will need a monitor that has an even higher refresh rate as it paints the screen at even higher refresh rates.

The important thing to know about line doublers/upscalers is that they can use any number of methods to draw a single progressive image. There are several methods used and each has pluses and minuses. Not all doublers/upscalers are created alike. You will have to judge for yourself, but this will explain why some console/VGA converters are inexpensive and others cost more.

There are two major options for upscalers. The first is a device from Japan known as the XRGB-2plus from a company called Micomsoft (**www.micomsoft.co.jp**). It's popular in import circles because it can accept input from a variety of sources all at once and input one of them to your VGA monitor. The inputs on the Micomsoft device include Japanese SCART, composite, and Svideo. If you hooked up via a Japanese SCART/RGB cable to your PS2, and then Svideo from your Xbox and composite in for your GameCube, a single device could upscale your entire console collection. The device gets good reviews. For more info on this device visit these excellent sites:

✔ To get the XRGB-Plus2 Device visit National Console Support (**www.ncsx.com**) or Upstate Games (**www.upstategames.com**).

✔ You should also read Jeremy Pallant's excellent set of articles on the XRGB box, which can be found at **www.tiptonium.com/videogames/reviews/ other/XRGB2-PLUS.htm**.

The next option is actually a suite of optional devices from the manufacturers mentioned in the following section. Of those, a new series of devices from **www.avtoolbox.com** called the HG 300 Series Hi-Res Gamers (**www.avtoolbox.com/ hg-series.htm**) are nice lower cost devices that directly connect to the console of your choice. You can pick one up for $49.

Viewsonic also makes a line of VGA monitor connection devices called NextVision. These are well-constructed video processors that enable you to hook up your consoles and other devices to higher-end VGA and HDTV capable monitors. The models offered include the N4, N5, and N6. The N5 sells for $150 and the N6 goes for $400 at the time this book goes to press. The N6 features a remote and inputs for RF, S-video, composite (RCA), component (YPrPb)(RCA), and RGB pass-through plus audio.

Video Gadgets Galore

As you get more into the world of audio and video, you'll learn that this is a world with a tons of gadgets, many of them black boxes with tons of ports. Some of these gadgets perform some funky stuff, but it's worth looking at them a little closer. You can do a lot more than you'd think once you know this stuff exists, and where you can get it:

Two of the most useful gadgets you'll probably be searching for are additional VGA and Component video converters as well as switchers that can connect multiple devices to the same monitors. Instead of organizing this gear by product I organized it by vendor because each vendor has different items worth discussing.

Audio Authority
www.audioauthority.com

Audio Authority makes several devices worth checking out. First is their component video to RGB Converter, which gets good reviews and sells for just under $200. Next is their VGA to component video converter, which can be useful for hooking up a PC to your TV, especially if you don't have a card that outputs to TV in a format better than composite video. Audio Authority also makes a few switchers for video and audio.

TV One
www.tvone.com

TV One makes an incredible range of devices in several categories. First is its series of first-rate scan converters which can convert VGA signals to various forms of NTSC and PAL via component, S-Video, and other outputs. These devices, which can get quite expensive, are great for potentially recording PC games out to video.

TV One also makes a huge series of up-converters which let you take in composite or S-Video and output it to VGA and HDTV resolutions. The highest-end product for their consumer line is the imageMAX which can output to various VGA settings: 480p, 720p, and 1080i resolutions. It sells for just under $500 and is distributed by **www.avtoolbox.com**. They also have a series of splitters, which are nice for displaying the same image on various monitors. This isn't needed for most living rooms but if you are running LAN parties or LAN centers, these devices can be used to output a particular PC both to its screen and to an overhead projector.

 You might want to check out Advanced Media Products at **www.advancedmedia products.com**. They sell the imageMAX for **$385** the last time I checked.

AV ToolBox
www.avtoolbox.com

AV Toolbox is a sister company to TV One and focuses more on consumer devices and products. They sell the aforementioned HI-RES line of console/VGA converters as well as higher-end upscalers. They also have some great downscalers and an excellent HDTV switcher that takes three different inputs to make it easy to switch between DVD, satellite, and your game console.

Key Digital
www.keydigital.com

Key Digital makes three converter products worth checking out. The first is its component to VGA adapter that can drive up to two VGA monitors. It sells for just under $300. The second is its VGA to component adapter with VGA passthrough which sells for just under $200. Finally, they offer an X-Blaster product, which sells for just under $200, and enables you to convert incoming component video to VGA format: RGsBHV for Xbox or Game Cube in Resolutions 480p/60, 1080i/60 or 720p/60.

Cabling

We've sporadically talked about cables. Now it's time to put a little more focus on cabling. We'll first discuss the great cable debate in general. This is the idea that better cables lead to better video and audio clarity. Taken at face value, this argument is misleading because in reality you're led to believe that a single cable is going to just flip every bit and turn the world upside down. Bunk. There are three types of cables out there: poorly made cables, basic cables, and high-end cables that promote a higher level of quality signal.

The first group is important because many times there are one-off cables offered in the console and home-video space that do something funky but necessary. An example of this could be a homemade Japanese SCART cable rewired by hand from a European SCART cable. The quality of these cables can be poor. That's why it's good to wait for reviews on the first batch of a new company's cable.

Basic cables are mass-manufactured cables that produce a nice signal and are of a decent quality. These would include vendor-specific component cables, and some of the better third party cables. Then there are the higher-end cabling companies. They make excellent cables, which are tougher, longer, and manufactured better than the basic cables. The critical issue is whether the marginal improvement they provide is really noticeable and worth the money. Unless you can see it with your own eyes, my feeling is save your money. On the other hand, if I spent $5,000 for a major new TV, I'd feel that spending $50 to $100 on a killer cable is probably worth the chance that the cable might give me a slightly better picture.

Here are a few sources for the best of the best in game cabling.

Monster Cable
www.monstercable.com/monstergame
If there is a better known brand in the high-end cabling business I'm at a loss for who it is. Now Monster Cable is expanding into the games business with a suite of products including well made video cabling for all the major console systems.

The key cables to check out are their GameLink 400, 300, and 200 series for the Xbox, PS2, and GameCube. (The 400 series is not available for the GameCube.) These cables are extremely well made and are very long (10ft in most cases), which comes in handy. In addition, the PS2 and Xbox cables feature an option to output the audio portion in full digital fiber optic for receivers that will accept this type of hookup. The cables run $30 to $60 depending on the model. The optional fiber-optic audio passthrough cable goes for $30. For Xbox fans, they offer a Monster made Ethernet cable.

Monster also manufactures the Powerstation 600 surge strip, which is made for consumer electronics equipment and includes a pass through for phone. Monster also offers a Dolby audio system and other accessories but I've not seen any reviews on them and I haven't tried them myself. The cables get great kudos from fans for their quality and length and are well recommended.

Straight Wire
www.straightwire.com
Straight Wire is another well liked cabling company. They offer very high-end S-video and RCA cabling that might be of interest to some gamers, especially those recording their games to video. Straight Wire only sells through dealers like 1888camcorder.com and they are not cheap. A single 6-ft high-end S-video cable is $180 on sale. I'm clearly in the wrong business.

Hook Up, Tune In, Drop Out

What's amazing about games is that we put so much stock in the visuals. There are entire games that don't need great visual to be fun, and for a long time, visuals weren't exactly the big selling point of games. But when a game has great visuals, we want to make the most of it. Yet, TV and console technology have not kept pace with the advancements in gaming. We need converter boxes, better-than-average cables, and more—all to create the perfect game-playing experience where we can just spend a lazy Sunday (and Monday, and Tuesday, and …) afternoon opening up a can of whoop ass on some main monster, or foe in Madden or SoCoM.

Component video, RGB video, and component RGB get bandied about along with YPrPb so it pays to know that these are all more or less the same thing in that cables are used to carry separate components of the core signal. YPrPb however is different in how it carries signals from a straight RGB signal. It combines the signals in a matrix that optimizes bandwidth. So when you see component video described as YPrPb you'll know it's this specific form as compared tp straight RGB. Modern HDTV sets and component hookup systems use the YPrPb form.

chapter 7

UNIQUE GAME GEAR: COLLECTIBLES AND MORE

Being a movie fan is in some ways easier than being a game fan. Sure we gamers have better magazines and great fan sites, but movie fans come out on top when it comes to collecting merchandise. The game industry just isn't the merchandising colossus that the movie industry is. I think this will change in the next five to ten years. Japan is already way ahead of the U.S. If you currently want to collect game-related merchandise for your favorite titles, you'll need to really hustle. And don't expect to get rich from your collectibles. Chances are strong that the Lara Croft poster you acquired five years ago is worth just a little bit more than whatever you paid for it. But don't be discouraged—there's a good chance that the value of game merchandise will increase as the fan base for gaming grows.

In this chapter we'll explore game-related merchandise and other media like books, music, and movies. You're about to read the best, most complete, piece of information on fan-related game merchandise that exists. I know because in researching this topic I didn't come across anything remotely comprehensive as this chapter. I've tried to cover all the big areas of game-related gear and collectibles including action figures, music, books, movies, posters, and apparel. There is a lot to cover, but at times the pickings will be sparse. That being said, let's go through the merchandise gauntlet!

Action Figures

Action figures are close to the top of the list of in-demand collectibles. The market has come a long way from my days with early Star Wars figures. Who knew back then that this stuff would increase in value? And what's this nonsense about not taking it out of the boxes to enjoy it? Videogame inspired figures are a recent addition to the entire action figure phenomena but a welcomed one for various gamers who want to enjoy the characters that the game world gives us.

Game-oriented action figures come from one of roughly a dozen companies. A few, such as Resaurus, are now out of business but are worth knowing about if you are searching on ebay or the Web in general. New companies pop-up with some frequency in the action figure market so you'll also want to look for new products from new companies. Table 7.1 presents the major companies that have released action figures based on games.

TABLE 7.1
Key manufacturers of videogame oriented action figures.

Manufacturer Name	Related Games	Email Contact	Comments
Toy Biz www.Toybiz.com 212-689-6360	Marvel vs. Capcom; Tomb Raider; Final Fantasy; Street Fighter; Resident Evil	N/A	Toybiz a division of Marvel Comics, has produced a few lines of toys on various games including the original Resident Evil.
Playmates Toys www.playmatestoys.com 852-237-7388	Tomb Raider; Turok	N/A	Playmates made two lines of videogame figures both of which are long gone but still might be found by scouring the Web and outlets like ebay.
McFarlane Toys www.spawn.com	Metal Gear; Solid 2; Soul Calibur 2; Onimusha 2; Ultima Online	Toys@ mcfarland.com	Todd McFarlane is the creator of Spawn but also runs an extensive toy company that focuses on figures. He's even designed some of the characters in Ultima Online and Spawn will appear in the upcoming Soul Calibur game.

(CONTINUED)

TABLE 7.1 (CONTINUED)
Key manufacturers of videogame oriented action figures.

MANUFACTURER NAME	RELATED GAMES	EMAIL CONTACT	COMMENTS
AnJon/Digital Leisure www.digitalleisure.com 888-8364383	Dragons Lair	Elizabethf@ digitalleisure.com	Based in Ontario, Canada, they only make products related to Dragons Lair line of games.
Kotobukiya	Final Fantasy X	N/A	Based in Japan, they produce some figures based on Final Fantasy X.
Artfx	Final Fantasy VIII	N/A	Based in Japan nut not much else known.
RadioActive Clown www.radioactiveclown.com	Unreal II	N/A	Newly founded company out of Texas. Unreal line is first for games.
Epoch & Joyride Studios www.joyridestudios.com	Gampro Line; Mech Warrior; Tekken; Legend of Zelda; SSX Tricky; Crazy Taxi; Sonic; Virtua Fighter 4; Mario Brothers; Cel Damage; Halo; Monkey Ball; Metroid; Command & Conquer; Jet Set Radio; Future; Medal of Honor; Dead or Alive	Chris@ joyridestudios.com	Probably the single biggest group that makes videogame-inspired action figures. Based in Glenn Ellen, IL.
Blue Box Toys www.blueboxtoys.com 212-255-8388	Soul Reaver; Perfect Dark; King of Fighters; Fighting Force	Bbusa@ blueboxtoys.com	Based in New York, they have made several lines of figures.
Toycom www.toycom.net	Metal Gear Solid; Kingdom Hearts; OniMishu; Diablo; Warcraft; Starcraft; Devil May Cry	N/A	You might find some of the series like Kingdom Hearts sold under the Mirage/ N2Toys brands given recent acquisitions.
NECA	Tron 2.0	N/A	N/A
Mirage Toys	Kingdom Hearts		Was known as N2 Toys but is now a sister company to Toycom based out of Japan.

(CONTINUED)

TABLE 7.1 (CONTINUED)
Key manufacturers of videogame oriented action figures.

MANUFACTURER NAME	RELATED GAMES	EMAIL CONTACT	COMMENTS
Resaurus	Crash Bandicoot; Street Fighter; Sonic Adventure; Gex; Mech Warrior		Resaurus went out of business but you can still find some of the lines they put out using ebay and other collectors site.
Palisades Toys www.palisadestoys.com 410.540.9090	Resident Evil; House of the Dead	Info@ palisadestoys.com	On their site they only show Resident Evil but they are doing House of the Dead and they did import some Lara Croft series from Europe when Playmates ditched them.
Milo's Workshop	American McGee's Alice; American McGee's Oz; EverQuest	N/A	This is a shop that makes really nice figures and the upcoming Oz line looks incredible.
Bandai www.bandai.com	Final Fantasy; Final Fantasy IX; X	N/A	One of many companies to pump out some figures based on the Final Fantasy series which are now hard to find.

You'll also want to check out some of the best action figure stores and sites on the Web that are listed in Table 7.2 to help you both monitor and acquire your collection. Periodic trips to the local toystore can also be useful, and many of the big retail chains carry some figures. As a final place to look, some of the importers listed in Chapter 3 also carry figures (and other videogame merchandise) as well.

You should also pick up a copy of *ToyFare* Magazine. It's simply the best magazine on action figures that you'll find. Unfortunately, they don't have a Web site but you can order it via Amazon's magazine section by going to **www.amazon.com/ exec/obidos/ASIN/B00006KZVP**.

The action figures collectibles market is pretty fluid and figures can easily appreciate in value, although it's hard to say if collectors really purchase them for an

TABLE 7.2
Best sites and stores for action figures and action figure news.

Site Name	Site URL	Comments
Raving Toy Maniac	www.toymania.com	Killer site for action figure information.
Entertainment Earth	www.entertainmentearth.com	Great shop for action figures of all kinds including extensive video game inspired figures.
Figures.com	www.figures.com	Extensive site covering the action figure industry and scene.
Action Figure Times	www.aftimes.com	Major news site,
Big Bad Toy Store	www.bigbadtoystore.com	Lots of figures for sale.
Hobby Link Japan	www.hlj.com	Good source for imported toys.
Treasure Island Sports	www.tisinc99.com	Mostly Anime inspired figures but a few video game lines are stocked as well.
Action Figure Express	www.actionfigurexpress.com	Major site for action figures.
Amok Time	www.amoktime.com	Large collection of game-based figures including Alice, House of the Dead, and Metal Gear Solid.
Yes Anime	www.yesanime.com	Slow site that offers some good sets for ordering, from Japan-based companies.
Wizzywig	www.wizzywig.com	99% Anime figures but a few hard to find older lines from Japan can be found here.
Explosion Toys	www.explosiontoys.com	Great site with lots of video game lines in stock for ordering.

investment. Prices are driven mainly by the availability of action figures. The market is so fickle that many figures are manufactured, sold out, and retired to the collectors market in a year or less.

Apparel

After I tell you everything I know about gaming apparel promise me I won't bump into you at E3 and find you covered from head-to-toe in gaming-related clothing. There are four key types of apparel you can find:

1. The first is SWAG (Stuff We All Get) which is given away as handouts at various conferences. I've got a closet full of t-shirts going back to the 80s that I've snagged from sales reps, at trade shows, and so on. Unfortunately this stuff

rarely ends up for sale barely anywhere. Unless you decide to go to E3 and stand in some long line, don't expect to find much.

2. The second category of stuff is official merchandise provided for sale by developers, publishers, or licensees. This stuff is not widely available although there are some key outlets you can scour to find stuff. Some of the stuff you see licensed is truly cheesy. As you might guess, there is a more availability of crappy kids stuff like Dragon Ball Z and Pokemon merchandise.

3. The third category of stuff you can find consists of vintage-oriented clothing having a focus on brands like Atari, Intellivision, Pac-Man, and so on. Retro clothing is big and often the brands represented might be sufficiently out of business so no one worries about copyright issues. However, I've found that most of the Atari t-shirts I see these days aren't licensed.

4. The final category of clothing consists of new designs which are influenced by games and gaming culture. There is some surprisingly great stuff popping up along these lines and it's great to see it. I hope it grows.

One of the cooler pieces of apparel comes from the time Sega sponsored the U.K. soccer team, Arsenal (2001 - 2002). As a sponsor, Sega's name was used the first year and the Dreamcast brand was used the second year on authentic Arsenal team jerseys (see Figure 7.1). You can still find the jerseys on the Web or on ebay. If you're in Europe, you can still find them in some shops. In the U.S. or Japan, try mail order from Soccer Plus (**www.soccerplus.net**).

FIGURE 7.1
Sega sponsored the well-known British soccer club Arsenal during its 2001-2002 season.

Tables 7.3 through 7.5 lists the actual stores, links and sources for cool game-oriented apparel.

TABLE 7.3
Licensed apparel.

Store	Link	Offerings and Comments
Xbox Gear Store	gearstore.xbox.com	As official as it can get.
PlayStation Official Threadz store	www.us.playstation.com/ purchase/featureditems	Lots of stuff for PS2 addicts. My personal favorite being the Parappa the Rappa orange knit ski cap.
Toy Destination	www.toyd.com/ playlicclotw.html	Small selection of licensed PS2 clothing and goodies.

TABLE 7.4
Vintage/retro apparel.

Store	Link	Offerings and Comments
Intellivision Lives Retropia Store	www.retropia.com	Great merchandise from the people who are officially bringing Intellivision software back to life for its fans.
Emerchandise	www.emerchandise.com/ browse/ATARI/ ALLPRODUCTS	Movie related merchandise store with large selection of the retro Atari shirts that seem to be everywhere these days.
80's Tees	www.80stees.com/Atari_ directory.htm	Another source for Atari retro t-shirts.
Y-Que	www.yque.com/a383.html	Retro shirt featuring old-school NES gamepad.
Atari Age t-shirt	www.atariage.com/features/ contests/tshirt	This killer enthusiast site for all things Atari designed its own shirt which will align you not only with Atari but with current day enthusiasts.
Krazy Shirts	www.krazyshirts.com/ supnincontsh.html	Sells a simple shirt with a SNES gamepad on it.

TABLE 7.5
Game influenced designs.

Store	Link	Offerings and Comments
Thinkgeek	www.thinkgeek.com/ tshirts/gaming	A number of original designs including an "All your base are belong to us" and my personal favorite "I see fragged people."
JoyStick Junkies	www.joystickjunkies.com/ pages/clothing.html	Dedicated to creating new game-influenced designs. Very cool stuff although the ordering system requires you to visit another site, choose them from a list and then shop.

All Hail ebay!

ebay is a gift from God for the merchandise collector. As I mentioned, there are many promotional shirts, buttons, and other merchandise often given away in limited supply at trade shows, in shops, or as part of special offers. There are also limited runs by licensees and other manufacturers that make it to market. Aside from ending up at the bottom of some closet or in a local thrift or goodwill store, this SWAG and other merchandise ends up on ebay. Table 7.6 lists some basic searches that turn up the good stuff.

Other keywords worth combining from time to time for unique searches include watches, wallscrolls, patches, mugs, mousepads, and glasses. You can also search for music but because there are some great specific game music sources on the Web I find this less of a need other than to bargain hunt.

TABLE 7.6
Guide to ebay searches for game-related merchandise.

BRANDS, WORDS TO USE	WORDS TO COMBINE WITH THEM	COMMENTS
Game, Videogame	Shirt, Hat, Poster, Backpack, Plush, Stickers, Figure, Postcard, Promo, Display	Universal game or videogame are good to use to find stuff that might not turn up easily in more specific searches like Robotron shirts, etc.
Xbox	Shirt, Hat, Poster, Figure, Postcard, Promo, Figures, Display	Xbox is less likely to turn up figurines, or kids stuff so far.
PlayStation, PS2	Shirt, Hat, Poster, Postcard, Figure, Plush, Promo, Display	Sometimes people just put PS2 vs. PlayStation.
Nintendo	Shirt, Hat, Poster, Backpack, Plush, Stickers, Figure, Promo, Display	Nintendo has more kids oriented stuff so things like stickers and plush generate decent returns here.
Gamecube	Poster, Shirt, Hat, Figure, Postcard, Promo, Display	Unlike Xbox and PlayStation, Gamecube and Nintendo are different and thus searches do turn up stuff listed under one brand but not the other.
Sega	Shirt, Hat, Poster, Postcard, Plush, Promo, Display	You can also try Dreamcast, Saturn, and Genesis which are key hardware brands of Sega also.
Final Fantasy	Shirt, Hat, Poster, Postcard, Figure, Promo, Display	Mixes in stuff from the horridly written movie also.
Tomb Raider, Lara Croft	Shirt, Hat, Poster, Postcard, Figure, Promo, Display	Mixes in stuff from movie too.

Wallscrolls are fancy posters that are printed on cloth or vinyl plastic as opposed to paper. If you didn't know this don't worry. Not being an anime freak, I didn't either.

Other major publishers and brands like Electronic Arts, Capcom, Metal Gear Solid, Tekken, Virtua, Mario, and others also turn up when combined with some of the most basic keywords. However, setting up searches for them is more work than what it returns. However, if you want to be extensive, add major series, publishers, and games to your list but don't combine them with every last keyword. Keywords like hat, poster, shirt, and promo will turn up most of the stuff available.

Automating Searches on ebay

If you're not familiar with ebay, you need to learn how to use its favorite searches option to track down stuff automatically each time you log on. Here are the steps to follow:

1. Create an account.

2. Under the search button, choose the favorite searches menu item. You will be greeted with a listing of all your favorite category searches, keyword searches, and sellers as shown in Figure 7.2.

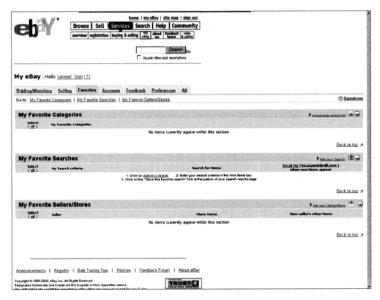

FIGURE 7.2
The My Favorite Searches system on ebay makes it easy to automate your monitoring of game-related merchandise.

3. Under the My Favorite Searches area on the right-hand side, click the Add New Search link, which will let you add a new search as shown in Figure 7.3.

4. In the Search Keywords field, type in the mix of words to use as outlined in Tables 7.3 through 7.5. You'll need to set one up for each of the basic combinations you wish to monitor. Leave the rest of the options at their default setting except for Sort. (I recommend you set this option to Newly-listed items first.)

5. Press Search and you will given the results of that search.

You're not done yet though! In the upper right-hand corner of the search results page you'll find an important link titled "Save this search." You must click this link to save the search to your "My favorite Searches" list. When that is done your favorite searches will update as shown in Figure 7.4. Now with a saved search you can do two more things. One is the easy Search Now link, which is self explanatory. The other is a check box under the email me column which will send an alert to your email when someone posts a new item relevant to the search you've saved.

Game Music

When games first debuted the music and sound quality wasn't exactly like a John Williams score. Music for a long time was a bit of a bastard stepchild. Today, however, game music has really come a long way. It has improved so much that a symphonic tribute to game music is being planned for the 2003 E3 Expo. In Japan,

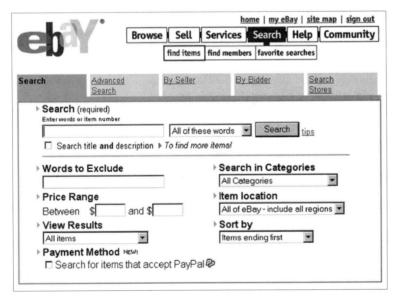

FIGURE 7.3
The basic item search page on ebay.

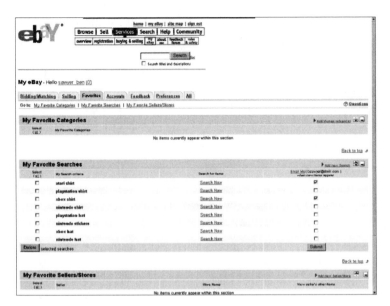

FIGURE 7.4
The My Favorite Searches feature lets you get email updates so you
don't miss out on good stuff.

game soundtracks are released regularly and sell in decent quantities. Ask any avid gamer and they're likely to tell you about several games that had amazing sound tracks. I remember I recorded the Score to Ultima IV and Ballblazer so that I could listen to them on my Walkman.

Occasionally, a game soundtrack will really breakout and the composers become household names for hardcore gamers. There are now enough soundtracks on the market that there are a number of sites devoted not only to game music but to selling it. Table 7.7 shows you the best sources for finding great versions of your favorite soundtracks.

You can occasionally find soundtracks packed into collectors editions, for sale in major chains and on ebay. In addition to CD-based soundtracks, a number of developers release MP3s of their soundtracks on their sites. It's useful to visit the various developer's sites to find them, and several of the sites above do let people know when such releases debut.

Posters, Wall Scrolls, and Post Cards
Most of the posters that that feature videogame subjects are not sold in stores. They are bound in magazines, included in games, or are used for promotional purposes at tradeshows or in retail stores. Thus, ebay is a great source for posters. Aside from

ebay, you can still find a number of game-oriented posters or wall scrolls available from a few select retail stores. Table 7.8 provides some good leads.

For postcards, two major original sources are available. The first are the publishers themselves who sometimes create postcards to handout at shows and stores as promos. The second are national postcard advertising companies like GoCard (**www.gocard.com**) that are used by a number of companies to advertise game systems or software.

TABLE 7.7
The best locations to find and/or order game music soundtracks.

SITE/STORE	URL	COMMENTS
Game Music	www.gamemusic.com	Probably the single best source on the Web for game music soundtracks. You don't need to go anywhere else.
Music 4 Games	www.music4games.net	More of an information site with links to retailers for soundtracks.
Game Music Revolution	www.gmronline.com	Giant database of all track listings for game soundtracks.
Soundtrack Central	www.altpop.com/stc	Meticulous soundtrack reviews.
Chudahs Corner	www.chudahs-corner.com	Site devoted to game music with lyrics database, reviews, news, and track listings.

TABLE 7.8
Best leads for posters and wall scrolls.

SITE/STORE	URL	COMMENTS
Treasure Island Sports	www.tisinc99.com	Mostly anime stuff but with an extensive collection of wallscrolls for sale including Final Fantasy and Resident Evil 3.
Toy N Joys	www.toysnjoys.com/wallscroll.html	Has large collection of wall scrolls including Metal Gear Solid and Final Fantasy.
Poster Parlor	www.posterparlor.com/3/n7823-video-games.html	Only three posters which shows you the sorry state of online retail poster availability for games: Spyro, Tomb Raider, and Gex.
Posters.uk.co	www.posters.co.uk/Acategory/1_Posters/144/3/Computer_game.html	Two rarer posters, one a promo promoting the WuTang Clans PS2 fighting game, and one of Lara Croft relaxing in a pool with her clothes on.
Post Age Collectibles	www.post-age-collectibles.com/pinball/flyers/flyers.html	Number of vintage posters/flyers for various arcade games.

There are dozens of card vendors around the globe but in the U.S. the biggest are Max Racks and GoCards. Others include Hotstamp, Brandaid, Eyecards, and Supercard. If you're ever in a big city like San Francisco or New York, you can usually find these racks in trendy bars, resturants, and places like Tower Records. I usually check a few of them whenever I'm going through New York and have picked up a few related cards like a Crash Bandicoot one that's pretty funny. If you can't find them yourself, I'd suggest checking out Ralph's Rack Cards which is on the Web at: **http://members.aol.com/rackcardking/index.htm**.

Ralph's is the best site on the Web for collecting rack cards and his prices are great. There are a number of cards from Nintendo and Sega which uses GoCard. Sony uses Max Racks and Electronic Arts uses GoCard dispensed through Tower Records. Ralph's site has an exhaustive listing and you can leave standing orders so if he picks up other cards you want, you can get them right away. Max Racks (**www.maxracks.com**) also has a customer bulletin board located at **www.maxracks.com/maxads/maxexchange.html** where you can leave posts if you're seeking certain cards. Ebay is also a good site to try to find some.

You can find other cards that have been distributed at shows and the like on the Web at: **http://rog.vcvgc.bc.ca/collectibles/postcards**.

Books and Novels

Games are still not widely recognized as an art form for their storytelling aspects. Yet some of the most complete and interesting worlds including Ultima, StarCraft or Lara Croft, have been developed. We've also got games like Theif, Deus Ex, and Shenmue that are interesting stories in and of themselves. It should be no surprise that there are a number of games that have been turned into, or extended through novels. Most of them are in the sci-fi and fantasy realms and some of them are actually pretty good reads. Table 7.9 presents the list of every major novel based on a cult game or game world that you might be interested in.

Non-Fiction Fan Titles

There are also a growing number of non-fiction books worth collecting. This includes *The Art of Warcraft* and *The Art of Final Fantasy*, which hopefully will lead to more art books being released if they sell modestly well. Table 7.10 presents the set of non-fiction titles.

TABLE 7.9
Novels based on games.

TITLE	AUTHOR	ISBN	PUBLISHER
Halo: The Fall of Reach	Eric S. Nylund	0345451325	Del Rey
Halo: The Flood	William C. Dietz	0345459210	Del Rey
Crimson Skies	Eric S. Nylund, Mike Lee, Eric S. Trautmann, Nancy Berman	0345458745	Del Rey
Brute Force: Betrayals	Dean Wesley Smith	0345458508	Del Rey
Neverwinter Nights	Philip Athans	0786918160	Wizards of the Coast
Myst: The Book of D'Ni	Rand Miller	0786861614	Hyperion
Myst: The Book of Ti'Ana	Rand Miller	0786881887	Hyperion
From Myst to Riven	Richard Kadrey	078686365X	Hyperion
Myst: The Book of Atrus	Robyn Miller	078688942X	Little Brown & Company
The Sea of Mist (Might & Magic)	Mel Odem	0061031631	Harper Entertainment
Shadowsmith (Might and Magic)	Geary Gravel	0345382935	Del Rey Books
The Dreamwright (Might and Magic)	Geary Gravel	0345382927	Del Rey Books
Legacy of Blood (Diablo, 1)	Richard A. Knaak	067104155X	Pocket Books
The Black Road (Diablo, 2)	Mel Odem	0743426916	Pocket Books
Kingdom of Shadow (Diablo 3)	Richard A. Knaak	0743426924	Star Trek
Diablo Tales of Sanctuary	Dave Land, Philip Amara	156971682X	Dark Horse Comics
Day of the Dragon (Warcraft 1)	Richard A. Knaak	0671041525	Pocket Books
Lord of the Clans (Warcraft 2)	Christie Golden	0743426908	Pocket Books
The Last Guardian (Warcraft 3)	Jeff Grub	0671041517	Star Trek
StarCraft #1: Liberty's Crusade	Jeff Grub	0671041487	Pocket Books
StarCraft #2: Shadow of the Xel'Naga	Gabriel Mesta	0671041495	Pocket Books
Speed of Darkness (StarCraft)	Traci Hickman	0671041509	Star Trek
Baldur's Gate II Throne of Bhaal	Drew Karpyshyn	078691985X	Wizards of the Coast
The Dig	Alan Dean Foster	0446603791	Warner Books
Machinations (Ultima: The Technocrat War)	Austen Andrews	0743403797	Pocket Books

(CONTINUED)

TABLE 7.9 (CONTINUED)
Novels based on games.

TITLE	AUTHOR	ISBN	PUBLISHER
Masquerade (Ultima: The Technocrat War)	Austen Andrews	0743403800	Pocket Books
Maelstrom (Ultima: The Technocrat War)	Austen Andrews	0743403819	Pocket Books
Centauri Dawn (Alpha Centauri)	Michael Ely, Robert Simpson	0671040774	Pocket Books
Sid Meier's Alpha Centauri: Dragon Sun	Michael Ely	0671040782	Pocket Books
The Forge of Virtue (The Ultima Saga)	Lynn Abbey	0445210656	Warner Books
The Temper of Wisdom (The Ultima Sage #2)	Lynn Abbey	0446362263	Warner Books
Tomb Raider, Vol. 1: Saga of the Medusa Mask	Dan Jurgens, Andy Park, Jonathan Sibal, Richard Isanove, Jonathan D. Smith	1582401640	Image Comics
Tomb Raider, Vol. 2: Mystic Artifacts	Dan Jurgens, Andy Park, Jonathan D. Smith	1582402027	Image Comics
Tomb Raider: Chasing Shangri LA	Dan Jurgens, Billy Tan, Andy Park, Francis Manapul, Sibal Jonathan, Jonathan D. Smith	1582402671	Image Comics
Tomb Raider: Volume 3	Dan Jurgens	1582402345	Image Comics
End Run (Wing Commander)	Christopher Stasheff, William R. Forstchen, Bill Forstchen	067172200X	Baen Books
Heart of the Tiger (Wing Commander)	William R. Forstchen, Andrew Keith	0671876538	Pocket Books
False Colors (Wing Commander)	William R. Forstchen, Andrew Keith	0671577840	Pocket Books
Action Stations: A Wing Commander Novel	William R. Forstchen	067187859X	Baen Books
Wing Commander: Freedom Flight	Mercedes Lackey, Ellen Guon	0671721453	Baen Books
The Price of Freedom (Wing Commander)	William R. Forstchen, Ben Ohlander	0671877518	Baen Books
Fleet Action (Wing Commander)	William R. Forstchen	0671722115	Baen Books

TABLE 7.10
Non-fiction titles based on games.

Title	Author	ISBN	Publisher	Notes
1,000 Game Heroes	David Choquet	3822816337	TASCHEN	A coffee table book with great color and printing to make all those characters look so good.
Digital Beauties	Julius Wiedemann	3822816280	America LLC	Not a gaming book per se but from the same publisher as 1,000 Game Heroes. Focuses on 3D female characters, some from games.
Game On	Lucien King (Editor)	0789307782	Universe Books	Interesting book of culture and historical articles about the games industry covering the Game On exhibit and travelling exhibit developed by Royal Museum, Edinburgh, which you can find on the Web at www.gameonweb.co.uk.
Lara's Book— Lara Croft and the Tomb Raider Phenomenon	Douglas Coupland, Kip Ward	0761515801	Prima Publishing	Written by well-known author who penned GenerationX and Microserfs.
Pac-Man Collectibles: An Unauthorized Guide: With Price Guide	Deborah Palicia	0764315544	Schiffer Publishing	Web site for book is at www.pacmancollectibles.com.
The Art of Final Fantasy IX	Dan Birlew	0744000505	Brady Games	Includes concept art and more from the making of Final Fantasy IX.
The Art of Warcraft	Jeff Green, Bart Farkas	0744000815	Brady Games	Includes artwork from all three games in the series.
The Making of FINAL FANTASY: The Spirits Within	Steven Kent	0744000718	Brady Games	Inside look at how they made the stunning animation for an awful movie.
The Official Book of Ultima	Shay Addams	0874552648	Compute	Out of print and printed before every last Ultima came out but with good inside stuff on the series.

Japanese Game Art Books

Books on game art are much bigger in Japan than they are in the U.S. and Europe. Unfortunately, for those of us outside of Japan we miss out on the amazing game art books. The trick is to scour the Web and local Japanese import shops and locate the books released. I've actually done this for you so check out Table 7.11. You can think of me as your personal game merchandise shopper! These are among the best art books covering games released thus far. The biggest publishers are Soft-bank (**store.sbpnet.jp**) and Digicube (**www.digicube.co.jp**). One other places of note concerning Japanese artbook imports are DMD Sales, which is a distributor. (If you want to resell the books in your store or something call them.) Their Web site is at **www.dmd-sales.com**. They are also good to scout out new books that are out so you can look for them at retailers.

Digicube publishes a list of its released book titles in English on its investor's relations Web pages located at: **www.digicube.co.jp/ir/title/index.php?cate=2&lang=2**.

TABLE 7.11
Japanese game art books.

Book Title	ISBN (Japan)	Import Place(s) to Find It	Potential Price
All About Capcom Fighting	488554676	www.animeoutpost.com/artbooks.html	$25 to $35
All About Final Fantasy Tactics	N/A	www.animeoutpost.com/artbooks.html	$20 to $30
All About SNK Characters	4939110109	www.animeoutpost.com/artbooks.html	$40 to $50
All About Street Fighter III	4885544734	www.animeoutpost.com/artbooks.html	$25to $30
Art of Metal Gear Solid 2	4775300652	www.tokyocentral.comwww.animeoutpost.com/artbooks.html	$26.00
Bouncer The Visual Arts Collection	4925075926	www.tokyocentral.comwww.videogamedepot.com	$26.50
Capcom Design Works	4757704127	www.animeoutpost.com/artbooks.html	
Chrono Cross Ultimania	492507573X	www.animeoutpost.com/artbooks.html	$20 to $30
Dawn: Final Fantasy	4871881350	www.animeoutpost.com/artbooks.html	$55 to $60
Devil May Cry - Memorial Album - Precious Tears	4887870558	www.tokyocentral.com	
Devil May Cry Graphic Edition	4047070718	www.animeoutpost.com/artbooks.html	$25 to $40
Final Fantasy - VII through X - Complete Works, Vol 2	4887870574	www.tokyocentral.com	$24.95

(CONTINUED)

TABLE 7.11 (CONTINUED)
Japanese game art books.

Book Title	ISBN (Japan)	Import Place(s) to Find It	Potential Price
Final Fantasy IX Visual Arts	4925075829	www.animeoutpost.com/artbooks.html www.videogamedepot.com	$25 to $30
Final Fantasy Japan - Yoshitaka Amano	4871883388	www.animebooks.com	N/A
Final Fantasy VIII Memorial Album	4925075527	www.animebooks.com	N/A
Final Fantasy VIII Original Soundtrack	4810863115	www.animebooks.com	N/A
Final Fantasy VIII Seal Book	4925075438	www.animebooks.com	N/A
Final Fantasy X Post Card Book Digicube Publishing	492075802	www.tokyocentral.com www.videogamedepot.com www.dmd-sales.com	$10 to $15
Final Fantasy X: Memorial Album	4887870280		
Final Fantasy X: Visual Arts	4925075829	www.animeoutpost.com/artbooks.html	$25 to $40
GRANDIA XTREME - World Guidance: Softbank Publishing	4797319828	www.tokyocentral.com www.videogamedepot.com	$24.95
Guilty Gear Draftworks Artbook	4757703015	www.animeoutpost.com/artbooks.html	$20 to $30
Legend of Soul Calibur Illustrations	4877196609	www.animeoutpost.com/artbooks.html	$25 to $40
Metal Gear Solid 2 Sons of Liberty Metal Works The Perfect Softbank Publishing	4775300644	www.tokyocentral.com	$25.00
Metal Gear Solid 2, The Making	4789718433	www.animeoutpost.com/artbooks.html	$27.50
Phantasy Star Online, Episodes 1&2, Materials Collection	N/A	www.tokyocentral.com	$29.50
The Bouncer Maximum	492507587X	www.tokyocentral.com	
UNLIMITED: SaGa - Visual Art BookDigicube	N/A	www.tokyocentral.com	$12.95
Vagrant Story ULTIMANIA	4925075756	www.tokyocentral.com	$16.25
Valkyrie Profile, Material Collection Softbank Publishing	4797313862	www.tokyocentral.com	$46.50
Virtual Beauties 2020	4758010072	www.animeoutpost.com/artbooks.html	$25 to $30
Xenosaga Episode 1 -Official Design Materials-Enterbrain	N/A	www.tokyocentral.com	$28.00

Using Amazon.co.jp

You can also order all of the above books directly from Amazon.com in Japan (a last resort if you can't find it elsewhere) but you'll need to know how to order via Amazon's Japan site properly. Amazon.co.jp works almost exactly like Amazon.com so if you're familiar with their interface, you'll be familiar with the basics of ordering from the Japan site. There is an In English button on the Amazon.co.jp site but that is really a route to shopping for imported English language books more so than translating the entire site. To search for books the best thing to do is to input the ISBN from above into the main search box on the homepage (see Figure 7.5).

Once you've done that correctly you'll get the product page and you can then add it to your shopping cart using the button on the right hand screen. If you have an existing Amazon.com account, it won't work here. You'll need to eventually create a new account for this site. So proceed to the checkout to do this.

When filling out an address by default it will assume you live in Japan. Look in the upper right-hand corner and click the International Address button to enter an international address. Amazon.co.jp offers two shipping options for International orders: International Economy, which is three to four weeks and International Express which is two to five days. Economy shipping will be ¥1500 (which

FIGURE 7.5
Find ISBNs for the book(s) you want and input them here.

is roughly $12 as of 2003) and ¥3000 for express shipping (roughly $25 as of 2003). In some cases shipping is more than the book. If you want to calculate the exchange rate use Expedia's currency converter located at (**www.expedia.com/ pub/agent.dll?qscr=curc**).

One final item you will encounter is signing up for a new user account, which threw me at first because I didn't know what they wanted in the Furigana field which will be displayed. From what I figured out it should be the basic user name you'll use when logging back in. Once you do that the rest is pretty self-explanatory and you should be able to check out.

Locating Out of Print Books

As a collector you're going to have to resort at times to finding books that are no longer in print. While you can find many of the books just listed on sites like Amazon.com and BN.com, not all of them are still in print. That shouldn't deter you because there are two excellent sites for finding out of print titles at great prices. The first is Abebooks.com (see Figure 7.6). Abebooks lets local used booksellers from around the world add their lists to a giant database that Abebooks maintains. You can search with title, ISBN, or author and find the books you want and complete the order directly with the merchant who will then ship your book. I've

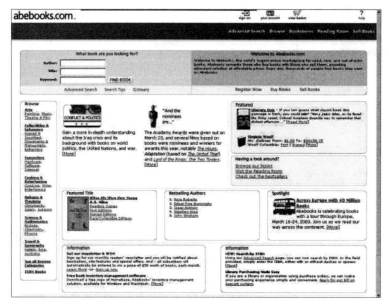

FIGURE 7.6
Abebooks is a great place to find books now out of print.

used it several times and it is really the first place I turn to find books no longer in stock at the major booksellers.

The other place to turn to is Powells.com, the site for the huge bookstore based in Portland, Oregon. Powell's (**www.powells.com**) specializes in used, and out of print books and is a good backup to Abebooks.

Movies and DVDs Related to Games

You could say I've saved the worst for last. Movies based on games have really sucked, other than a few movies which essentially weren't great but didn't suck. It's a wonder any movie producer even goes near the damn things. Talk about career suicide for a producer! It's like the kiss of death for a movie to be based on a game. If you can sit through all of the movies listed in Table 7.12 without wanting to gag at least three times, you might be a candidate to work at the CIA. I hear they need people who can withstand rigorous torture.

TABLE 7.12
Movies based on games.

Movie	Basic Details	Comments
American McGee's Alice	The re-interpretation of Alice as a stark raving lunatic from the game makes the leap to the big screen.	Wes Craven opted this movie so it's got a real chance of being a stellar production. With McGee now working on a Wizard of Oz remake there is good pressure on Craven to make this into a potential franchise.
Battle Arena Toshinden	Anime title out of Japan based on the characters from the PlayStation 1 hit.	Reviewers considered this to be more involved than the game (as if that was hard). Features decent animation that could appeal to video game fans.
Crazy Taxi	Optioned by Richard Donner (Lethal Weapon) and in early phases of production planning.	What is it with Richard Donner and crazy taxi movies? First he directed Mel Gibson as a crazy cab driver in Conspiracy Theory then this. Is Crazy Taxi going to be a sequel? Maybe they could reunite the cast from D.C. Cab. I haven't a clue how this is going to work.
Deus Ex	Optioned by Columbia Pictures and being currently lead by Laura Ziskin who spearheaded Spiderman for the studio.	Could be very cool for any number of reasons. Spiderman was a pretty good adaptation and designer Warren Spector seems involved enough to help it avoid a catastrophe.
Doom	Optioned by Warner Brothers. They need to start work on it or id gets the rights back.	Who knows what this will be like. It could be as good as Aliens or it could be as terrible as Aliens 3.

(CONTINUED)

TABLE 7.12 (CONTINUED)
Movies based on games.

MOVIE	BASIC DETAILS	COMMENTS
Double Dragon	Billy and Jimmy vs. the world.	Vanna White in a cameo appearance. Alyssa Milano. Need I say more?
Duke Nuke'em The Movie	Duke's in space trying to save the earth when he should be back on earth trying to finish the damn game.	Duke was originally optioned to be a movie years ago. Both the movie and a true sequel to the game have been AWOL ever since. The guys behind this now are Dimension Films and the producer of the Mortal Kombat movies so it stands a chance of being mildly good.
Fatal Fury Movies	Anime films from Japan.	They get ok marks from fans from what I can see. Never seen them myself.
Final Fantasy: The Spirits Within	I'd try to explain the plot but you'd only laugh. There are spirits in the Earth (Gaia) and some kook scientist and his daughter need to stop some other wack job from doing something that might destroy the Gaia Spirit (I think).	The animation was amazing and it's worth owning on DVD for that aspect, but the story is so bad I'd recommend watching it MST3K style with the volume down while you and friends make up your own lines. This movie actually caused Square Pictures to fold, and was a financial disaster for Sony/Columbia which backed it.
Final Fantasy Anime Videos	There were two Final Fantasy anime titles released on VHS in either dubbed or subtitles English. Called Legend of the Crystals (volumes 1 and 2) which you can find on Amazon.com among other places.	If you're an FF freak they might be worth watching. Fans seem to like them for what they are. I've never seen either one but almost anything can have a better plot than The Spirits Within.
House of the Dead	Still in production but almost out. Is supposedly a prequel to the games (there was a plot in the games??!?)	Maybe director Uwe Boll is the next Ted Rami, or Wes Craven but I'm betting he's not.
Max Payne	In production planning at this time.	The person behind it has worked on the cool FX series, The Shield, as well as Angel but also worked on Life with Louie. Let's hope he took this job because he was starving. Dimension is doing it so this has a chance.
Mortal Kombat 1&2	The first film sets up the premise of Mortal Kombat and the Outworld tournament. Spawned a sequel.	This first one wasn't half-bad and had a decent soundtrack too. The characters were well represented and the story held together okay. But if this is what we're holding up as a "good" game movie it shows you how bad the rest really are.

(CONTINUED)

TABLE 7.12 (CONTINUED)
Movies based on games.

Movie	Basic Details	Comments
Panzer Dragoon	Anime movie out of Japan sure to get renewed interest with the release of Panzer Dragoon Orta for the Xbox in 2003.	According to the reviews, this is one of the poorer anime movies around. Save your cash.
Perfect Dark	Supposedly in development as a series and/or a movie.	Like everything else it could be good if the right people do it which more often than not with game movies is NOT.
Pokemon Movies	A new Pokemon goes awry and forces young kids all over the world to buy Gameboys and trading cards.	Which came first? The game, or the movie? Does it really matter? They're all awesome, at least that's what the subliminal messages told me to say.
Resident Evil	Lab accident spawns zombies, and Milla Jovovich shows up to kill them.	Haven't seen this but I've heard it's not that bad when compared to other game-based movies. When compared to other great horror flicks or the game itself it's nothing to write home about. Soundtrack is supposed to be good.
Shenmue	An animated film edited and comprised from all the cutscenes from Shenmue I. Released in Japan as a movie and on DVD and included in the Xbox release of Shenmue II.	If you played the game, the DVD is an amusing way to relive a game that had 0 replay value. I wonder if we'll see more DVDs like this in the future.
Sonic The Hedgehog: The Movie	There was a series which sucked, but did you know there was a movie too?	I can't do better than the quote found on IMDB.com that someone posted, "What the producers did to this franchise is the equivalent of taking a chainsaw to a Monet painting."
Street Fighter	Guile played by John Claude Van Damme fights against M. Bison played by Raul Julia.	An exquisite performance by Van Damme; Oscar caliber and not to be missed. He could be the best video game actor ever. As for poor Raul Julia he must have needed the paycheck to appear in this crap. Don't forget pop sensation Kylie Minoque either who plays Sammy!
Street Fighter II (Animated)	More Street Fighter because you didn't get enough from the games or the live action movie or the animated series.	This is what happens when the live action is so bad—you're relegated to animated status after that.
Super Mario Bros.	It's Bob Hoskins as Mario and John Leguizamo as Luigi who try to save Princess Koopa.	Could possibly be the worst video game movie ever made? Wait don't answer that!

7

(CONTINUED)

TABLE 7.12 (CONTINUED)
Movies based on games.

Movie	Basic Details	Comments
Tekken: The Movie	There are two Tekkens around. First is an anime movie out of Japan and the second is a reported live-action Tekken in development.	The anime movie gets so-so reviews. Worth it if you're a true fan I guess. The live-action flick is anybody's guess. At least with Mortal Kombat the bar is not set terribly high just adequately high enough.
Tomb Raider	Lara Croft must capture artifacts that control the fate of time before the bad guys shoot everything in site.	Like Mortal Kombat it's not bad, it's just not that great either. Did well enough that we get a sequel now! Oh Joy! I'm begging George Lucas to make another Indiana Jones flick to remind us how it's really done.
Wing Commander	Here's the idea. If the game had so many movie segments why not take out the game and just leave in the movie? Cast many of the same folks, and do a basic save the world plot.	Set back the ambitions of any game developer ever directing a full-feature length movie 1,000 years. There was an animated series too—Wing Commander Academy, which was actually pretty good.

Other than game-based movies, movies have been made that incorporated games as an integral part of their plot. Again, not much to say here, although a few were big hits. These include Tron, Wargames, Last Starfighter, The Wizard (ugh), Cloak and Dagger (double ugh), and Joysticks (kill me now). In terms of TV series, Saturday morning television is the usual space for game influenced media and the results there are about as bad as the movies. So bad I doubt you'll be seeing many DVD releases of shows like the Pac Man cartoon (**www.classicgaming.com/ pac-man/Cartoon**) or Earthworm Jim (**www.bcdb.com/pages/Universal/ Television/Earthworm_Jim**).

 A great site covering the intersection of games and movies is the Games in Movies pages located on MameWorld at: **www.mameworld.net/movies**.

This site covers a ton of instances where video games are seen in parts of various major movies complete with stills from the films

Loving Games Goes Beyond Playing Them

As you can see from this chapter, games have spawned a number of media and products, some of them even worth the money you pay for them. I think we'll see a lot more novelizations, action figures, and licensed apparel and hopefully some better movies and shows too because it can't get any worse than what we have now. Still, if you love games your interest in all things related to games is probably pretty good. You probably already have a figure or two, maybe even a shirt sporting the logo of your favorite console, you might have even put a gamepad down long enough to read a book too. If you don't and you want to call yourself a monster gamer you need to scarf some cash and go get some. But like I said, don't necessarily walk around town decked out like someone who snuck into E3 and grabbed all the SWAG they could find and put it on.

7

chapter **8**

Everything You Need to Know about Competitive Gaming

You probably can beat the pants off of your computer, or at least you don't get beat very often if you're a hot monster gamer. So the best of us seek head-to-head play, one-on-one or in teams. Despite its ignorant critics, gaming can be a highly social activity and the advent of the Internet and network games has made gaming immeasurably more social. As few as eight years ago no gamers would have envisioned that competitive gaming would have expanded as it has. Today we have mega-competitions, professional leagues, and sponsored gamers from huge companies like Intel, NVIDIA, and CompUSA. Some gamers are so good that they get paid $1,500 per month and a percentage of their winnings, as well as all the pizza and soda they can inhale. (I don't know about you but free pizza gets me every time!) One hot competitor won a Ferrari and last year another won a customized Ford Focus. Some tournaments offer prizes (or purses) as high as $100,000. The emergence of LAN parties, tournaments, and the Cyberathlete Professional League (CPL) are probably the coolest new developments to the gaming scene in many years.

Back when I used to have major Intellivision sports tournaments at a friend's house, I never realized how big (and fun) the world of competitive gaming could be. So in this chapter we're going to cover *as much as possible*. You'll learn how to become a true Cyberathlete, find cool tournaments and parties to attend, and host your own. By the end of this chapter you'll be an expert on it all. Now if only you could be as good at Quake...

The Landscape of Competitive Gaming

The landscape of competitive gaming is fairly vast so let's map out the territory. The types of competitive gaming venues available to you include:

✔ **Informal competitions at home**: Your friends come over and you beat them to a pulp.

✔ **Informal competitions online**: You go online and play on a variety of servers waxing everyone in site as much as possible.

✔ **Formal/Organized online competition**: You compete in online leagues, ladders, and other tournaments competing for fame and fortune.

✔ **LAN Parties and Mega-LAN Parties**: You take your computer to a site, set it up, and try to kick major butt. Mega-LAN parties are huge events built around hundreds or even thousands of participants. Sometimes prizes are given out.

✔ **Organized In-Person Tournaments**: These are more formal events that are structured a bit more rigorously, with extensive rules and prizes. Some even will go so far as to standardize the equipment that is used for some or all portions of play.

✔ **Amateur and Local Leagues**: These are set leagues but they don't offer any level of pay and may be held offline or online. There are also a number of local "regional" leagues starting up. I've tried to list as many as I found.

✔ **Professional Leagues**: Right now there is only one major professional off-line league, the CPL, but other leagues may be coming as the sport grows. Professional leagues will feature the most formalized rules, specialized schedules, and established teams and gaming rules.

Becoming a Professional Gamer: Inside the CPL

The penultimate form of competitive gaming is professional competitive gaming. A few leagues or major tournaments have been formed but the biggest and most professional is the Cyberathlete Professional League (**www.thecpl.com**). The CPL is the brainchild of Avault.com founder, Angel Munoz. Launched in 1997, the CPL is a bona-fide league that hosts a series of tournaments. But don't confuse it with various annual tournaments like QuakeCon or Lansanity or with online leagues like the World Online Gaming League. The CPL is an in-person, professional league that takes its structure and cues from real-world sports leagues like the NBA or NFL.

Online tournaments can't be fully standardized like in-person tournaments can in a way to create a true level playing field. This is a key distinction between any LAN event and an online tournament. The CPL does have an online component, however, which is called the Cyberathlete Amateur League (CAL). CAL operates online but it does not offer prizes. It provides a venue for people to build the skills and notoriety to bring them to a sanctioned CPL regional or national event.

INTERVIEW WITH ANGEL MUNOZ, CPL PRESIDENT

The CPL has been around for several years now. Looking ahead, where will the CPL be in three or four years?

The market for professional computer gaming is growing quickly. In the immediate future the scene will be divided among a number of international players, but in the end the organization that is truly leading the industry will survive. We think that organization is the CPL. Our plans are to add team sanctioning, league membership, and joint sponsorship agreements with the league's top teams and third-party event sanctioning and licensing. The industry will mature and the novelty will wear out, but the sport will quietly continue to grow as long as gamers are interested in being the best and going pro.

The CPL has mostly been about first-person shooters but now it's branching out into other game genres. What are the next major types of games?

The CPL has in fact concentrated on FPS games, but we have recently started using WarCraft 3 at the CPL Europe events with some success. We think that our focus is directly proportional to our longevity and changes in genres will occur slowly over the next few years.

Standardized equipment is used for CPL games, does that include pads, keyboards, and mice or are athletes allowed to use sanctioned devices of their choosing?

The CPL was the first organization in the world to implement standardized computer equipment at gaming tournaments. Back in 1997 when we launched the concept of all computers and monitors being exactly the same, we realized that a bit of flexibility on our part was also needed. Therefore, we allowed the following variable peripherals: mouse, keyboard, mouse pad and headphones/headsets. This allows the gamer to choose his sport gear as a tennis player chooses his racket of choice or a baseball player chooses his glove or bat of choice.

We also realized that as the industry grew some companies would want to cater to the professional gamers by making superior products for them. In fact over the years

8

(CONTINUED)

INTERVIEW WITH ANGEL MUNOZ, CPL PRESIDENT (CONTINUED)

several companies have introduced products that cater exclusively to this hardcore market, including Intel, Razer, Plantronics, and Logitech.

In terms of spectators, what sort of growth are you seeing for gaming as a spectator sport? What is the CPL doing to enhance the spectator experience?

When we ran our first event, the spectators were mostly just the competitors between their matches. At our next event we had 700 competitors and over 2,000 registered spectators. Furthermore, Intel and CompUSA are giving out an additional 10,000 free spectator passes for the next event. The growth obviously has been phenomenal. Offering people a diversity of activities during our events and making the matches easy to follow enhances the spectator experience. Matches are displayed on large projection screens and narrated by members of the CPL staff. CPL events also attract tens of thousands of online spectators that track the events via IRC, SHOUTcast, HLTV, and streaming videos.

What's your advice about people wanting to compete as a team? The path for single player competition seems easy to see, but teams have their own wrinkles don't they?

Love the game and care for the people you want on your team. The challenges of playing and practicing on a team are very different from those of the solo player and if you do not love the game or care for the team members, you are doomed from the moment you start.

Getting to the Professional Ranks

With the CPL, you must be at least 18 to play in the professional tournaments. If you are under 18, you can participate in CAL and in the BYOC gaming events at CPL but not in sanctioned CPL tournaments. IDs are checked so don't think you can grow a beard and sneak in.

Teams must also be incorporated entities. The CPL does not pay prize money to individuals or clubs so teams that don't have a legal structure can't compete. To obtain a legal structure for your team, you should organize into an entity with its own bank account and business name. You can do this by forming a corporation or LLC. You may also affiliate yourself with a corporate sponsor who can accept payment for prizes on your behalf. If you have a great team that you want to incorporate, go talk to a lawyer. (Just remember to leave your checkbook at home.)

To establish your company, I suggest you visit a few online sites. My favorites include www.mycorporation.com, www.corporate.com, and www.instacorp.com. To set up a bank account in the U.S. you'll need to provide proof of your corporation and some sort of Tax ID number. You might also want to get an accountant to help you file returns if there are any winnings and a lawyer who can file updates to your corporation to keep it in good standing. Because all of this "bookkeeping" might seem like a pain in the ass, some competitive gamers find corporate sponsors to deal with it all.

All CPL events are open-format like some professional golf and tennis events. Eventually, some tournaments may require a certain level of pre-qualifications or acceptable rankings for a team to make the initial cut. For now, available slots are on a first-come first-serve basis and cost $75 for individuals and $250 for teams. If you think you're good enough to compete, you can sign up. If you're not as good as you think, you'll get bounced out in the first match.

The CPL now hosts two major North American events. the CPL Summer Event is held in later July, early August in Dallas, TX. The CPL Winter Event, also held in Dallas, takes place before Christmas. The CPL also holds local qualifying tournaments at major CompUSA CyberStore locations around the country. There are currently 20 of these and you can find links and information about the qualifying tournaments at **gamefixx.compusa.com/tourney/cpl/default.asp**. The CPL also has a European league (**www.cpleurope.com**) which is running both FPS, and RTS tourneys. Several events have been held so far, and more are on the horizon. An Asian league is forthcoming but as of this chapter's writing **www.cplasia.com** is a still a work in progress.

Becoming a professional requires real skill. You can get this by constant practice. Try to participate in as many LAN tournaments as you can as well as online games through CAL and others. However, as CPL President Angel Munoz points out, just being good isn't good enough. He says you've got to attend tournaments as part of your training. The pressure of being on a new computer, under the lights with the huge crowd, noise, and other distractions is critical to being a true cyberathlete. The best may be good, but the best-of-the-best are good at the game in a stadium like atmosphere.

Getting a Team Together

Teams usually have four to six players. In the future I think we'll see all sorts of team-based competitions from two-man teams to much larger teams. In any case, the dynamics of forming a team, and holding it together are key aspects of the competitive gaming landscape. So how do you do it?

The first thing to consider is joining an existing team instead of starting a new one. There are plenty of clans/teams trying to add to their ranks and placing yourself in an existing one is a good way to start. Whether you're starting your own clan or looking to join one the best place to start is **www.Clanbase.com** which is dedicated to listing Clans and helping your organize them.

The basic issues for forming your own team are as follows:

✔ **Find some friends**: The nucleus of most teams includes a core group of people who know each other—remote friendships found online or friends from school or around the block. Chances are you have some people you already play with who will join your team.

✔ **Get a name**: Nameless teams don't get very far. You should check long and hard to see if your name is already taken. Most clans/teams also create a team logo.

✔ **Set up a Web site**: On your site you should have a way for people to see the games your clan focuses on, what your rules are, how to join, and how to contact you for sparring matches. For more on setting up a good Web site, see Chapter 11.

✔ **Promote your team**: List you clan/team on sites like Clanbase.com so others know you exist and can interact with you to setup matches, or join as members. For places to list your site see Table 8.1. You can find listings for specific games as well on major fan sites for those games.

✔ **Practice**: You have to practice to be good. Team members need to know their roles and develop shorthand for how to coordinate. Some of the best teams are locally based so they can actually get together physically and play as a team. For all the good of Teamspeak and RogerWilco, there is something to be said for being in the same room.

Other Tournaments

In addition to the CPL, there are other tournaments that are well known and frequented. These tournaments offer additional chances for cash winnings, and overall fun. Table 8.2 lists some of the major in-person LAN tournaments operating as of spring 2003.

Online Tournaments, Leagues, and Ladders

In addition to offline tournaments, there are many forms of online tournaments. These tournaments attempt some level of organization for fun, and a few do also offer prizes. Some online tournaments are routinely run one right after the other, while some are annual or semi-annual events.

TABLE 8.1
Resource sites for teams/clans.

Site	URL
ClanBase	www.clanbase.com
ClanWorld	www.clanworld.com
Clan Yellow Pages	www.clanyellowpages.com
GamerClans	www.gamerclans.com
Global Clan Directory	www.globalclandirectory.com
Clan World Network	www.clannetwork.com

TABLE 8.2
A sampling of key LAN parties for competitive gaming.

Tournament/ Event Name	Held Where & When	How Many Expected?	Comments
QuakeCON	Dallas, TX	3500+	www.quakecon.com
LanSanity	Seattle, WA	~200	www.lansanity.com
LanTactics	Chicago, IL	N/A	www.lantactics.net
WWCL	Germany	N/A	www.wwcl.net
WCGUSA	Various	700+	www.wcgusa.org
Fragapalooza	Edmonton, Alberta	2000	www.fragapalooza.com
Million Man Lan	Louisville, KY	1000+	www.millionmanlan.com www.lanwar.com
Stompfest	Indianapolis	250	www.stompfest.com
GDFest	Seattle	500+	www.gdfest.com
The BadLans	Rhode Island	200+	www.badlans.com
i-series	Newbery, England	800-1000+	www.multiplay.co.uk
The Gathering	Norway	Lots	www.thegathering.org
IGL Winterlan/ Springlan	Beverly, MA	100+	ladder.iglnet.com/iglans
The Electronic Sports World Cup	Poitiers, France	400+	www.esworldcup.com
MPCon	Dearborn, MI	150+	www.mpcon.org
DreamHack*	Sweden	5000+	www.dreamhack.org

* Dreamhack is a demo tournament which also features heavy BYOC gaming tourneys.

8

Most tournaments and leagues use a ladder-style system, or match scoring system for play. Clans, teams, or individuals sign up on a ladder system. The system develops matches from that (or you can sometimes issue challenges) and each clan, team, or individual has to show up on a server at the right time and place to play or risk forfeiture. Then, the winner logs back in and declares victory and moves up the rankings as a result.

Another form of online tournaments you're starting to see are single online tournament servers that run multiple sessions through-out the day for prizes. You pay to play in a specific game and winner takes all. Table 8.3 lists some of the more popular online tournaments.

Keep an eye out for tournaments run by the companies themselves. These tend to be right around the time a game comes out. Check the official sites of your favorite games. Also be on the lookout for tournaments run at stores like CompUSA, which offers many of them and works with the CPL. The big sports game publishers like EA, Microsoft, Sega, and others tend to run tournaments in stores and at other venues.

Hey, Where Is My Site, Party, or Tourney?

Ok heckler, read the table headings nicely. Note the word "sample." I don't have enough room to include every last party, major gathering, league, or tourney. However, if you visit **gaming.dmill.com** you can send me a note to add yours to a large list I'm compiling.

The Dark Side of Online Tournaments

Whether you play games like CnC Generals, Madden, or Battlefield 1942, you can have hours of enjoyment (sometimes 24 in a row!) competing online against others. But the dark side to this play has to do with playing in more serious tournaments held online for cash. The problem is with the Internet itself. The quality of server connections and the integrity of other players are all questionable whenever you play and compete online. Because of the risks, some competitive players simply won't compete online (at least not publicly).

Competing online it's a bit like gambling. This can be reduced (if not eliminated) by playing in a LAN environment, especially one in which you can play on a standardized set of equipment that some of the major tournaments like CPL use. Does this mean you shouldn't play online, or even in online tournaments? No. If you just want to have fun and improve your skill, go ahead. Just realize that you are not playing in a standardized environment for competing and if cash is involved that

TABLE 8.3
A sampling of the better-known and frequented online tournaments, and leagues.

Site/Tournament/ Event Name	Basic Details	URL
Battle For Europe	Generals order you into battles strategically but you and your team fight it out with WWII FPS games to see who wins each skirmish and thus ultimately the war.	www.battleforeurope.com
Clan Ladder	A ladder system run by Clan World Network.	www.clanladder.com
Cyberathlete Amateur League	The amateur and online league division of the CPL.	www.caleague.com
Firing Squad League	Online tournament and league started by Thresh, one of the first major CPL champions.	firingsquad.gamers.com/ fsleague
ILAN Gaming League	Runs online ladders, matches, and tourneys but also a LAN event as well.	ladder.iglnet.com
Leaguez	German League.	leaguez.gamigo.de
Squad Games	Ladders and tourneys.	www.squadgames.com
Stronger Than All	Clan Warfare league and site.	www.sta-league.org
Team Warfare	Hosts many leagues and tournaments for team based FPS games.	www.teamwarfare.com
The Combat Zone	Hosts ladders on major combat games.	www.thecombatzone.net
The Proving Grounds	A top site for ladder based competition and tourneys.	www.provinggrounds.com
United Gaming Clans	Well run league focused on CounterStrike and TFC games.	www.ugcleague.com
World Online Gaming Leagues	Hosts number of tourneys and ladders.	www.worldogl.com

puts your cash at risk based on something other than your skill. If you really want to compete to win money, you should be careful. Some online tournaments might fall victim to online gambling laws and regulations. If so, it means you you'll have to play on offshore servers, and transferring money to such servers could violate the laws in your country. In the U.S. it could get ugly if such wire transfers are seen as violating the U.S. Patriot Act.

If you still think this could be fun (and safe) you might want to check out **www.YouPlayGames.com**. This site offers servers (based in the Antilles so it can be 'legal') that you can pay to join. You then get paid extra if you rack up more frags against opponents than they do against you. The site has a lot of requirements, and I'm not sure it will work 100% but it definitely shows how much the competitive gaming scene is expanding.

Game Servers for Hire

Want to play a game against another clan but no one's got a good server or acceptable ping? Many players are turning to rented game servers to offer them clean pings, great response, and excellent admin. A bunch of companies and Web host providers are popping up to provide these services. Here are some worth checking out:

✔ www.apexsun.com

✔ www.barrysworld.com (UK)

✔ www.clanservers.net

✔ www.games-world.net (UK)

✔ www.xgamingservers.com

Many of the major sites I've listed here will point you to others. Also, try searching Google using "Hosted Game Server." Prices will range from $40 and up depending on the number of simultaneous users but you may find some cheaper alternatives as well. Many server providers will have a host of options including Roger Wilco or other voice support, easy access to various mods, and support for features like Half-Life TV. Private servers should cost less than public ones.

Esports Sites

If you're going to be a part of the competitive gaming scene you definitely need to check out the various esports sites. There are five major sites that track the scene fairly thoroughly:

www.sogamed.com

This is a text-based site that is sponsored by Samsung, which along with Intel is one of the biggest sponsors of competitive gaming. The site is published out of Europe giving it more of an international flavor. It contains a ton of news and information on the scene.

www.gamers.nu

This is a site based out of Sweden. It features many movies of various matches that they collect and post.

www.gotfrag.com

This is one of the leading U.S. based esports sites with extensive coverage of many of the major online and off-line tournaments and matches.

www.cached.net

The first big site in the esports arena and is still considered to be one of best with lots of good articles and event coverage.

www.shackes.com

Run by the same people behind the popular news site, Shacknews.com. ShackES is its esports division and it provides basic coverage of many major online and offline events.

LAN Parties

Not every competitive outlet is a mega-event or huge tournament with $100,000 purses. The majority of events gamers attend are basic BYOC LAN parties or events held at local LAN centers. You can think of these events as great fun for an afternoon or weekend, or they can remind you of backwater pool halls like in "The Color of Money." In either case, LAN parties are quickly becoming one of the major activities for monster gamers. So where can you find good LAN parties? Start by looking at the sites listed in Table 8.4. Here you'll find most of the major places to locate LAN parties. The largest is **www.LanParty.com**.

TABLE 8.4
Places to find LAN parties.

WHERE TO LIST	URL
Bawls Gaming*	www.bawlsgaming.com
Blues News	www.bluesnews.com/cgi-bin/lanparties.pl
Clan Yellow Pages	www.clanyellowpages.com
Gamersport	www.gamersport.com
Lan Addict	www.lanaddict.com
LAN Party Coalition	www.lanpartycoalition.com
Lan Surfer	www.lansurfer.com
LanParty.com	www.lanparty.com
Planet LAN (German)	www.planetlan.net
So Gamed	www.sogamed.net
UK Lans	www.uklans.com
Xbox Lan Central	www.xboxlancentral.com

* This is a site sponsored by the Bawls Guarana caffeine drink company. They list qualified parties and if you're sponsored you may get some free Bawls stuff to give away.

Before participating in LAN parties, you should read the section in Chapter 2 on gaming etiquette, which includes LAN party etiquette. Make sure you also call the day before the event to ensure everything is in order. Smaller LAN parties can sometimes fall apart once Johnny's mom realizes he just advertised the family basement to 10,000 monster gamers she doesn't know.

You also might want to get some aids to help you tote your gear to a party in style. The first are carry straps for your CPU. The two best I've seen are made by Xbags (**www.xbags.com**) which makes a strap and integrated bag system and CaseAce Products (**www.caseace.com**) which makes several tote and bag systems for CPUs, monitors, and other hardware under the GearGrip brand. These straps cost between $25 to $50. You can find a low-end straps-only carrying system called PC Tote at www.pctote.com which runs around $15. Some people also buy PC carts with casters to make it easy to roll their PC through the hotel lobby to their location as well. If you want something sort of cool for your laptop, check out the bags offered by **www.LoopNYC.com**. They make a brand of bag called Version that is pretty cool compared to your normal executive style laptop bag.

Last but not least, make sure you install basic security on your machine. Check that your rig has the latest OS patches and it has virus-checking software.

Be sure to label everything you bring to some extent. You can protect your gear by labeling it so a hub, mouse, or patch cable doesn't get confused during breakdown or setup.

Setting Up Your Own LAN Party

LAN parties are one of the centerpieces of the esports/competitive gaming movement. If you'd like to throw your own LAN party, there are some critical things I can help you with. We'll first start with the planning process and then I'll give you some tips from the trenches.

Creating a Basic Plan

Before you do anything think hard about your plan. Are you just going to have a few friends over and patch everything together? Or, are you going to have a come-one, come-all approach? Are you going to charge for admission or will your party be free? If you charge, will the charge include prizes? If you offer prizes how do you ensure that the process of giving out prizes is fair? How are you going to deal with security of the room if you have kids under 18 in age? And you thought planning was easy! Once you consider all of these issues, jot down a simple plan on paper before you do anything else.

Obtaining a Space

Once you've got a plan you'll need a space for your LAN party. You can select a private space like someone's home, a place of business, or a public space that you acquire or rent. Spaces you rent fall into two categories: spaces that are regularly rented for event functions like banquet halls, hotels, local schools, and civic centers, or places like the YMCA.

The other group consists of non-traditional spaces that are worth checking out. Most are large vacant retail spaces. Because they're not currently rented, you have a chance to get these spaces fairly cheap and many might offer parking. I used to rent spaces like this for campaign work I did and I could usually find a broker or owner who would set a short term lease (even a few days). You can find these spaces by simply driving around and jotting down numbers on the for-rent signs. Then, just call them up and say you want to rent the space for one or two days for an event and name a price you think is fair. Some places won't want to deal with you but eventually if you call five to -ten places you can find one.

Here are a few tips to consider for acquiring a location. First, make sure the owner understands what the heck a LAN party is. Explain the types of people who will be coming, the equipment they'll be unloading, and the noise your event may generate. (Make sure you find out what's acceptable.) Go over power requirements, furniture needs, food, and other issues.

Preparing for Power!

As someone who has set up large groups of computers for people (not LAN parties but very similar events), I can tell you it's easy to underestimate the power requirements. Today's machines eat a lot of power and a room jammed with machines requires lots of power and a strong setup. Before you sign a lease or pick a spot, do a walk-through with the maintenance people and make sure you have the power you'll need and that you have enough power strips for people to plug into.

You also need to know how the circuits are laid out because most circuits will only support a set amount of computers and support equipment. Here's a rule of thumb to follow: You can hook up seven computers for every 20 amps of power. Otherwise, you'll have problems. You also need to be able to extend power and distribute it to the various power-strips you use.

Getting power to all of players who attend your LAN party requires using *good* equipment. You'll need thick power cables properly rated for extending power to strips that will draw enough current. You can get these types of extension cables

> easily at most hardware store. Tell the clerk how much stuff may be on the other end. For power strips, you want industrial strength ones that can actually support other strips themselves. These are not your common $9.95 power-strips. Go to a good hardware store and you'll find them. Tripp-Lite is one of many manufacturers.

Get all of the basic power cabling done before much setup begins. Don't skimp on the duct tape and do it right. Label everything and as people set up make sure you and others are around to properly supervise.

Basic Setup and Security

Depending on the size of your LAN party, you'll need to deal with the basic setup beyond the core power situation, and the network setup. This means tables, chairs, restrooms, food, and security.

Tables, Chairs, and Furniture

To have a good LAN party you'll need comfortable seating and enough space to set up computers. You can get furniture from the facility you are renting or rent them separately. Get good sturdy tables that can withstand some knocking around and the occasional "fist of frustration." Don't forget chairs for spectators, parents, and others who might drop by.

Restrooms

If you forget about restrooms you're toast. If you rent a place like a vacant store-front make sure you pay some attention to the restroom situation. Make sure they're clean, and don't forget you might need to be the person who brings the TP, soap, and paper towels. Cleaning tools might also be a useful.

Food

You can have a great network, plenty of chairs, and clean bathrooms, but if you screw up the food logistics expect to hear about it. Most LAN party how-to's recommend that you find a location that is in the vicinity of convenience stores and restaurants. You also want to have some level of on-site food and drink. You can optionally charge for this but try to make it available. Beverages should include an assortment of sodas, juices, and coffee. In terms of food, keep it simple. Offer some basic snacks or pizza.

If you're holding the event at a hotel or other event center, food catering might be available. In fact at most of these places they really make their money from their food service. Hotel catering can be expensive and they don't usually let you bring outside food into their facilities. If you host an event at a hotel or banquet center, check the rules concerning food carefully.

If you're providing food at your event advertise what will be made available and if it will cost extra. Events that require people to BYOB should also be well advertised. Another option (if deliveries are allowed to your facility) is to make copies of local fast-food menus available.

Music

LAN parties have downtime during setup activities and at breaks. Music can be a useful addition. The best parties actually bring in D.J.'s to spin during the event. I'll leave you to determine the play list and equipment you're going to use but don't forget this key ingredient.

Security

Security is important and involves a number of factors that can be easily overlooked. Your goal should be to limit your liability for problems and provide a safe environment for your attendees. Here are the issues you need to consider:

✔ **Insurance**: God forbid someone trips over a stray power or Ethernet cable and breaks something. Another nightmare could be parents who send you a threatening email because their son played games at your event that he or she wasn't supposed to be playing. It also bites to hear someone may be holding you responsible for a blown power-supply or stolen mouse. There are some simple steps you can do to protect yourself and your event attendees from scenarios like this. You can also get event cancellation insurance. You should consult with your local insurance agent. Two places that are frequently used in North America are K&K Insurance (**www.kandkinsurance.com**), and well-known broker, CSI (**www.csi-coverage.com**).

✔ **Security Personnel**: Security is important when it comes to protecting your attendees and equipment. You have a few options here depending on your goals, the size of the event, and your worries about the crowd itself. If you need physical security (for large events), you should contact a local security company, which has trained and bonded security guards. Security should not be your two friends who have black belts in Jujitsu. Bonded security guards are insured for liability. If Rocco beats the crap out of some guy, it's not your issue.

✔ **Signage**: Signage can be important, especially for well-attended events. This includes disclaimer signs such as "we are not responsible for lost, stolen or damaged equipment or personal effects." You also might need signs for items like Food, First Aid, Exit, and Restrooms. Make these well-marked signs in big letters.

✔ **Disclaimers/Permission Forms**: The final piece of security issues you might want to consider is having a simple form for attendees to sign, including parents. This would be a standard issue form that absolves you from lost, stolen or damaged equipment. It might also include a form that allows people under the age of 18 to compete. If you're going to have kids under 18 compete (the CPL does not for several reasons), you may want to require a parent's signature for the child to compete. This is especially important if you charge a fee for you party. The parent should acknowledge the child is playing games that may be rated by the ESRB as mature only games, and that the event organizers are not responsible for the child's safety or return home. You might want to adapt the Gaming Café permission form I describe in Chapter 11 for your own use.

✔ **Secure Check-in**: You might consider having a volunteer or two who before someone connects to the network, insures that a person has installed up-to-date virus software. Have a few CDs with the latest version of shareware virus scanning software available for someone who doesn't bring a machine that is inoculated properly so it can be installed on site. Once the volunteer approves the machine, the user can connect to the network.

✔ **Prevent Equipment Theft**: Security is all about good planning and prevention. This means having a good system for labeling equipment (yours and others). This can be done by stickering everything with labels and making some labels and pens available to everyone attending who didn't do this at home. You should also make sure all exits are clearly marked and that you and the volunteers have a fire escape plan in place. Also, make sure that people admitted to the LAN party are there to play. To accommodate people who aren't there to play, create a separate roped-off spectator area. To protect equipment at an overnight party I suggest having several volunteers who can also join optional hired-security people to ensure that no equipment is touched.

✔ **Other Items**: Other helpful hints for security are to make the volunteers standout. Have them wear the same color shirts or hats. Have nametags that identify them and give them a means to communicate easily with one another if you have a big space. A couple of volunteers with $50 walkie-talkies is ideal. Another thing to have on hand is a simple first-aid kit. And by all means have a sheet of paper in an easy to find place that has the numbers for local police, fire, and ambulance. Also have a number for the building management. A cellphone or two should be on hand if landlines are not possible.

If you're having a really large event, say 100 or more people, you might also meet with the local police and let them know of your plans. (Just don't tell them you're playing Grand Theft Auto.) They'll appreciate that greatly and might even offer to send someone by now and then to check in on things. In some local jurisdictions off-duty police can be hired out (in uniform) as local event security as well. The police may also be required to help ensure parking and other local ordinances are properly followed.

Networking

After acquiring a space and providing basic event logistics, you'll need to make sure your LAN is operational and bug-free. No LAN no LAN party. If you're the organizer, the responsibility of having an easy setup, reliable operations, and easy breakdown is squarely on your shoulders. This means you have to be Mr. Failsafe. You have to ensure that all of the necessary equipment is on-site. Even if you're asking others to bring hubs, switches, or cabling you should consider yourself the last line of defense.

Hubs and Switches

The two types of equipment that enable you to hook up multiple computers in a network are hubs and switches. A *hub* is basically a dumb repeater. It connects everyone to a network and broadcasts one message to everyone else on the network. Your computer sorts out the data that is useful and the data that was meant for someone else. Hubs are stupid but that makes them cheap. Most people should be running 100mb Ethernet cards but because so many 10mb cards are still used you probably wants hubs that support both 10/100mb modes. A 16-port hub costs less than $100.

A *switch* is a smart-hub. It intelligently routes information around a network making sure only the information related to a certain computer actually goes to that computer. This is a cleaner, faster form of networking and can be a great way to hook up many computers. The price for switches are all over the map but you can find good unmanaged switches for under $250 for a 24-port switch.

Internet or Not?

Offering Internet to your users isn't necessarily the biggest deal for many LAN parties. Sure it's really useful for downloading patches and so on but it's not a necessity for the core process of playing other people. The downside with bringing in the Internet is that you can invite all sorts of mischief and headaches. If you decide to have Internet connectivity you should set up a firewall and set rules of conduct. You also need to decide if you're going to allow people to compete remotely over the Internet. Furthermore, you'll need to get some sort of deal with an ISP to support an entire network of machines on a network. Some people have had good success partnering with a local ISP for support and promotion.

As a middle ground, some parties make available a 4-port setup to a broadband connection available separately for people to connect to for checking email or getting patches.

IP Addresses

To setup a private network using IP addresses you need to know how to map that out for everyone so it works well. You could use a central server system using DHCP that automatically assigns people numbers or do it manually. I don't have the time or space to help you with either of these so check out a good article on this at: **www.theadminpage.com/SettingUpaLAN.htm**.

The best document for understanding private IP addresses is the IANA (Internet Assigned Numbers Authority) document RFC1918 that explains it all which you can find a copy of at: **ftp://ftp.isi.edu/in-notes/rfc1918.txt.**

Cables

Relying on people to bring, or remember to bring networking cables is a recipe for disaster. Thus, you should have an assortment of cables available. The uber-geek, though, goes further. They use multi-color cabling, one color is used to hook up all the intranet cabling between hubs, and so on. Another color is used to cable over to machines that may be acting as a central server or Internet gateway and the rest is used to patch people into the network.

Charging Fees

Most LAN parties that charge fees do so to break even or make a small profit that is plowed back into the next LAN party. A few parties try to make more serious money, however. You can do either but the important thing is don't forget to have fun. Whatever approach you take, be prepared to take a loss. If you can't absorb a loss, you shouldn't be throwing a LAN party bigger than having a few friends over to your house. Don't be afraid to start small and build up from there.

To determine your break even point, take your expected costs, divide them by the number of seats you expect to sell, and multiply by 1.2, which will give you a 20% "profit." This protects you if your attendance is lower than you expect. If you're going to offer some cash prizes to winners I suggest two things. First, make sure you set aside those funds and don't use them for anything else. You'll look like an idiot if you can't dish out the prize money at the end of your party. Second, make sure everyone gets a set of the rules and disclaimers and that they sign a form spelling them out. You need to protect yourself against accusations of unfair rules or play. You should also have a plan for how you'll deal with cheaters and how you'll deal with disputes. As an example, you could have any disputes settled by votes from the participants present. You could also appoint an odd number of referee judges who will render opinions that participants signed.

To collect fees, you can accept cash or credit cards, if possible. Credit cards are run through specialized merchant accounts and getting one is a pain-in-the-ass. Talk to your local bank if you're really that interested. If you can't get a merchant account, setup a PayPal account, which you can use to charge online before the event or during the event if an Internet connection is available. Pretty much everyone knows about PayPal these days so running payment through PayPal is pretty easy. To get a PayPal account you only need to have a checking account. If you do charge, offer people a receipt. You can either print them out or buy a receipt book at a local office supply store.

Promotions and Partners

Getting people to your party means promoting it well before the party date. Good party promotion starts online with a Web site for your party. Whether it's one page or multi-page, you need a site showing the time, location, and details. Fancier sites can include a registration form and payment capabilities (if you're charging) and links to download any patches for games that you're going to play. Once you have a site you can start getting your party listed by visiting the best sites for LAN party promotions. That list is the same list for finding LAN parties I presented in Table 8.4.

Also, as part of your promotion make sure you had a good signup sheet during admission where you obtained player's email and snail-mail addresses. The best parties grow due to repeat visitors. Putting posters around your town isn't a bad idea. Local schools and colleges should help draw a bit of a crowd, as well as coordinating with any local arcades or land centers.

If you can talk to a local ISP about sponsoring some service, the best is local DSL or cable broadband folks who want to hype their services. A local computer store or LAN center is also a good partner. Try to get them to put up some cash per attendee to sponsor, say a few dollars per expected attendee. At the very least get some free services or co-promotion. Sponsors also usually like to tie their sponsorship to something, like free soda provided by Jack's LAN Center. They should want some signage at your event or inclusion of their logos on your flyers and Web site.

Breaking Down Your LAN Party

Don't forget about the breakdown phase. Make sure everyone is given a warning before closing time. You'll need to kill the power to the hubs to stop the action, otherwise it'll keep going—trust me. I'm bringing this up in this section on planning because it's easy to forget about important breakdown tasks. Make sure volunteers are present and working to help breakdown the LAN and equipment. Make sure the vendors who you may have rented stuff from are coming on time to get their stuff. Ensure the place is cleaned up and everyone gets their equipment back safely and if people have lost equipment take their name and number in case something turns up. Plan your breakdown ahead of time and you'll be very happy you did.

Hardware for Competitive Gaming

The best competitive gamers try to use the best equipment and while there are some debates as to which mouse pads and mice are the best, there is some general feeling as to who at least is competing for the hearts, minds, hands, and wallets of monster competitive gamers:

Mouse Pads

There are four major types of mouse pad surfaces that get attention. The first is cloth, loathed by some but still liked by others including CPL champion, Fatality. The second is a plastic/acrylic-like surface. The third is glass and the fourth is steel, which is quickly gaining a hardcore following. A ton of companies push their wares to monster gamers.

I can't tell you which one to choose over the others because they all have their particular strengths and weaknesses. Steel pads seems to be getting a lot of the hot buzz now, but I've yet to see any one pad really take the world by storm. You might try a few to find the one that suits you best—some may even be too sensitive. At the next LAN party you attend, see if there are some new ones to try.

Here's a quick rundown of the pads getting the most use:

Func Industries
www.func.net
There latest design is the Func 1030 which features multiple surface types, a clip to keep your mouse cord from getting in the way, and a textured rubber surface to prevent slippage. The pads sell for $20.00

Everglide
www.everglide.com
The Everglide pad is a large plastic pad that sells for $12.95 to $18.95. There are specialized pads sold for optical mice as well.

IceMat
www.icemat.com

The Icemat, from Germany, is made out of glass and has two versions. A clear one and a black one specifically made for optical mice. The price is about $30 give or take currency fluctuations and about $10 to $15 for shipping.

FatPad
www.fatality.com/fatstore

This is a giant cloth pad sold and endorsed by Fatality who is the reining champ of the CPL.

3M Precise Mousing Surface
www.3m.com/ergonomics/precisemousepads.jhtml

From the people who brought you Scotch Tape is a surface that is anything but sticky and worth a look. You can find it at buy.com among other online retailers for about $12.

Steelpad
www.steelpad.com

Finally, there is the Steelpad from Germany, which is made of Aluminum (doh!) and is quickly becoming one of the more popular pads around because it is super-smooth and it is sturdy and won't move as you use it. Two models are offered—the 3S and 4S (one is bigger than the other). Ordering is done via the Web and will run you with shipping $40 to $60 depending on currency fluctuations. The site also offers a steel cord holder (like a mouse bungie but different) and Steelpad Padsurfer tape similar to mouse skatez.

Compad
www.com-pad.com

Yet another pad, which has gotten good reviews that is made from a composite material. It is available in many colors, but check the compatibility chart for best results based on your mouse brand and type.

Ratpadz
www.ratpadz.com

Look for the Ratpadz GS (for gaming surface). This is a well reviewed pad that features a smooth glide and good optical pickup. It sells for $10.00.

X-Trac Pro HS
store.yahoo.com/pcxmods
Many optical pads feature a random dot pattern to help optical mice pick up movement well. The Xtrac goes a potential step further by using a hexagonal pattern in addition to random dots to create what it feels is an ultra accurate optical surface. The Pro HS model is quite large and sells for $12.95.

Mice Skatez
www.mouseskatez.com
Mouse Skatez, available from Everglide, are slippery surfaces you can apply to the feet of your mice to reduce friction. They sell enough material for two mice for $4.95. Be sure to clean your mouse thoroughly before you apply the tape to it.

Mice

Your two options for mice are trackball and optical. Among the trackball camp, BoomSlang made a small name for itself and you can still find them, although only a few players really swear by them. Today, most of the action is with optical mice.

The two major mice manufacturers left in the world competing tooth-and-nail for your attention are Microsoft and Logitech. Microsoft initially took the lead because its early optical designs were solid. Gamers have quickly moved up to the latest models from both companies as they improve the optics. As of this writing, the Logitech MX 500 seems to be getting a lot of attention. (Logitech also makes an MX 300 which is good for lefties.) One thing to note here is that Logitech earlier brought out a "dual optical" mouse, which had two optic sensors. The thinking here was that two sensors would be better than one but Logitech returned to a single optic sensor for the MX line. Maybe one is good enough! All gamers prefer non-Bluetooth/wireless mice since no player wants to risk someone screwing with their wireless connection in a major tournament

Keyboards

In addition to having a good mouse, you'll also want a killer keyboard. There are a few options but most are made by either Microsoft or Logitech. I prefer the natural keyboard myself because I type so much (as this book attests) and many gamers seem to prefer it as well. Logitech also makes some good models. Lately, however, gamers looking for every edge have been going back into their garage, ebay, and elsewhere to find old IBM "Selectric" style keyboards that shipped with early IBM PCs. Why? Because of the weight of the keyboard, which gives it a solid feel and keeps it from shifting around during play. One other source of these hard-to-find relics is **www.pckeyboard.com**. Cost is about $50.

Another keyboard device some gamers are learning to favor is Nostromo n50 Speedpad (see Figure 8.1). This is a hybrid keypad-style device that sells for $35 from their site at **www.Belkin.com**.

Finally there is the Zboard from Ideazon (**www.ideazon.com**) which is a totally customizable keyboard designed for gaming. You really have to see it to understand it but essentially you can program keys and rearrange layouts and such to totally customize the keyboard to the game you're playing.

Software for Competitive Gaming

When it comes to software for competitive gaming there are a number of various utilities for players and server operators. I'll focus on a few player utilities and a smidgen of server items. On the server side, there is a lot more to cover than I can possibly do in this book. Much of this has to do with tools for operating specific games on specific servers. So if you plan on running your own server make sure you really spend time learning about all the additional tools and utilities geared toward your application. Be sure to visit the key fan sites for your favorite games be they Half-Life or Return to Castle Wolfenstein.

FIGURE 8.1
The Belkin Nostromo n50 Speedpad is a hybrid keyboard pad some gamers are favoring these days.

Half-Life TV

Half-Life TV is a great modification to Half-Life (and Half-Life based mods) that I think we'll start seeing built into almost every online game system going forward. HLTV is essentially a proxy system for Half-Life games that allows people to watch a match without gumming up the main server. To use it, a server operator connects as a spectator using HLTV to an in-progress game. They then open up slots on their server to spectators so everyone is watching via proxy. HLTV servers can also daisy chain themselves as well making it easy for a number of spectators to be served. HLTV is part of the latest upgrade of Half-Life. You can find a well-written tutorial on it at Pro Half-Life (**www.pro-hl.com/hltv.shtml**).

 Unreal Tournament also has a TV system which you can download at http://utv.clan-sy.com/ and Quake3 has a TV system for it. You can find information on GTV for Quake3 at **http://q3ctfcup.clanbase.com/ec4_gtv.php**.

Broadcasting Matches via Shoutcast and Streaming Video

One of the more interesting things you will see in the realm of competitive gaming is the use of Nullsoft's SHOUTcast radio system to deliver audio commentary on matches in conjunction with the use of Half-Life TV. This gives players some serious play-by-play and color commentary as well as a video feed of the action.

To listen to SHOUTcast broadcasts, you need an MP3 player which can listen to SHOUTcast streams. The best is Winamp made by Nullsoft. Download it at **www.winamp.com**, although I bet most of you have it already.

There are two major broadcasters going right now and I'd expect more. WSBN.com is home to the Web Sports Broadcasting Network and mostly focuses on Tribes and a few other games like Jedi Knight 2 and Return to Castle Wolfenstein. Team Sportcast Network, available at **www.tsncentral.com**, covers a lot of other games. You can send a request in to TSNCentral to cover your matches as well.

To be a broadcaster, you need to be able to setup a SHOUTcast server. This takes some effort (I know I wrote a book about it but that's another story and another publisher). Start out by visiting **www.shoutcast.com** and downloading the server and broadcasting tools. One important tip here is that you will need a version of Winamp 2.X not 3.X to broadcast using SHOUTcast. Visit both the download page and the documentation page. You'll also want to get a microphone. Use a low bandwidth setting (no need for voice to be sent out in 128bps) and find some people to set up relays and you'll be in good shape. If you're smart enough and have some bandwidth to spare you should be able to get something setup inside an hour or so.

If Half-Life TV isn't possible for your game (or something similar), other tournaments have actually broadcasted via streaming video their matches. This usually involves outputting from a VGA card into a live capture feed on another PC and then streaming the output via video over the Net.

Voice Chat Software Systems

Many teams use voice chat to coordinate their actions online against other teams. If you can't all be in the same room, this is the next best thing. There are four major products that offer voice chat for you and your team:

Roger Wilco

Roger Wilco lets you voice chat with other gamers. This tool is now offered by GameSpy Industries. There are two major downloads you should know about. The first is the vanilla Roger Wilco application, which can be found at **rogerwilco.gamespy.com/products/downloads.** It's available for PCs and Macs. You can download the free trial version from the link and pay $19.95 to upgrade it. The other app is the Roger Wilco Base Station, which is used to make it easy to tune into a Roger Wilco stream instead of calibrating it individually. This is especially important if everyone on your team uses ISPs that don't assign static IP addresses. The Base Station app can be placed on a system with a static IP and it will act as the central connection for everyone on your team. You point your client to the address and the software handles the rest. If you're using Roger Wilco, check out the add-on apps section, **rogerwilco.gamespy.com/products/ addons**, where you can download an app to make it easy to control Roger Wilco from within Quake 3.

BattleCom

Battlecom was put to rest officially in June 2001 when Microsoft acquired its creator, ShadowFactor. (Microsoft used the software as the basis for their Game-Voice product.) Battlecom lives on in its last updated form unofficially on the Web through user generated support. Since it is free in this unofficial version, many people still use it while others have moved on to purchase the Microsoft GameVoice system. To access the community support and download site, visit **www.battlecom.org**.

GameVoice

Microsoft saw game voice chat as important part of the gaming world and has chased after it hard with both Xbox Live! and its PC-oriented GameVoice product (**www.gamevoice.com**). You can download the client and server software from the GameVoice Web site and Microsoft also sells a hardware headset and command console as the Sidewinder GameVoice system. The problem is that as of March 2003 the extra features enabled by the hardware system weren't compatible with DirectX 9 so people were having problems and Microsoft didn't do so well with the product and the support has been iffy. I suggest you check out the software first and see if it serves your needs before you spend the extra bucks on the hardware.

TeamSpeak

TeamSpeak (**www.teamspeak.org**) is a new community-developed tool created by some gamers who wanted a low-bandwidth solution. Version 1.0 is available and the team is now hard at work on Version 2.0. The product can be downloaded for free download at the Teamspeak Web site.

Software for Finding Servers

Many games now have built-in systems for finding servers and players. This wasn't always the case and so a product, GameSpy (**www.gamespy.com**) was born that helped people find servers, check ping rates, and sign-on users. GameSpy now licenses this code to many other games. This has accelerated the amount of built-in game servers that can locate other servers. People still use the third-party systems, however, because they offer extra features.

There are several third-party systems used and many players have opinions on which is best for what. The big drawback for GameSpy is that it takes a long time to load up its lists because it insists on pinging every server. This gives you much more accurate lists but on a dial-up with a big server list, you might as well take a long trip to the fridge. You can improve performance by upgrading to the registered version, which also gets rid of the built-in ad banners. GameSpy also has had a tendency to freeze in the past. At the same time GameSpy is supported by many games and it includes other chat and program features that continue to make it a major piece of software used by gamers.

The next most popular package and one gaining a lot of hardcore usage is All Seeing Eye (ASE), which is available at **www.udpsoft.com/eye**. What people like about ASE is that it's really fast. What they don't like is the overall interface that isn't as easy to use as some would like. Still people who use it and like it defend it in a zealot like fashion so it's certainly worth the download. You can upgrade ASE to the registered version for $10.

HLSW is another major server finder from Germany, and is available at **www.hlsw.org/index.php?language=English**. Short for Half Life Server Watch, the program supports nearly twenty server systems from Neverwinter Nights to SoF2 to BattleField 1942 to Quake and CnC Renegade.

Two Web Based Systems that work well are Serverspy.com, which is fantastic, and GameTiger.net, which is just ok. They let you search for maps, mods, people, or other server specifics and then you can log on to those games.

We've Come a Long Way Since Pong

In Chapter 1 I told you about my first competitive gaming experience playing my mom's friends for Pong at our camp in Maine. Since then we've come a long way. I mean I used to win a quarter or a nickel and today leading competitive gamers are winning cars and enough cash to take early retirement.

Furthermore, the competition is fun, and people seem to be enjoying themselves whether they win or lose. Sure I know the chapter says *everything* but I mean isn't 10,000+ words enough? There are more leagues, tourneys, LAN centers and parties then I could possibly fit in this book. So I'm going to probably have to write another one just on competitive gaming (hint, hint). I hope my publisher is listening.

Competitive gaming is thrilling enough to make me want to stop writing and jump online and compete a little more. Now if I could only find that blue plastic piggybank I had when I was a kid so I had a place to stash my winnings…

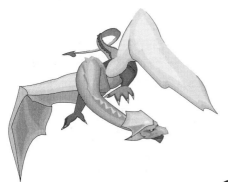

COMPLETE GUIDE TO GAMING ON THE GO

If you travel a lot, take extended trips, or just take long bus or subway rides to school or work, don't deprive yourself from enjoying a little interactive entertainment. As the world becomes more wireless and mobile, we'll likely travel more and be away from our plush living rooms and computer dens more often. I don't know about you, but spending the rest of my life as a house bound agoraphobic isn't exactly my goal.

In this chapter we'll explore *everything* about gaming on the go. If you think this just means having a GameBoy and a copy of Advance Wars II, you're highly mistaken. Wireless entertainment is booming, with new technologies being released constantly. I'll cover the various mobile platforms and experiences you can have. You'll also find in Chapter 15 some references to places you should travel to as a gamer. Monster gamers should be world-savvy travelers heading around the globe enveloped in gaming goodness. So pack your bags, batteries, and other gear and don't forget to lock the doors.

Mobile Gaming 101

The first stop in our travel adventures is mobile gaming. The five main platforms for mobile gaming include pocket game systems, cellphone systems, PDA gaming, laptop gaming, and "mobilizing consoles." Let's briefly discuss each one, and then we'll explore each one in more depth.

Pocket Game Systems

The GameBoy line from Nintendo dominates this group. A few others have been released like GameGear from Sega, NeoGeo Pocket, and the new one coming soon is the game system/cellphone hybrid from Nokia called the N-Gage.

Cellphone Systems

The huge push for mobile gaming comes in the form of a variety of cellphone platforms and technologies, which feature the ability to run programs like games. Forget the venerable SNAKE game you find on most Nokia phones, we're talking major games equivalent to what we were playing on NES and Genesis systems in the late 80s, early 90s.

PDA Gaming

The two major forms of PDAs include WinCE and market leading Palm OS systems. PDAs have attracted a number of games include ports of games like SimCity, and new games like Hyperspace Delivery Boy. PDAs are open platforms and fairly easy to develop for, not to mention gaining in power.

Laptop Gaming

Laptops were the first mobile gaming platform, if you don't count the classic Mattel, Nintendo, and Coleco games we used to play as kids. Today we have some really cool choices because some manufacturers are making laptops specifically for people who game extensively. Coupled with the rise of Wi-Fi technology, mobile gaming with laptops is going to grow in significance I think.

Some of those classic Mattel games were recently re-released. You can find them at better toy stores and on Amazon.com. Football (which I pretty much played for hours when I had it) and baseball were the two released.

"Mobilizing" Consoles

Taking your console on the road is not out of the question any more because of the various adapters and other hardware available. More cars are being outfitted with TVs in the backseats (to shut up the kids) and the amount of people taking consoles with them on trips is exploding.

Where Things Are Headed

Among the pocket, cellphone, and PDA games system, I think you'll begin to see the emergence of devices that basically combine all three under one roof. That is epitomized by the debut of Nokia's N-Gage system (see Figure 9.1), which is a PDA, cellphone, and gaming system.

 The N-Gage is definitely making a splash in 2003. You can learn more about it by visiting **www.n-gage.com**.

To give you a sneak preview of the future we can look at the current specs for the N-Gage device. It weighs 137g (with battery) and is a bit bigger that the Game-Boy Advance. Major games will come on game cards and through downloads. The system features J2ME as well as native Symbian applications. Included in the system are basic PDA functions like a calendar, to-do list, and contacts. The backlit screen has a resolution of 176x208 and the device provides 3.4MB of user memory. Musically, the N-Gage can record and playback digital music, and includes stereo FM radio. You'll also find full support for multimedia messaging, email (IMAP4, POP3, SMTP, MIME2), and a full featured XHTML browser with WAP support. It also has a USB port and it supports MP3, AAC, Midi, and WAV ringing tones. Music files can be download from compatible PC over USB cable and the system features a 64 MB memory card for music and a hands-free speaker for

9

FIGURE 9.1
The Nokia N-Gage is a neat looking device that is a sign of things to come in the mobile gaming space.

music listening as well as headphone. The system supports most major forms of wireless phone connectivity, as well as Bluetooth which can be used for connectivity to other devices and players.

I played with the N-Gage recently at a show and was impressed, although I felt the system was a tiny bit slow with the games I played. The control was responsive, but overall it was a bit under-powered—something I think will be better either once production starts (so check it out yourself) or the next model or two debuts after the initial release.

All Nintendo has to do is cellphone-enable a GameBoy SP and it has got the same thing (perhaps with a simple contact list and calendar for core-PDA needs). We may see these five categories for a little while but I'd expect standalone PDAs to drop off significantly as cellphone or combo devices usurp this market. I also expect more gaming devices to have phone capability and vice-versa.

Location Based Entertainment

The complete mobile gamer isn't just a player who can stuff a GBA SP in his or her pocket or take a killer Wi-Fi laptop on the road. The complete monster gamer seeks experience only possible by travelling, or knows a few places he or she can drop in on to get a gaming fix satisfied.

LBE sites encompass three major groups: traditional arcades or amusement centers, virtual reality rides/game centers, and gaming cafés (e.g., PC Bangs in Korea). Other than that you're still apt to find the oddball suite of arcade games in various movie theatres, bowling alleys, and even a bar or two.

Arcade and Amusement Centers

In North America there was a time when you could find several arcades in every town, even in smaller towns. Today we're left with a bunch of Starbucks on every corner. (If you haven't been to New York lately you might be surprised to see some intersections with a Starbucks on at least two of the four corners.) In other parts of the world, especially Japan and some cities in Europe, you can still find arcades. Ideally there should be a nice listing on the Net for all the major arcade locations in the world, but there isn't. I'll list two that are worth knowing about.

Dave and Busters
www.daveandbusters.com
Dave and Busters is a grown up Chuck-e-Cheese. It is a killer chain of bar/ restaurants that feature pool, other games, and a lot of arcade games. It has over

30 locations in the U.S. I suspect that they will add locations and become the major chain of restaurant/bar/arcade centers in North America.

Gameworks
www.gameworks.com

Gameworks has over a dozen locations (mostly in the U.S.) and each one offers a number of arcade games on site. A few locations offer specialty made games like Seattle——a shooting game where you ride up and down a four-story chair lift. It's not the best game but if you make it to the top when the game ends you get a cool rush hurling back down to the first level.

VR Centers

Immersive virtual reality centers were the rage in the U.S. and elsewhere at one point. They sort of stalled out because the technology was wickedly expensive. Many players also got bored with the specific games that were available. There are, however, a few centers around and some like FighterTown (**www.fightertown.com**) and Virtual Worlds (**www.virtualworld.com**) still thrive. To find VR gaming centers near you or near a town you might be travelling to, check out the VR Centers World Wide page at Atlantis.com (**vr-atlantis.com/lbe.html**). The list is a bit dated but it is still the most comprehensive one available.

Sony Metreon and Disney Quest

In the mid 90s both Disney and Sony opened up complexes they called "urban theme parks." Sony's was opened in San Francisco and is called the Metreon. It functions more like a mall but does include a big arcade, and at one point had some VR games (that sucked). Disney opened up two called Disney Quest, one in Florida and one in Chicago that later closed. Disney's center is a multi-story indoor theme park and arcade, complete with lots of games, specialized Disney VR rides, and other games. After pulling out of Chicago, Disney may eventually open more centers in North America.

PC Bangs and Gaming Cafés

The craziest location based entertainment centers include Game Cafés or PC Bangs. (*Bang* is phonetic for room in Korean and the double entendre seems on purpose.) Gaming cafés are the arcades of the future and I think they're cool, even if they're not necessarily always the classiest of joints. (Hey, neither were arcades when I was growing up.) They have taken hold in Asia providing a place for young people to hang out and play games. There are over 20,000 PC Bangs in Korea according to recent reports where the phenomenon is greatest.

Want to set up your own PC Game Café? I cover some of the basic issues in Chapter 11, *Putting Your Game Habit to Work*. Check it out.

Right now there isn't a great way to find PC game rooms outside of Asia. (In Korea and parts of Asia just walk a block or two and you'll find one.) In other parts of the world finding one is a bit of work. I suggest you use Google, email local gamers you might know in the area, or look up some of the Internet Café directories. Netcafeguide.com is one of the better sources. Clanbase.com also lists a few European-based gaming cafés in its links section.

Here's a tip from the Teach Korea Web site where an author related his experience with PC game rooms that should hold true for other countries where English isn't always spoken. He writes, "Most game room employees do not speak English, so if you have any Internet problems, you usually have to puzzle them out yourself. If you do find one that has an English-speaking employee (or owner), be sure to talk with him/her a little every time you come in. I completely believe in helping Koreans to believe that foreigners are interested in talking with them." Remember that these establishments give you a great chance to meet other gamers as you travel. Use the opportunity. You may meet people who can join your clan when you're back online at home someday.

Tournaments and LAN Parties

Tournaments and LAN parties are also part of the gaming-on-the-go experience. However I've covered these activities in Chapter 8. If you haven't read Chapter 8 by now you're commanded to do so. One thing to keep in mind when you do travel is that you should check to see if there is a local league, party, or tournament going. If you've got a killer gaming laptop, you can join in the fun.

Pocket Game Systems

GameBoy Advance is the leading pocket game system so let's discuss it first and then we'll look at some other systems. The two GameBoy Advance devices available include the original GameBoy Advance and the new GameBoy Advance SP (see Figure 9.2). The big difference between these two devices is the packaging design. The SP has a slick looking clamshell design, a backlit screen (which we all screamed for when the first GameBoy came along), and a rechargeable battery system.

There are two flavors of other pocket gaming systems, those that have been around for a while but still have some fans and some new ones you probably haven't heard

FIGURE 9.2
The GameBoy Advance SP offers a much needed backlit screen.

of yet. Table 9.1 lists the key older systems and some links so that you can learn more about them. I've left out a few systems. If you want to learn more about the various mobile systems throughout the years check out **www.pelikonepeijoonit.net/ articles.html**, which has a FAQ and a large exhaustive list with links to many I've omitted like the Tiger Game.com device and many vintage systems.

In terms of contemporary systems, some might praise the Neo Geo Pocket and WonderSwan. These systems are still pretty active among a few diehards. A new system called the Game Park 32 (**english.gamepark.com**) debuted from Korea and is an interesting device. It uses smart cards instead of cartridges and features a USB connection. You can actually download games for it. The sites **www.PlayAsia.com** and **www.lik-sang.com** carry the devices and you can get more information at the GP32news.com Web site and GP32 Extreme (**www.emu.pl/gp32**). Because the Game Park 32 features open development, a cult community formed around the device is growing around the world. Another available device includes the Cybiko system, which is a hybrid wireless device aimed squarely at kids. For more, visit **www.Cybiko.com**.

The Future of Pocket Systems

The future of pocket systems sits in the hands of Sony, Microsoft, and cellular phone makers like Nokia. Another factor influencing the expansion of PDAs is the

TABLE 9.1
Older and established pocket gaming systems.

SYSTEM	COMMENTS	LINKS
Atari Lynx	Originally developed at Epyx, an early and popular 8-bit computer game development firm run by Dave Needle and RJ Mical. These guys helped design the Amiga computer system. Lynx was a color machine with good graphics and sound but ate batteries and was pretty big for a portable. It didn't last long either.	*Good Info:* LynxFAQ (www.atari-history.com/lynx.html) *Find Stuff (other than ebay):* Game Masters (www.game-masters.com) United Game (www.unitedgame.com)
NEC Turbo Express	This device plays PC Engine games in a portable format. One of the first of a new wave of portables when it debuted. It flamed out quickly as NEC got out of the game biz. Featured 16-bit graphics, optional TV tuner, and link cable for multi-player games.	*Good Info:* TG-16 FAQ (www.classicgaming.com/museum/faqs/tg16faq.shtml) *Find Stuff (other than ebay):* Turbo Zone Direct (www.tzd.com) 1-818-706-2051
NeoGeo Pocket	The pocket cousin of the NeoGeo console system from SNK. Like the Wonderswan, it had a short period of popularity among hardcore gamers and then pretty much died.	*Good Info:* NeoGeo Pocket Shock (ngpc.roarvgm.com) NeoGeo For Life (www.neogeoforlife.com) *Find Stuff (other than ebay):* Play Asia (www.play-asia.com) GameChoice (www.gamechoice.com.hk)
Sega GameGear	Color system with backlit screen that played 8-bit Sega games. You can still can find titles for it in some stores. Sega sold the rights for the Game Gear to Majesco at one point, who sold a cheaper unit (not compatible with the TV tuner cartridge). If you buy one on ebay ask for the specs before you spend your dough.	*Good Info:* Game Gear FAQ (www.classicgaming.com/museum faqs/realggfaq.shtml) *More Info* (Ryangenno.tripod.com/sub_pages GameGear.htm) *Find Stuff (other than ebay):* (www.sega-parts.com)

(CONTINUED)

TABLE 9.1 (CONTINUED)
Older and established pocket gaming systems.

SYSTEM	COMMENTS	LINKS
	The Sega system also had what was known as the "Master Converter" which let you play Sega Master System games on it. Like the TV tuner cartridge, it is rare and best found on auction sites. It runs around $30 to $40 from what I've seen.	1-888-271-5678 Amazon.com/Toys R' Us (Has Majesco units and software) (www.aplusvideogames.com)
Sega Nomad	Basically a portable Genesis. This system is very rare and didn't fair that well.	*Good Info:* It's pretty much a Genesis so just search for the many links on thatfor that device. *Find Stuff (other than ebay)* It's extremely hard to find the hardware. Ebay has been the best bet.
WonderSwan	A black and white system put out by Bandai that eventually went color. It had some following in Japan and a bit in the U.S. for a while but pretty much failed to catch fire against the GameBoy juggernaut.	*Good Info:* Bandai (www.bandai-asia.com/wonderswan) FAQ (http://db.gamefaqs.com/portable/wswan/file/wonderswan_a.txt) WonderSwan World (www.wonderswanworld.co.uk) *Find Stuff (other than ebay):* Lan Kwei (Hong Kong) (www.lan-kwei.com) NCSX (www.ncsx.com) GameChoice (www.gamechoice.com.hk)

active group of developers who want to create games for a portable that isn't closed to outside development. As I mentioned before, I think the next generation of GameBoys will also have some sort of wireless functionality. Perhaps they won't have phones (although don't count this out) but they likely will incorporate something like Bluetooth or Spike. In fact, a company called X-tra Fun (**www.x-trafun.com**) has recently demonstrated a Bluetooth add-on for the GameBoy SP.

Gaming via PDAs

PDAs are not as universal as you might think since they are mainly used in North America. In Europe and Japan, core PDA features (phone books, notes, calendar, and so on) are being merged into phones. The number of hybrids, such as the Nokia Communicator (see Figure 9.3) or the Palm-powered phones from Handspring seems to indicate that PDAs are becoming more like mini-computers. Still a lot of people have classic PDAs and some of the latest models like the HP/Compaq iPAQ pack enough power to do 3D graphics and power games like Doom, Age of Empires, and Need for Speed.

MAME and Other Emulators for PDAs

One of the super cool things about PDAs (and eventually phones I bet) is the potential to run MAME and other emulators on them. There are several flavors of MAME ports for WinCE. One of the best is found at **www.mameworld.net/mamece3**. You can also find an alternative iPAQ version at **www.mameworld.net/imame**. Both work with the existing MAME ROMs but may not be as perfectly current as the core MAME app for PCs.

FIGURE 9.3
The Nokia Communicator, a hybrid PDA.

There are also other decent emulators available for PDAs. Being a a monster gamer you'll want to play with many of them and enjoy some retro gaming fun on the road. Table 9.2 presents the other major emulators. Note that many are for iPAQ devices. Clearly, emulators will be a force on mobile devices.

Linux for Your PDA

Linux is everywhere these days and your PDA can run Linux too. There are specific Linux-flavored PDAs and there are sites that show you how to get Linux onto higher-end PDAs like the iPAQ. The site to visit to learn everything you'll want o know about retrofitting and working with Linux on existing PDA hardware is **www.handhelds.org**. There is also the Sharp Zaurus that is now a Linux-based PDA from Sharp (**www.myzaurus.com**).

Finding Publishers and Developers of Major PDA Titles

Since the PDA is not a huge market for games, most major publishers have stayed away from the PDA market. Instead they license their games and properties to skilled PDA developers and publishers. In addition, there are a few budding PDA

TABLE 9.2
Cool Emulators for PocketPC Devices means access to more games.

NAME	EMULATES	WORKS ON	LINK
Pocket //e	Apple IIe	Multiple PocketPC/ WinCE platforms	www.pocketgear.com/ software_detail.asp?id=2701
Pocket Atari	Atari 8-Bit	Multiple PocketPC/ WinCE PDAs	pocketatari.retrogames.com
Pocket Engine	PC Engine	IPAQ	pocketengine.retrogames.com
Pocket64	Commodore 64	Multiple PocketPC/ WinCE platforms	www.clickgamer.com/ moreinfo.htm?pid=4 ($6.95)
PocketColeco	Colecovision	Multiple PocketPC/ WinCE platforms	Pocketvcs.emuunlim.com/ coleco/coleco.html
PocketNES	Nintendo Entertainment System	Multiple PocketPC/ WinCE platforms	pocketnes.retrogames.com
PocketScumm	LucasArts SCUMM Games (e.g. Monkey Island)	Multiple PDAs WinCE, PocketPhone	arisme.free.fr/PocketScumm
PocketVCS	Atari2600	Multiple PocketPC/ WinCE platforms	http://pocketvcs.emuunlim.com

9

developers that are bringing out commercial quality new content. The first place you'll probably start are with a variety of freeware/shareware titles, MAME, and a few other emulators. If you want to grab some very cool state-of-the-art stuff for an upcoming long plane or road trip, check out the sites listed in Table 9.3.

Gaming via Laptops

If you have a job or you are a student, you probably have access to a laptop. But chances are that the laptop you use for your job is probably not tweaked for games. So let's discuss, as quickly as possible, the keys to buying a kick ass gaming laptop.

The company that leads the pack for gaming laptops is Alienware. They offer a few models including the Area 51-M and a newer Hive-Mind version. These laptops, and other gaming specific rigs, provide the extra memory and best laptop capable graphics possible. If you plan on hitting a lot of game cafés and LAN parties, you'll want a souped-up gaming laptop like this. The downside is the weight of these rigs. I travel around a bit with my 5lb rig and I'm screaming for the day when I can trade down to a nice slim 2lb sub-notebook.

TABLE 9.3
Best sites and publishers to use to find great PDA games.

NAME	TYPE	LINK
Gameloft	Publisher/Developer	www.gameloft.com
Handango	Online Retailer	www.handango.org
Hexacto Games	Publisher/Developer	www.hexacto.com
MonkeyStone	Publisher/Developer	www.monkeystone.com
Nomad Games(French)	Enthusiast Site	www.nomadgames.com
PDA+	Enthusiast Site	home.no/entie
PDArcade	Enthusiast Site	www.pdarcade.com
Pocket PC Fanatic	Online Retailer	www.pocketpcfanatic.com
PocketGamer.org	Enthusiast Site	www.pocketgamer.org
PocketGear	Online Retailer	www.pocketgear.com
PocketPC Spiele(German)	Enthusiast Site	www.pocketpc-spiele.de
PocketRPG	Enthusiast Site	www.pocketrpg.com
Public Pocket Games	Enthusiast Site	www.publicpocketgames.com
Wireless Gamer	Enthusiast Site	www.wireless-gamer.com
ZioSoft	Publisher/Developer	www.ziointeractive.com

To combat the heat that many high-end gaming laptops produce, you should check out Postworx Speedball products (www.postworx.com), which you can find at a few online retailers like www.madsonline.com or eshop.macsales.com. These removable balls connect to your laptop to lift it off the ground giving it more air flow.

If you need to travel light, a sub-notebook might be your best option but you'll have to make some sacrifices, like high-end graphics. Fortunately, by end of 2003 the best sub-notebooks will probably be able to push 30 to 40 frames a second on previous generation 3D games (Quake II/III, Unreal II, and so on). You could consider using a portable that runs on a Transmeta chip, which is used to power some of the coolest and slimmest portables around. Transmeta's chips don't just give you longer battery life but also reduce heat. Their first chip was the Crusoe, which hit speeds of around 1GHz. By the time this book is out their new Astro processor chip should be available. Intel has responded with the Centrino processor, which includes built-in Wi-Fi and improved power management.

The other big problem with sub-notebooks is CD drives. Many forgo them figuring people will use a CD at home via a cable or use the Internet itself to install most of their software. This sort of hurts the process of installing games if you're going to have to need the CD to start them up. Fortunately, not every game starts this way. To get around this, pick up a copy of Farstone Software's GameDrive which lets you fool the game into thinking you have a CD installed by installing the entire CD as an image to your harddrive. For more info, visit www.farstone.com.

To find the coolest in portables and ultra portables, you need to go to Japan. Since not all of us can, you can turn to the number one importer of Japanese laptops in the world—Dynamism.com (see Figure 9.4). In Japan, it is not uncommon for a manufacturer to release a portable designed for a market as small as 25,000 units. So the creativity of the machines is much higher as is the frequency of new models. Dynamism works to locate better products and then brings them to North America and Europe. You can buy them from Dynamism and they will update the OS to non-Japanese Windows. They also will provide full warranty and support.

Mobilizing Consoles

I'm often surprised at how many people take their consoles on the road, and I'm not just talking about people with little kids. There are two situations with mobilizing consoles to consider. The first is using it in a car, boat or non-outlet setting

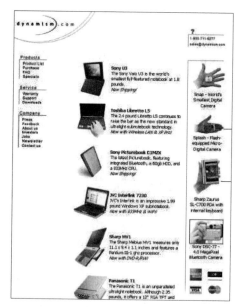

FIGURE 9.4
The coolest notebooks from Japan are found at Dynamism.com.

and the second is using it in other quarters outside your home. Mobile platforms require that you also have a place to secure the console from bouncing around.

If you use your console in a vehicle you'll need a display (unless your vehicle comes with one). Elite Interactive (**www.elite-interactive.com**) is bringing out a new line of mobile monitors by the fall of 2003. A new company in Florida called Intec (**www.inteclink.com**) has brought out some mobile monitors that are sold at bigger chains including Wal-mart.com, Best Buy, and Toys R' Us. They make screens for all the major consoles.

Since all consoles use optical/DVD type drives, and the Xbox also has a harddrive, you need to keep these drives from skipping. This means securing the console in place and protecting it from bumps. I recommend using a good blanket in a secure location and placing on top of that a simple acrylic cutting surface to keep things flat. Give it enough cushion underneath and it should be in good shape. You may need to turn things off if you're on a particularly bumpy rural road. And don't be an idiot and take your gaming system on a four-wheel driving adventure. Monster gaming and monster trucks don't mix well!

POWER IN MOBILE SITUATIONS

Cars, boats, and other vehicles use batteries that provide DC current. Every day devices, like your Xbox, mobile screen, or laptop use AC current. This means you have to convert the current. (Yes you can do a DC to DC conversion but please don't waste my time with this "superior" geek crap.) All inverters provide a certain amount of wattage. If you use an inverter that offers less wattage than the equipment you need, it may not work, or at least it will get very hot which is not good. Your cellphone, small boombox, and so on aren't high wattage affairs. But the Xbox and other devices eat much more power. An Xbox needs as much as 100 watts to operate and you want to have some extra. (When devices fire up they sometimes like a bit more juice to start, and you're going to need some room for those mobile screens too aren't ya?) GameCubes and PS2 need a little less (40 to 80 watts). Thus, you could sneak by with a 100 to 150w inverter but I would suggest having more like a 300w inverter.

APC is one of the best power accessory companies for computers used in cars. They make a 350w adapter that works with your cigarette lighter for $80 (U.S.). You can find it on their site at **www.apc.com**. Tripplite is another trusted manufacturer that makes a 300w system. You can find them online at **www.tripplite.com**.

For boats, I'd check with the local marine supplier you use and they'll hook you up pretty easily, although the thought of being at sea with a dead battery because someone left the PS2 on all night makes me nervous.

In terms of camps, or other venues where you might need some portable power outside of the car, try Xantrex which makes some great portable rechargeable power packs. They're on the Web at **www.xantrex.com**. A 300W model should set you back $100 or so. Higher end gas/oil generators can be found at **www.colemanpowermate.com**.

Gaming via Cell Phone

I saved the best for last. The world has gone crazy over cellphones. In Japan more people access the Internet through their iMode phones than they do through their PCs. In Korea broadband wireless makes phone gaming really rich and fast. In Europe phone games are more popular than in the U.S. but North America is catching up as networks upgrade, better hardware is released, and more game technology hits the market.

In Japan, gaming and doing things other than talking is so popular that many people have two phones—one for talking and the other for gaming and entertainment.

The Basics of Cellphone Games

Cellphone gaming requires two things: the capability of the handset and the capability of the cellular service provider you're using (especially speed and reach).

Those two capabilities create the specific platform for gaming on handsets. Support for various OS technologies that enable games on cellphones is also critical. There are four major platforms and several minor ones enabling games and other applications on cellphones:

- ✔ **J2ME** (Java 2 Micro Edition): This is one of the main platforms going, if not the most popular.

- ✔ **BREW** (Binary Runtime Environment for Wireless): This is a runtime environment for phones developed by Qualcomm aimed at services running Qualcomm-based CDMA networks. BREW is lead by Verizon in the U.S. and is also very popular in Korea.

- ✔ **PocketPhone**: This is essentially Windows CE for phones and is used by a few manufacturers.

- ✔ **iMode**: This is the format used by NTT/DoCoMo in Japan and AT&T's mLife service in the U.S. Because it was one of the first major services with interactivity, it has gotten a lot of press. iMode is essentially J2ME but with a number of tweaks layered on top of it.

- ✔ **Symbian**: This is an OS favored by some phones in Europe, especially Nokia and it is the OS that drives the Nokia 9112 Communicator phone and the N-Gage device.

These platforms are important because, as with different console platforms, they allow access to different games. Depending on the phone you get you will support either J2ME/iMode, or the other operating systems I just mentioned. Because of the nature of J2ME, it could also be used on phones featuring BREW or Symbian OS (as it is with the N-Gage). Don't be shocked if you hear about phones with J2ME in addition to other platforms on it. In these cases, games will be available for the native OS as well as for J2ME. Macromedia is also trying to get Flash/Shockwave running on phones, which will open up games made for that platform to the entire mobile phone space as well.

Depending on the capabilities of the service, you will access games via direct download through the service provider using the data/Internet functionality of the phone. Some phones may also have the ability to sync with your PC, like PDAs do, and receive content through that link as well as memory sticks/cards.

Finding Games

Games for your phone can be found using three direct methods. The first is via on-phone menu systems that interact with the service provider and provide you a menu of titles to acquire and play. Some services and phones will also give you an independent way to locate games and download them. You can also visit some of the top cellular game sites on the Web to find news and links to new games. I've listed some of the best sites for cellular gaming news and downloads in Table 9.4.

Wireless Communication

As the mobile device world grows, especially cellphones, it is important to understand the basics of various wireless technologies and how they fit into the entire gaming on the go spectrum. The world of wireless communications is split into two main groups: wireless networking technologies led by Wi-Fi/802.11 standards and BlueTooth, and cellular technologies which include a variety of flavors lumped under GPRS, 3G, and CDMA2000.

All About Wi-Fi

Wi-Fi, also known as WLAN, is essentially the brand name for the 802.11b wireless networking standard. It will also be used for an updated, and faster version known as 802.11g that is coming of age right now. Wi-Fi is without a doubt the most important major PC technology since 3D accelerated graphics. As a gamer, the big thing about Wi-Fi is that it will let you access online games while you're sitting in a Starbucks or waiting for a plane at the airport. To use Wi-Fi you need a Wi-Fi compatible card, an Intel Centrino equipped laptop (which includes Wi-Fi built into the core chipset of the machine), or any laptop with built-in Wi-Fi. When you get this be sure to configure it properly, especially the security features. Using Wi-Fi for gaming isn't necessarily as great as a fast low-latency Ethernet connection but when roaming the world, and given the lower-latency of the Net to begin with, Wi-Fi is pretty decent overall.

9

TABLE 9.4
Major sites for news and pointers to various mobile phone games.

NAME	TYPE	COMMENTS	LINK
Wireless Gaming Review	Enthusiast Site	The best site if you ask me. Very comprehensive coverage.	www.wirelessgamingreview.com
Midlet Review	Enthusiast Site	A good site but not as extensive as WGR.	www.midlet-review.com
Radio Gamer	Enthusiast Site	In English and German	www.radio-gamer.com www.radio-gamer.de

To learn everything you could want to know about Wi-Fi check out Jeff Duntemann's Drive-By Wi-Fi guide available from Paraglyph Press (**www.paraglyphpess.com**).

The problem isn't getting Wi-Fi equipped hardware, it's finding locations in the world that support Wi-Fi access. Known as hotspots, locations that support Wi-Fi are growing rapidly. Hotel chains, bookstores, airports, coffee shops, and fast food locations are among the first wave of aggressive organizations adding Wi-Fi support. Of course some of these places are charging for access (and some aren't!) either separately on-site, or as part of networks run by aggregators like Boingo! Wireless. If you travel a lot and find yourself in airports and other major hotel chains, you may find it worthwhile to check out Boingo.com or CometaNetworks.com, which are two of the biggest aggregators going right now. The way Boingo! works is you download a client application from their site which gives you a means to locate nodes to visit, and then has a simple app to use to sign on to them if there is a node which requires you to be a Boingo! member to access.

The biggest chain in North America to offer Wi-Fi access is Starbucks which offers service through T-Mobile's HotSpot service. You can sign up for it at **www.t-mobile.com/hotspot** but check out Starbucks.com first because they may have free promo offers. Schlotzky's Deli is another major chain rolling out Wi-Fi and you can find locatons at **www.cooldeli.com/wireless.html**. Borders Books & Cafés is also close to rolling out a major Wi-Fi network.

Visit **www.wi-fizone.org** to learn even more about Wi-Fi and use their search engine to find Wi-Fi Zones.

Wi-Fi and Warchalking Signs

One way to find local establishments using Wi-Fi is to look for the Wi-Fi or Wi-Fi Zone logo (see Figure 9.5a). This symbol denotes that an establishment might be using Wi-Fi. Another useful series of symbols are the Wi-Fi community created warchalking symbols (see Figure 9.5b) which is used to denote the type of Wi-Fi node that is present (open, secure, and so on) and key details about how to log onto it. To learn more about warchalking specifically, visit **www.warchalking.org**.

All About BlueTooth

BlueTooth is known as a *PAN* or *personal area network* technology. It was developed for several reasons including as a way to get rid of all those messy cables that we

FIGURE 9.5a
Wi-Fi Zone logo.

let's warchalk..!	
KEY	SYMBOL
OPEN NODE	ssid)(bandwidth
CLOSED NODE	ssid ◯
WEP NODE	ssid access contact (W) bandwidth
blackbeltjones.com/warchalking	

FIGURE 9.5b
Warchalking symbols.

all deal with. It has also been pushed by cellphone vendors who see it as a way for various mobile devices to work together. Bluetooth headsets, for example, make it possible to have a headset for your phone that isn't actually connected to your cellphone. A PDA with Bluetooth could talk to a phone and download content through it or automatically sync with your computer once it was within the same room with it.

In terms of gaming Bluetooth could be used for mini-ad-hoc head-to-head or group games with no cable needed. Imagine battling complete strangers only a few seats away on the train into work. The Nokia N-Gage device features Bluetooth that can be used for just this purpose.

All about Spike

Spike is a little known wireless protocol which is garnering some attention because of its videogame roots. It is a technology from Eleven Engineering that is used to power wireless game controllers. Unlike Bluetooth—a standard run by a consortium, Spike is wholly developed by Eleven Engineering who plans to license it to various videogame companies, controller companies, and consumer electronics companies. The system has a lot of similarities to Bluetooth but it is more geared to a real-time environment and it's much cheaper to implement. This has a lot of people speculating it could become a bigger deal not just for videogames but as an alternative personal area network system. Meanwhile, Spike game controllers

9

are expected to be compatible in such a way as you only need one controller for all your devices that support Spike wireless controllers. Now wouldn't that be nice!

Have Travel Will Game

The biggest problem with gaming while traveling is the image. When you're 30+ and you're on a coast-to-coast flight you might not feel encouraged to take out your GBA and play a few hours of Advance Wars or Final Fantasy Tactics. This says that gaming isn't perfectly accepted as adult entertainment. On the other hand I've used my laptop to play games, or played games on my cellphone and no one bats an eye. The issue is not the games you play but the hardware you use to game by. Overtime, I think this will change. The new GameBoy Advance SP looks a lot more "adult" in its design for a reason.

What will make mobile gaming really fun is when Bluetooth, Wi-Fi, and Spike make it possible for us to game in ad-hoc networks against each other as we sit amongst ourselves on a train, bus, or in a local coffee shop. I can't wait to see this happen because mobile gaming actually has the potential to make gaming much more social. We can't be nearly as social with gaming when we're cooped up in our homes.

Another thing that will make mobile gaming interesting is when we utilize the real world as part of the game itself. This is already happening in small forms now. *Geocaching* (**www.geocaching.com**) is a growing phenomenon and companies like Bandai have released games that change based on barcodes from products you scan into the game. I've also seen phone games that use phone cameras integrated into the games. The possibilities of games in mobile environments are very interesting and dynamic. If you're truly a monster gamer, you need to get involved now.

chapter 10

THE COMPLETE GUIDE TO RETRO GAMING

One day I was sitting idly at my computer (I mean I was busily writing this book) and an email came in from a friend. He usually sits idly at his computers all day (I mean he busily trades stocks for his Wall St. firm) but occasionally he sends me a funny chain-email joke. Recently he sent one that really caught my attention. It recounted how the writer used to lament his parents' nutty stories about how they would trudge ten miles through deep snow in bare feet to their one-room school-house before slaving away at a factory to make ends meet. Then the writer began to think about today's kids and how he had similar stories to tell them about how tough life was when he was a kid. There was a particularly poignant part about video games worth sharing:

> "We didn't have any fancy Sony Playstation or Xbox video games with high-resolution 3D graphics. We had the Atari 2600. With games like Space Invaders and Asteroids, the graphics sucked butt! Your guy was a little square! You had to use your imagination! And there were no multiple levels or screens—it was just one screen...forever! And you could never win! The game just kept getting harder and faster until you died! Just like LIFE!"

Ah, the good old days. Any monster gamer over the ripe old age of 28 likely remembers plunking actual quarters (not tokens) into the arcade game at the corner store or local pizza joint. I can't tell you how many dives I spent time in just to play a game like Mr. Do, BurgerTime, Galaga, Sinistar, or Defender. But what are our kids going to do? How will they get the experience of playing the games we played when we were kids? How can we take a trip back in time to play these games that are still fun today? I defy a monster gamer to tell me the occasional game of Joust, Tempest, or Defender isn't still fun. Thankfully, there is an entire support network for retro gaming. In Chapter 3 I explained how you can buy and restore old cabinet-based arcade games. But how many of us have the cash, space, or technical capacity to do this? Luckily, there are programs called *emulators* available to re-run old software on new hardware. For example, you can now run an old arcade program like Robotron 2084 on your PC in all its original glory.

Emulators have been around for a while. In this chapter I'm going to show you how to use them to support your retro gaming habit. Eventually one piece of hardware becomes much faster and powerful than older generations and it can emulate lower-end hardware with room to spare. Emulators fool software that runs on one chip into thinking the old chip is still in the system. In reality he emulator operates just as a translator as it sends the translated commands to the real CPU, which recreates the output. Much overhead is involved so until one CPU is significantly more powerful than the one it's emulating, it can't offer much. Emulators are neat things, and they occupy a space of programming that is especially popular for programmers, especially those who like machine code and assembly.

The King of Emulators—MAME

Back in 1996 a programmer named Nicola Salmoria decided to build a single hardware emulator in software. The idea was to run a plethora of different code under a single roof. That project grew to become known as *MAME*, an acronym for Multiple Arcade Machine Emulator. The first version was released as open source on February 5, 1997. Since then, the project has grown to see a number of contributors and it has expanded to support over 2,000 games. MAME has been ported to a number of operating systems and platforms and is probably the single biggest achievement in keeping old classic games alive for people to play.

As defined by the MAME team, MAME's purpose in life is to help people explore the inner workings of arcade machines and to preserve the old arcade games. Here's what they write in their documentation:

"MAME is strictly a non-profit project. Its main purpose is to be a reference to the inner workings of the emulated arcade machines. This is done for educational purposes and to prevent many historical games from sinking into oblivion once the hardware they run on stops working. Of course to preserve the games, you must also be able to actually play them; you can consider that a nice side effect. It is not our intention to infringe on any copyrights or patents on the original games. All of MAME's source code is either our own or freely available. To operate, the emulator requires images of the original ROMs from the arcade machines, which must be provided by the user. No portions of the original ROM codes are included in the executable."

Someday when you have kids (if you don't already) you'll probably use MAME to show them what video games were like before they were played on six-foot HDTV screens with life-like graphics. Then, they'll realize that the games didn't get easier and you never did finish them—they finished you!

MAME is not the only emulator for retro gaming but it's easily the biggest, best, and most popular. We'll cover some others later, but the focus of this chapter is learning how to master MAME. MAME exists for several platforms. For purposes of this chapter I'll focus on the Windows flavor of MAME that has a built in GUI, known as MAME32QA.

MAME is the king of arcade emulators but another one that is quite popular is RAINE, which can be found at **www.rainemu.com**. Unfortunately, I can't cover it as much as MAME but for true enthusiasts you might want to check it out. You can also find several other arcade emulators at **www.emustatus.rainemu.com/emu.htm**, which let you play some other games not covered by MAME or RAINE. At the end of this chapter I cover other emulators to enable playing of old home console and computer games on your PC.

Downloading MAME

Table 10.1 lists the available versions of MAME on the "ports" page of its main Web site. This specific Windows version we are interested in is available as a .exe download at Classicgaming.com (**www.classicgaming.com/mame32qa**). To download it, you'll have to register with GameSpy to get access to the latest version since Classicgaming.com stores it on GameSpy's Fileplanet service. So take a few minutes to lie about yourself and your household income to GameSpy and get registered for the free version of Fileplanet. (A paid version is available which gets you priority access to their download archive—something worthwhile when things are particularly busy.)

TABLE 10.1
The flavors of MAME.

- MacMAME
- Xmam for various flavors of Unix
- Advance Mame (a version with specific support for arcade monitors)
- Xbox (AKA MAME-X)
- Dreamcast (MAMEDC)
- OS2

- Amiga
- BE
- PocketPC
- Zaurus
- PSION/EPOC32
- Nokia 9210

The program is really simple to install. It just asks you to specify the directory where you want to stick it. If you need help with that, return this book and get the Dummies guide to being an idiot or the Idiots guide to being a dummy. Once you run it, you'll be greeted with the main Mame32 display. This flavor of MAME marries a well-designed interface with the core MAME32 engine. To do this it builds a well-designed database that lets you manage your games and their launch characteristics. It also lets you set up a database of imagery to spice things up. To master this program, we'll need to discuss two things:

✔ The core issues concerning using MAME to play games.

✔ How to configure and tweak the setup.

But first (after things are up and running), you'll want to grab some ROMs to use to play some games.

Steal this ROM

Last time I checked the police listings in the newspaper, they had more important things to do than bash down doors and investigate people for having images of ROMs on their computer they never owned. Technically speaking, it's illegal to posses ROMs that you don't own. It's even more illegal to distribute those ROMs to other people. Of course, not everything in the land of retro gaming is black and white, as you'll see. Here's the gray area: Most of the games emulated by MAME are no longer available—some were even created by companies that went belly up. At the same time, unlike used games and other forms of piracy, you're probably not hurting a developer who is expecting to cash in on a dinosaur game. Last I checked, Noah Fahlstein, one of the people who developed Sinistar, wasn't still cashing his royalty checks from that title. In many cases if you combine MAME with a love of arcade board collecting you're definitely in the clear because you are allowed to posses copies of ROMs you own yourself. However, not many of us are going to do that are we?

On the flip side, you shouldn't think that these games don't have value any more or are just going to be left entirely on the scrap heap. Because of technologies like handheld gaming and cell phones, publishers are realizing that there is some value left in their old ROMs. Activision, Namco, and others have re-released game packs of their classic titles for not only the PC, but consoles, GameBoy Advance, and some cell phones. The next time you see some guy weaving down the road in his SUV, don't just assume he's yaking on his cell phone and not paying attention. He might be doing some retro gaming with an old Activision game.

So here are my rules on acquiring ROMs, which you can use to gauge your own feelings and actions:

1. **If there is a legal and cost-effective way to acquire ROMs, do it**. By fair cost I mean no more than $50—the top cost of any console game. A fairer price should be $5 to$6 because most "classic collections" give you 4 to 5 games for $20 to $30, which establishes the market value for most classic games. Most arcade boards are going to cost more than this because you're buying a lot more than the ROM so don't take this to mean I think arcade boards should cost $50.

2. **Do not under any circumstances pay for CD-ROMs or downloads of ROMs that are clearly not from anyone licensed to do so**. As tempting as it is, this *rewards* piracy and keeps your money from going where it should. Conversely, don't sell ROMs on the Internet.

3. **Consider buying the classic game packs that are available if you've obtained ROMs from those products to use with MAME**. Unfortunately, not all games are available in this format. This is *not* a legal loophole however; a game pack like NAMCO museum is not the same as legally owning the ROMs from those games.

4. **Don't redistribute ROMs to other people**. While this could eventually choke off their availability, you really should leave this role to those people who feel brave enough to do it themselves. Doing this is just asking for legal trouble.

5. **If publishers begin to offer MAME downloads for a fee, support them**. If you don't, you're taking advantage of the situation and not being a good, card-carrying supporter of classic games.

6. **You might even consider writing letters and emails to publishers encouraging them to provide a legal means for obtaining their ROM images.**

Some people will say obtaining ROM images for MAME is stealing and illegal. In reality, they're right. But when viewed through certain moral prisms there is a case to be made for obtaining ROM image files if you can base your motivation on a love of games and a lack of a legal means to properly and fairly obtain them.

In the land of movies there is often a totally legal and affordable means to obtain almost every major movie made in the past 30 years or more. This makes it even more immoral to steal a movie since you have little to stand on except the basis that it makes the expense cheaper. In terms of music there is an entire back catalog available, some of it easy and cheap to acquire. The games industry, on the other hand, seems to ignore the interest in older titles, but simultaneously whines when those of us who want them resort to scavenging for them. If my little rant hasn't scared you away from acquiring ROMs, here is a clip from MAME's Web site that might scare you a little:

> "Remember, it is **illegal** to possess a ROM file unless you own the original circuit board containing that ROM. It is highly unlikely—probably impossible— that any one person could own the circuit boards for all 3300+ of the games MAME supports. Possessing a ROM file from a game you don't own is punishable by up to five years in prison and a fine of up to $50,000 for *each* violation. (Although no one is being prosecuted at this time, the law is in place.)"

The Real Solution

The ultimate solution is that someday the companies will find a way to create a downloadable super archive of all their classic games. We'll pay a special fee, maybe $9.95 a month and that will get us "all-we-can-eat" access to various ROMs and other image files. The publishers that own the properties will get to earn some royalty revenue from it and we'll all be able to play MAME until the cows come home. Of course I once predicted pigs would fly (they can you know), and I still think the Red Sox would win the World Series before my life is over.

Finding ROMs

Other than saying they're out there, I can tell you that a simple search on Google or other major engines will help you find some. But good luck, I'm not going to say any more. The MAME ROM scene is one very similar, albeit a bit more blatant and less policed than the MP3 scene. You will come across many empty archives, lots of pop ups, several or more ads for porn and gambling sites, and then eventually you'll find some ROM sets. Right now I'm going to turn my back for twenty minutes and let you go search for some ROMs for the arcade boards you better own.

Installing a ROM Set

I'm back; how was your trip to the local ROM shop? I bet they had a lot of good ROMs all nicely organized. And you paid for them right? You even sent a nice check directly to the publisher. Maybe you even included a note thanking the publisher for making it so easy to legally buy old games you still would be willing to play.

To install a ROM set with MAME32, you download the zipped archive and keep it intact. Then, put it into the ROM's directory as shown in Figure 10.1. Once it's there you can launch it and run MAME but you can also tweak its run time variables.

The properties dialog is found by right-clicking on the game you want to tweak and choosing Properties from the resulting menu (see Figure 10.2).

The Properties dialog, as shown in Figure 10.3, has seven tabbed areas that allow you to get or set various information. Lets roll through each one:

✔ *General*: This is the basic information tab about the game. It displays when the game was manufactured and by whom. It also tells you what CPU was used (many early games used a Z80 processor), and lists the basics on screen colors and size.

✔ *Audit*: This tab does a quick check in the ROM's directory to see if you have a proper ZIP archive of the ROM and whether it passes inspection (see Figure 10.4).

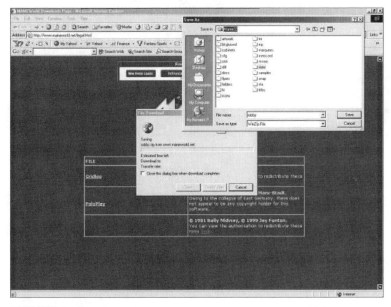

FIGURE 10.1
Putting your zipped ROM files in the ROM's directory.

■ 4-D Warriors		4dwarrio	Raster	No	0	Coreland / Sega	1985
■ 600		600	Raster	No	0	Konami	1981
■ 64th. Street - A Detective Story ...		64streej	Raster	No	0	Jaleco	1991
■ 64th. Street - A D	Play 64th. Street - A Detective Story (Japan)		Raster	No	0	Jaleco	1991
■ 720 Degrees (set	Play and Record Input...		Raster	Yes	0	Atari Games	1986
■ 720 Degrees (set			Raster	Yes	0	Atari Games	1986
■ 800 Fathoms	Add to Custom Folder...		Raster	No	0	Amenip (US Billiard...	1981
■ Ace	Remove From This Folder		Raster	No	0	Allied Leisure	1976
■ Acrobat Mission	Custom Filters...		Raster	No	0	UPL (Taito license)	1991
■ Act-Fancer Cyberr			Raster	No	0	Data East Corporat...	1989
■ Act-Fancer Cyberr	Select Random Game		Raster	No	0	Data East Corporat...	1989
■ Act-Fancer Cyberr			Raster	No	0	Data East Corporat...	1989
■ Adventure Quiz 2 Hatena Hate...	Properties		Raster	No	0	Capcom	1990
■ Aero Fighters		hatena	Raster	No	0	Video System Co.	1992
■ Aero Fighters (Turbo Force hard...		aerofgt	Raster	No	0	Video System Co.	1992
■ Aero Fighters (Turbo Force hard...		aerofgtb	Raster	No	0	Video System Co.	1992
■ Aero Fighters (Turbo Force hard...		aerofgtc	Raster	No	0	Video System Co.	1992

FIGURE 10.2
Choose Properties from the menu.

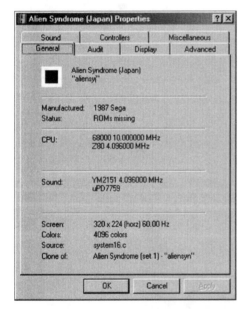

FIGURE 10.3
The Properties dialog.

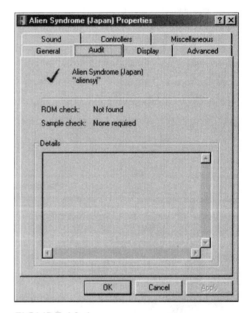

FIGURE 10.4
The Audit tab.

✔ *Display*: The display tab has a number of options, as shown in Figure 10.5, which include:

   ✔ *Run in a Window*: Determines if the game runs in a window on your desktop or full screen.

   ✔ *Start Out Maximized*: If this is checked and you are running in windowed mode, MAME will launch the Window at the maximum size.

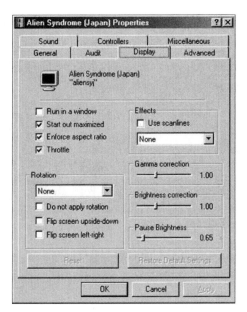

FIGURE 10.5
The Display tab.

✔ *Enforce Aspect Ration*: When in windowed mode, if this is checked the aspect ratio of the Windows is enforced. If you uncheck it and play in windowed mode you can create funky looking windows and play games in tall and fat mode. MAME will stretch the graphics to fit the shape.

✔ *Throttle*: When checked it slows the game down to its original playable speed. For most of you, this will make the game to run way too fast.

✔ *Rotation*: This feature lets you set various rotational and mirror image characteristics for your MAME system. If you build your own MAME cabinet (see below), this features can be handy; otherwise, you probably won't use it. You can use it to create a vertical orientation for some games that might be better played that way (think Galaga or Galaxian for example) and you can use the flip screens for systems that utilize a mirror system for their projection capability.

✔ *Effects*: This feature lets you add a variety of scanlines to enlarge an image to fill more of a screen.

✔ *Gamma Correction*: Lets you raise or lower the gamma ratio for your screen.

✔ *Brightness Correction*: Raise or lower the brightness level for the game when it's being played.

✔ *Pause Brightness*: Affects how much the screen is darkened when you pause the game.

✔ *Advance* The Advance Tab, as shown in Figure 10.6, presents a number of additional graphics features. Almost all of these revolve around the use of Direct-Draw (which for everyone reading the book should be enabled). The Use DirectDraw feature has nine key sub-features:

✔ *Triple Buffering*: Provides the smoothest looking graphics MAME can render. Selecting this option slows down your machine, however.

✔ *Match game refresh rate:* This helps MAME match the original refresh rate of the game itself. When used with triple buffering, you get the best graphics capability.

✔ *Sync to monitor refresh*: This causes MAME to sync its graphics to your current monitors refresh rate. If it is greater than 60Hz, it could result in game play that's too fast.

✔ *Wait for vertical sync*: This forces MAME to wait until there is a refresh before redrawing the screen. This option helps keep things from tearing or otherwise looking bad.

✔ *Stretch using hardware*: This will cause any stretching of MAME's display to use hardware acceleration for that purpose. There is a problem, though.

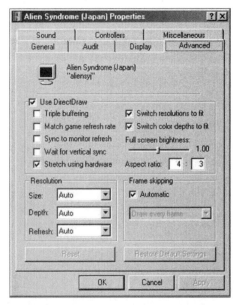

FIGURE 10.6
The Advance Tab.

Many times hardware-based stretching results in some blurriness as the card compensates for jagged edges. MAME's documentation recommends looking for an RGB sharpness setting in your particular cards control panel to compensate for this problem.

✔ *Switch resolutions to fit:* This allows you to use the resolution settings in MAME32 to resize the game to any number of output sizes. If not on then MAME draws to the current desktop size and settings.

✔ *Switch color depths to fit:* Same as *Switch resolution to fit* except for color. If you toggle it on, you can explicitly set the color depth. If turned off, it launches at the current color depth of your desktop settings.

✔ *Full screen brightness:* Some hardware cards alter the brightness of the screen when they enter into full screen mode. This setting lets you fight that tendency.

✔ *Aspect ratio:* Gives you more control over the setting of the aspect ratio.

✔ *Resolution:* This feature lets you set the resolution used to display the game. If any of these menus are grayed out it's because you've chosen to run MAME in a window back on the Display tab. If you've left that option unchecked, you can set the resolution, bit-depth for graphics, and refresh rate for the graphics here.

✔ *Frame skipping:* This lets you decide on how many, if any, frames should be skipped to maintain an acceptable speed for game play. Since most of us are running a fast rig this shouldn't be a problem.

✔ *Sound:* The Sound tab lets you turn the sound on and off and force re-sampling if the sample rate of the game is lower than the threshold you set.

✔ *The Volume Attenuation:* I haven't a clue what this does.

✔ *Controllers:* If you have a game pad or joystick active on your system, this will let you set up support for those devices. Some games also support mouse or light-gun input. Enabling Steady Support enables rapid fire key presses but can cause the game to be more sluggish.

✔ *Miscellaneous:* This tab includes support for options like backdrops, bezels and overlays, as well as using keyboard LEDs as game indicators. You can turn off and on game cheats and instruct the emulator to conserve CPU time wherever possible.

TIP If you overdo the configuration for your game at any point you can hit the Restore Default Settings tab to turn things back to the initial settings or hit Reset to set them back to the last applied changes you made.

✔ *Vector:* For games that were vector-based titles, you'll see an optional tab (see Figure 10.7) that controls vector-based options. This feature lets you tweak the display of games like Battlezone, Star Wars, and Tempest.

    ✔ *Draw antialiased vectors:* This feature improves the drawing of vectors by using some keen anti-aliasing to make the graphics look super smooth.

    ✔ *Draw translucent vectors:* This adds the effect you see on other vector games by utilizing a slight translucency and bright points where lines intersect.

    ✔ *Beam width:* Lets you set the beam width in pixels to create wider vectors.

    ✔ *Flicker:* When checked, this feature adds a small flicker effect on lines which mimics an effect that these games had because of the monitors they used.

    ✔ *Intensity:* This slider sets the brightness/intensity of vector lines. The higher the value the more the "bright glow" effect of vector monitors.

Organizing MAME32 for Windows

The next important part of your configuration is the MAME GUI itself. This can be as simple as making a few small choices to a more complex procedure where you download all of the associated icons, cabinet artwork, flyers, and more that are non-essential but still a wonderful part of the full MAME experience. You'll want

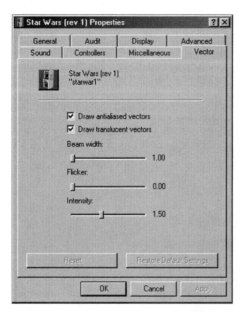

FIGURE 10.7
The Vector tab.

to download the newest versions every now and then because that automatically updates the ROM database. Other than that, customizing it is fairly simple. You can start by downloading all of the various graphics sets available.

 When you download a new copy of MAME32QA it will overwrite your MAME\folders\favorties.ini file so be sure to make a backup copy of it before overwriting it.

You can find these sets at **www.classicgaming.com/mame32qa/down.htm**. Each set comes with a small set of "add on" packs that you can install as well. Each set is organized into a series of downloads. The main zip file(s), such as Icons.zip, Title_01.zip, or Title_02.zip are the downloads that get you all the associated artwork for games supported by a specific version of MAME. There are also download links to files associated with newer versions of MAME as well. To get everything, you'll want to download the main files plus the update file for your version.

With the exception of the ICONS.zip file, which can be kept in the icons directory in zipped form, the other files must be unzipped to their respective directory to install. You may also need to start and stop MAME32QA to make it work once installed. Table 10.2 shows you which artwork type goes in which directory.

Additional Support Files

The additional support files for MAME that you can install include Marquee files, and the Hiscore.dat and History.dat files. The Marquee files are shots of the main marquee used on the cabinet for various games. These files used to be easy to find because they were distributed on one official site. The .dat files are installed in the root \MAME32 directory. When properly installed they will show you "official" hi-scores for MAME games. The official History.dat file is kept on **fandemame.emu-france.com**. When installed, the history facts will show up on your MAME32QA screen and in the game when you pull up the history setting from the in-game menu control (see Figure 10.8).

Configuring External Audio Files

Some MAME games store the sounds used in external files because these files were analog audio files or the sound chip hasn't been properly emulated. The byproduct of this is that samples can be replaced and tweaked as well. The place to find samples is on the official MAME distribution site at **www.mame.net/downsamples.html**. Download the files and place them into your MAME32/samples directory.

10

TABLE 10.2
Where to place MAME files.

ARTWORK TYPE	DIRECTORY TO UNZIP FILES TOO
Icons	\mame32\icons
Screenshots	\mame32\snap
Titles	\mame32\titles
Backgrounds	\mame32\bkground
Flyers	\mame32\flyers
Cabinets	\mame32\cabinets

FIGURE 10.8
Game History is shown after
you install the History.dat file.

Configuring Your Favorites

To add a game to a subfolder from the master list, you right click on it and choose the "Add to Custom Folder…" option. A small dialog appears, as shown in Figure 10.9, that lets you choose a place to put it with one of them being Favorites. By placing it in your Favorites directory you can easily click the Favorites folder from the leftmost list of folders on MAME32QA and get access to your games.

If you install an update to MAME32QA you will overwrite your Favorites folder so make a backup!

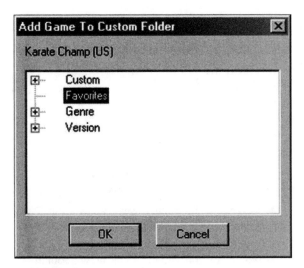

FIGURE 10.9
Choosing a folder.

MAME Command Line

At its core MAME is actually a command line program. MAME32QA puts an interface over that command line system. However, I'd be remiss if I didn't highlight where you can learn all of the command line instructions for classic MAME because on other platforms there may be a need to operate MAME via a command line. The best doc here is MSDOS.txt which comes with MSDOS binary downloads of MAME and can be found on the Web at **www.mame.net/ readmedos.html**. You might also check out MAME World's DOS pages at **www.mameworld.net/dosmame/main.php** for more help.

Playing MAME

Jeez after over a half-dozen pages of text we're finally at the point where we can talk about playing a game with MAME. Once you launch a MAME game you need to know the various keyboard shortcuts to make it work. Table 10.3 covers all of the major shortcuts.

More about Controls

Table 10.3 only tells part of the story of how to use MAME32 once it is running. Let's run through the entire process a bit and I'll point out a few critical items. First, you should understand how MAME loads your game. As far as the game software is concerned you've just booted up the arcade game for the morning. Thus you may

TABLE 10.3
Keyboard shortcuts for MAME.

KEY	SHORTCUT NAME	EXPLANATION
5	Insert Coin	This is the equivalent of inserting a coin and thus adds a credit to the game. Once a credit is in, you can hit one or two player buttons.
1	Start a single player game	Starts a single player game.
2	Start a two player game or add the second player	Depending on the game, starts a two player game or adds a second active player to a game.
3	Start a three player game or add the third player to the game	Depending on the game, this will allow a third player to enter the festivities. Think specifically about games like Gauntlet.
4	Start a four player game or add the fourth player to the game	Depending on the game this will allow a fourth player to enter the festivities. Think specifically about games like Alien Syndrome.
Cursor keys	Directional Controls	Up, down, left, right or combination thereof.
LEFT CTRL	Primary "fire" button	Shoot! Jump! and more…
LEFTALT	Secondary "fire" button	Jump! Shoot! And more.
Tab	Internal Menu	Brings up internal menu system for MAME32.
~	Onscreen Display	Brings up the onscreen display functions of MAME.
P	Pause	Pauses the game.
T	Tilt	Slam that machine when it screws you over.
F3	Reset	Resets the game.
F4	Display Game Color Palette	Shows the game's color palette.
F7 + SHIFT F7	Load and Save Game State	An effective but not 100% way to save and load games you're in the middle of.
F9	Change Frameskip	Cycles through frameskip needs. If you're experiencing sluggish behavior, use this option in the game to improve its framerate.
F10	Throttle Toggle	This turns the throttle off or on. If you throttle up on most modern machines the game will run really fast (almost unplayable in many cases).
F11	FPS Toggle	Cycles through various frames per second settings. Use this feature to improve sluggish games.
F12	Snapshot	Takes a snapshot of the screen.
ESC	Exit MAME	Back to work!

see some tests and initial diagnostics, the ability to set some dipswitches, and so on. You might also see some accounting information for the owner of the arcade game. If you're running a new ROM set for the first time, MAME also requires that you legally acknowledge its disclaimer as shown in Figure 10.10. To get by this, you have to type in OK, which is designed to properly absolve the MAME creators from your illegal use of ROMs (not that you would do that!).

Next MAME may provide some other messages such as known problems with the game. As an example, Figure 10.11 tells you there are some problems using the

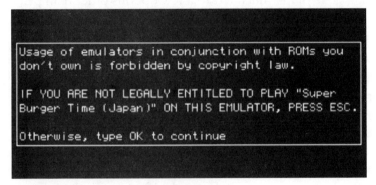

FIGURE 10.10
MAME's discloser.

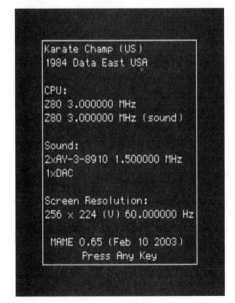

FIGURE 10.11
The MAME initial status screen.

game in "cocktail" mode, which refers to rotating the screen. Again you are asked to type in OK to move forward to the next screen.

Finally, MAME will show you a quick status screen for the game, which tells you the CPU and the audio chips for the game. Also shown is the date the game came out, screen resolution, refresh rate, and the version of MAME you are using. Press any key after this screen and the game will proceed to boot up.

In-Game Options

Once the game is running you're pretty much left to a few options other than playing the game. The first is the in-game menu (brought up by pressing the ~ key). The in-game menu is a small section at the bottom of the screen that lets you set the volume for any of the multiple audio channels. You can also use it to set video options including brightness and gamma. To cycle through the options here, press the up and down cursor keys. To change any setting, press the left and right cursor keys. Press Esc to return to the game.

Game Menu Items

The other major menu within MAME is the Game Menu, which you can bring up by pressing the Tab key. The menu, as shown in Figure 10.12, contains the following items:

FIGURE 10.12
The Game menu.

✔ *Input (General):* This area, as shown in Figure 10.13, lets you set all the general inputs that map to various joystick, trackballs, dials, or buttons that any of the games MAME emulates would have. When specific inputs are mapped to a game, these general inputs will take precedence. You can define an overall file for these items as well, which I'll cover in a bit. To change an item here just highlight the area using the cursor keys to move between the various options and press Enter to begin changing an option. Once you press Enter the key setting selected will be blank. The next key you press will then re-map to that item. You can press other keys as well (up to three) to map multiple keys to the same control. In general you'll find most of the general and game-specific key mappings to be well designed.

✔ *Input (This Game):* This area, as shown in Figure 10.14, lets you change settings for the specific game you're playing if those items have been remapped. Setting key-mappings here is no different than the previous Input (General) area.

 Although the general configuration setup can be edited by hand by changing settings in the controller file (see later), any settings changed in the specific game menu can't be changed outside of the game itself. The configuration file is not stored as plain text (don't ask me why this is). If you don't like the configuration file (and thus you

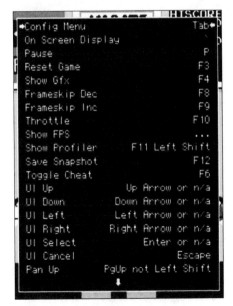

FIGURE 10.13
Input area of MAME's game menu system.

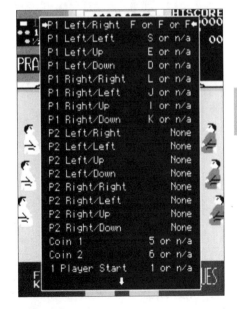

FIGURE 10.14
Changing settings for a specific game.

want to start), you can go into the MAME32/cfg folder and delete the relevant .cfg file. This is handy for those times you screw up and re-map the in-game menu key from the Tab key and forget what it is.

✔ *Dip Switches:* In ye-olden times Arcade games provided various tiny switches to control certain settings, such as setting the game to hard or normal, the amount of coinage needed, and soon. MAME lets you set these same settings using the in-game menu as shown in Figure 10.15. Highlight the area you wish to change with the up and down cursor keys. An arrow on each item points left or right or both. This lets you know which left and right cursor keys will switch the setting.

✔ *Bookkeeping Info:* This brings up a bookkeeping screen that will show you in some games the cash you've taken in while the machine was on (see Figure 10.16).

✔ *Game Information:* This shows you the basic game information screen you saw back when the game was turned on.

✔ *Game History:* Brings up a text history of the game if it was included in the ROM set you obtained.

✔ *Reset Game:* Resets the game entirely.

✔ *Return to Game:* Returns you to the game.

FIGURE 10.15
Using the dip-switch settings in MAME.

FIGURE 10.16
Viewing bookkeeping information.

Editing Default Controls

MAME provides an initialization file that makes it easier for you to tweak its control settings. This file is named STD.ini and it is located in the MAME32/cfg folder. You can open this file in Notepad, as shown in Figure 10.17, and edit away to create the configuration you like.

If you take five seconds to look at the file you'll see that it is easy to edit. The right hand column lists the basic controls a game may or may not have. For example, P1_Joystick_Up is the code for pushing the first player joystick up. Next to that is a quoted string of characters that lets you determine the key to map to it. For example KEYCODE_R means the 'R' key. Be careful about confusing case specifies. For example, to map a control to a "capital letter" you would insert LSHIFT, SHIFT, or RSHIT into this mix as in "KEYCODE_LSHIFT_R." Using the | character lets you add multiple entries that trigger the same event. You can also include mouse and joystick codes using the MOUSECODE and JOYCODE operands. MAME32 for Windows ships not only with the standard mapping file but also with some custom map files for use with various arcade controllers you can use specifically with MAME.

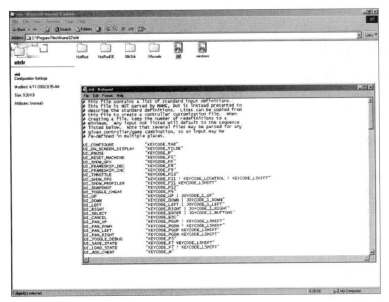

FIGURE 10.17
Editing the default control INI file with Notepad.

Saving States

Remember playing a game and doing so well that you wanted to save it and come back. One day I was kicking butt in a game before school that I missed the first two classes. This wasn't high school so "cutting class" was a bad thing. I got a great score and ended up in huge trouble. MAME, fortunately, provides a rudimentary save system to keep you from missing school (or work). It's called "state saving" and it works by saving the entire state of any game to a file. When you load that file in the game you can pick up where you left off. Well, this is how it's supposed to work. In reality this feature doesn't always work perfectly with all games. To save a state, find a good safe spot (look for a new level change or a specific safe position on a level) and press Shift+F7. MAME will respond with a window at the bottom of the screen that says "save position to" along with a number 1 through 9. Game play will quickly resume after that. Figure 10.18 shows an example of the save feature in action.

To restore a position press F7 and then MAME will respond with a window at the bottom of the screen that says "load position from." Provide the corresponding number you want to load in from and the game will reset to that position and play will quickly resume.

FIGURE 10.18
Using MAME's save state.

Recording and Playing Back Input

Recording a game is a cool way to not only evaluate play, but to show others how to get past certain obstacles in a game. It's also a great way to verify high-scores. MAME32QA helps you invoke the record game system MAME supports really easily. First, choose the game you want to play from the game list. Then, from the File menu, choose Play and Record Input. A standard Windows Save File dialog will pop up. Provide a name for your saved game and then hit Save. The game will load and all of your commands will be saved to a file.

To playback a game simply select Playback Input from the File menu and then choose the file you want to play. MAME32QA will load the game and pass the input file along and the MAME engine will replay the game exactly as you previously played it. Very cool!

Better Controls

Once you play with MAME you'll get hooked. You'll want more ROMs and a better setup. To play better with a real arcade control system, you can try some of the various arcade controllers available that support MAME.

X-Arcade
www.x-arcade.com

The X-Arcade stick is pretty cool and comes in both one player and simultaneous two player setups (see Figure 10.19). This stick is not only compatible with MAME but it's also compatible with your Xbox, GameCube, and others through adapters you can purchase.

FIGURE 10.19
Using the X-Arcade controller.

The Devastator
http://www.tomheroes.com/Devastator/devastator.htm

True MAME nuts will want to check out the Devastator stick if they deal with its less than stellar look (see Figure 10.20). The boards are hand-made by Jim Krych. The cool thing about them is they include a spinner (good for Tempest and games that require that) and a trackball too. This makes one of the ultimate MAME controllers because it's ready for any type of game except Star Wars, driving games, or other games with slightly more tweaked controls. The system sells for just under $400 as this book went to press.

The Slick Stick
www.slikstik.com

These guys go all out. They have several units including a Quad Unit (great for games like Gauntlet) which I've shown in Figure 10.21. Given the industrial design over the Devastator the prices are not cheap running from $250 to $700 for a quad unit. They have blank units for those who prefer to build it themselves.

Mame Compatible Lightgun
www.act-labs.com/scripts/proddetails.asp?pid=92

The best MAME compatible lightgun around is from ACT Labs and is called the ACT LABS PC USB Light Gun. It sells for about $30.

Building Your Own MAME Cabinet

You can also build your own MAME cabinet setup to give you a more arcade-like experience. There are several expensive and inexpensive solutions to consider.

FIGURE 10.20
This setup gives you almost every controller you'll need for MAME.

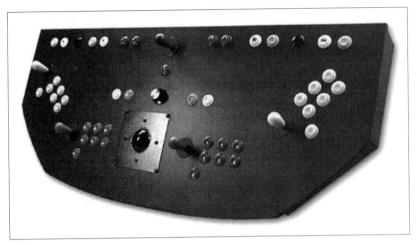

FIGURE 10.21
Anyone for a round of Gauntlet?

X-Arcade Universal Cabinet
www.x-arcade.com
This is a cabinet setup that's made to be easy. It includes shelving for a 27" television set, and shelves for games, and consoles. The $999 package includes a two-player X-Arcade controller plus adapters for PC, and two consoles of your choice.

Arcade Shopper MAME Cabinets
www.arcadeshopper.com/mame
These cabinets aren't cheap; expect to spend as much as $4,000. You can also purchase kits for $500 or less, but they don't include a CRT or controllers.

MAMEROOM.com
www.cybertechdesign.net/mameroom
These guys have an amazing array of kits and other MAME cabinets. They also feature links to a lot of other MAME cabinet resources.

Do-It Yourself
Cabinets aren't cheap but you can save money (and have some real fun) by hacking up something yourself. Some people get the home improvement bug, buy old arcade cabinets, retrofit them to hold their PCs and CRTs, and rig them up to play MAME games. If you type "MAME Cabinet" into Google and look around you'll find several dozen pages where people either show off, or even provide step-by-step instructions on how they did it themselves. If you're the type who can wire a few controls together, and can tinker enough to fit the square peg in the round hole, this is a viable course of action.

10

Two good sites to check out for do-it-yourselfers are: **www.arcadecontrols.com/ arcade.htm**, which has a number of tutorials, and **www.mameworld.net/ pc2jamma**, which shows you how to build a MAME cabinet project out of a standard JAMMA-compliant arcade cabinet.

Most cabinets use PCs that don't run Windows. They boot directly to DOS and load up a DOS-based front end. Thus, you'll probably want to check out not only the DOS binary for MAME but also EmuLoader, which you can find at **www.mameworld.net/emuloader**. Emuloader is one of the best front-ends for DOS-based MAME.

MAME Resources

I've told you almost all you need to know about MAME, but wait there's more! You can drop down to MAME's command line level to perform troubleshooting operations, find out more about ROM sets, and do other things that could cause you to blow a gasket. Here are several important MAME resources you should eventually check out to become a real MAME expert:

www.mame.net

The official site for MAME provides much info but the most important worth-while reading is the MAME FAQ located at **www.mame.net/mamefaq.html**.

www.mameworld.net

One of the Best MAME fan sites on the Web. They host a lot of other fan sites about MAME so be sure to spend a lot of time here. A day here will make you a MAME expert for sure.

www.clrmame.com

This is a special utility to help you manage your ROM collection across various emulators, especially MAME. It's useful for those of you who have a big ROM collection. The program isn't easy to use so you'll want to spend time with it and really understand the entire ROM and MAME scene first.

More Emulation

MAME is the place to start for retro gaming but there are other kids on the block. You'll find other emulators for various retro systems including Intellivision, Atari 2600, and others. There are also emulators for older computer systems like the Apple II, Atari 8-bit, and Commodore 64. To complete our discussion of retro gaming and emulation, let's run through the options available for emulating each major platform up through the first couple of generations of consoles.

Atari 2600

www.classicgaming.com/pcae

John Dullea's PC Atari Emulator (PCAE) is available at **www.classicgaming.com/pcae**. This emulator is a DOS program so you'll have to spend time reading the extensive and well-written docs to learn the commands necessary to get your games to run. You'll find links to various ROMs (stored in a .bin format), which are easy enough to find. Remember that even old Atari 2600 games are protected by copyrights, although you should be able to find old cartridges (you may even have some in your attic) so that you can claim proper ownership of the software.

Intellivision

www.gotmaille.com/nostalgia/nostalgia.html

pcae.vg-network.com/intv/intvdos.html

The two major emulators for Intellivision fans (I am a huge one) are the Nostalgia and the INTV emulator. Nostalgia has a really amazing interface. The INTV emulator was written by some of the people affiliated with the original Intellivision software development team and drives the Intellivision Lives! Product lines.

Intellivision Lives

www.intellivisionlives.com

Unlike other emulation paths where you grab the emulator and then scrounge for ROMs, the Intellivision Lives project has certified Intellivision games for free download and a number of collections for $30 that are guaranteed to work and are legal to own.

ColecoVision

www.classicgaming.com/vcoleco

At one point in the annals of gaming, this platform pounded all others into the pavement. It didn't last forever and it took an entire company down with it. Even with its super weird controllers, ColecoVision had some incredible stuff including ports of some big Nintendo games like Donkey Kong. Virtual ColecoVision is considered the best emulator for these games.

Atari 5200 and 8-Bit Systems

www.chrislam.co.uk

One of the best emulators for Atari comes from Chris Lam. The Rainbow emulator can emulate all Atari 8-bit platforms, which includes the Atari 5200 system—an 8-bit Atari computer disguised as a console (sort of the original Xbox when you think about it). Lam sells the emulator for both Mac and Windows but you can grab a demo from his site and later upgrade to the full version if you want for $20.

Atari 7800
www.atarihq.com/danb/a7800.shtml#emulation

One day when I was in grade school in New York City a teacher came in and asked me if I wanted to demo a new videogame unit from Atari's HQ? Why did they even bother to ask? So I go downtown and they show several of us this new system called the Atari 7800. I was hooked for life. They showed us all the games for it including two new games from George Lucas' company, which I'd never seen before. The games were Ballblazer and Rescue on Fractalus, which were amazing. I can still remember screaming when I heard the music for Ballblazer. We played the games and ran demos for the visiting press. Talk about having wicked fun, Atari delayed the release of the 7800 for two years and it flopped big time. Anyway if you want to emulate the 7800 and see some of its games, check out Dan Boris' emulator. It takes me back to those wonderful days of being a kid in New York.

Atari Lynx (Handy)
homepage.ntlworld.com/dystopia

Handy is considered to be the best Lynx emulator. I bought one of these systems when it first came out because I thought it'd be really cool. It was fun and some of the games were brilliant but like many of my console choices (Intellivision, Dreamcast, Lynx, and so on), I choose the system that seemed cool than the one that sold well. Handy is available for the Mac and Linux, in addition to other OS flavors.

Nintendo Entertainment System
www.emuxhaven.net/nesemu.shtml

I usually like to just point to one or two of the best items when I do a roundup. Because there is at least one NES emulator for each time Michael Jordan has retired from the NBA, let's look at others. This site provides links to all of them and the best seem to be Nesten. Another good one not listed here is Nesticle (which on the name alone has to win some sort of demented prize). You can find it on its homepage at **www.bloodlust.zophar.net/NESticle/nes.html**.

Super Nintendo Entertainment System
www.snes9x.com • www.zsnes.com

These are two very good SNES emulators, which are available for a number of platforms including Windows, Linux, BSD, and so on. The SNES9X team for bandwidth reasons had to take their download section offline so search Google for someone else who's posted the files.

Sega Master System/GameGear

www.smspower.org/meka
www.smspower.org/martin/esms

Meka is one of several Sega Master System emulators. The Sega Master System was also the basis of Sega's GameGear portable system. ESMS is a Windows based emulator that is also pretty good. For Mac fans there is SMS Plus available at **www.bannister.org/cgi-bin/link.cgi?sms**.

Sega Genesis/MegaDrive System

bloodlust.zophar.net/gen/genecyst.html

Genecyst is considered to be the best Genesis emulator around. There is also a well thought of Genesis emulator for Macs called Genem available at **www.bannister.org/software** and you can find some others for the Mac at **http://emulation.net/megadrive**.

TurboGrafx 16/PC Engine

www.magicengine.com

This was in some ways a cool system and was quite popular in Japan despite its limited run in the U.S. I remember a few friends who had it and loved some of the games. The Y's franchise got its big start on this platform. The best emulator around for it is the Magic Engine, which requires a $16.00 registration for the full version of the software.

Sega Saturn

satourne.consollection.com

The Dreamcast may have not fared well for any number of reasons but the Sega Saturn as you know was an unmitigated disaster for Sega. Because it was a Sega platform there were some very memorable games developed for it including Knights and Metal Slug. Satourne is considered to be the best Saturn Emulator going at the moment.

Nintendo 64

www.pj64.net/iedefault.htm

For a while the best Nintendo 64 emulator was UltraHle but it's not been updated for a while and it required a 3Dfx card to work or the ability to get a "Glide Wrapper" to fool the program into thinking your card was a 3Dfx card. Yuck! Project 64 is a newer emulator that works well with most nVidia cards and newer ATI cards. Check out the homepage for more information.

Virtual Boy
They do exist but why on earth would you want it?

Computer System Emulators

With the exception of the Rainbow emulator, we haven't discussed computer system emulators. So let's wrap everything up with a basic discussion of emulators for the four or so computer systems we really still care about: the Apple II, Commodore 64/128, and the Commodore Amiga. These are the systems we've grown up with and they featured some incredible games we may still have lying around on disks somewhere even if we dumped the hardware on a scrap heap some time ago.

Amiga

For the Amiga, the WinUAE homepage (**www.winuae.net**) is the first place to go. The WinUAE emulator is based on the DOS version available at **www.freiburg.linux.de/~uae**. There are good docs for WinUAE at **www.blizzard.u-net.com/uae_setup.html**. There is also a commercial Amiga emulator which is state-of-the-art and is available at **cloanto.com/amiga/ forever**. This emulator is officially licensed by the company that holds the Amiga brand. It costs about $60.00.

Commodore 64/128

For the Commodore 64 there are several emulators. CCS64 (**www.ccs64.com**) is considered one of the best for DOS/Windows. Frodo is another, which is available at **www.uni-mainz.de/~bauec002/FRMain.html**. This emulator works on a plethora of platforms. Mac users should check out Power64, which is available at **www.infinite-loop.at**.

Apple II

For the Apple II, Macintosh users should check out the ultimate Apple II Mac emulation site at **www.zip.com.au/~alexm/faq/emu1.html**. The site also has a good resource on Apple II Dos/Windows emulators at **www.zip.com.au/ ~alexm/faq/emu4.html**. The best emulator is considered to be AppleWin which has a homepage at **www.jantzer-schmidt.de/applewin**. There is also an AppleWin 2.0 site going **pages.ripco.net/~wizwom/applewin/about.html** which seeks to improve on the original.

Why not Gameboy, Gameboy Advance, PSX/PSI, and others?

In all honesty these are viable going platforms and while you can find emulators for them I'd say that unless a system is entirely discontinued then it doesn't qualify as a "retro" gaming platform.

Back to the Future

The funny thing about retro gaming is that it reminds me just how much time I wasted not playing games. I mean there are just so many games I didn't get to play because I was doing stupid stuff like working, going to school, making my bed, eating, sleeping, and playing football outside. With emulation I can make up for lost time (and an allowance that was too meager to really support my habit). Thankfully, with emulators like MAME, classic game shops, other emulators, and ebay, I can spend the rest of my life knowing I won't have to miss a particular game I never got around to playing.

10

chapter 11

PUTTING YOUR GAME HABIT TO WORK

If you really love games, you'll love reading and talking about them in addition to playing them. In this chapter we're going to look at how you can put your habit to work. This isn't about turning a few tricks to pay for your latest game fix, it's about using your passion for games to get something back. Sometimes you might even score a bit of fame and maybe a free game.

There are several courses of action you can take to exploit your habit. You can write about games, work for a retailer, set up a Web site, or create a gaming café. These are all easy goals to achieve depending on your own personal situation and they all let you feed your habit or meld it with work. In this chapter I'm going to describe several of these outlets for your gaming experience in detail. You can also go on to design maps, modifications, and total conversions for your favorite PC games, or you can even try and get a job in the industry. We'll talk more about these options later in this book. For now let's focus on some alternative outlets for your addiction. As a final note, there are volunteer opportunities for the Game Developer's Conference (**www.gdconf.com**) and opportunities to volunteer at major LAN party or competitive gaming events as well that you might want to consider. For more on LAN parties and competitive gaming, see Chapter 8.

Writing About Games

Do you have some writing skills? If you do, you can stoke your habit and give something back by writing about games. There are essentially five areas you can write about:

✔ Articles or reviews for a gaming Web site

✔ Articles or reviews for a gaming publication

✔ Articles or reviews for non-gaming publications

✔ A book about games

✔ Topics for your own Web site

The basics of writing are simple. You need to be able to cobble together whole sentences (which I do on rare occasions). You also need to be able to communicate in a fun and entertaining way. Depending on the publication, you also will need a good command of grammar. As someone who isn't exactly an English major by birth, I can sympathize with those of you who find it hard to write at a level on par with *The New Yorker* or even *TV Guide*. Fear not. There are a few ways you can improve your skills.

First, take your time and read and rewrite your stuff over and over before submitting it. Second (and this is a bit easier), find a friend to serve as a copy editor. You can also hire someone if you don't have a friend who has such skills. There are tons of English majors who need a few extra bucks to pay the rent. You can easily find copyeditors online. The going rate is about $2.50 to $5 a page, and maybe more for small pieces. Considering you might get paid $50 to $100 or more a page (yeah right), that's a decent investment. Even when you do submit a good piece, an editor will likely copyedit you work some more, but at least you'll submit something that won't embarrass you.

The easiest platforms to write for are game Web sites. You can find lots of them and they're hungry for content if it's good and fits their style. Contact the editors or managers for these sites and submit a sample or new piece you wrote to see if they like your stuff. Most of them don't pay for pieces, although some do have staff positions that pay. Writing for these sites is a good way to break in and have fun. Just don't expect to get much more than the occasional freebie game, or pass to E3.

Writing for an actual publication is much tougher. Magazines like *Computer Gaming World* used to have lots of open spots for reviews and other features. Unfortunately, in-house writers now write most reviews and articles. To find a job as a freelance reviewer you can write good reviews for some of the Web sites and then submit a letter and some samples to various publications and see if any bite. There are also several openings each year at most of the publications for staff positions. All will want writing samples and they'll want to verify you know games well. Most want college degrees or equivalent experience.

Writing for non-gaming publications may actually be easier because the universe of outlets is much bigger. At the same time, your local newspaper or community weekly may not want to publish game reviews, let alone pay for them. Many also use syndication services available from the AP and Reuters. Still, if there is a local publication, be it a community weekly or local daily, you might take some of your reviews (shorten them to 500 words or less) and submit them to the editor. Ask if they'd like a column or an occasional game review. Again, it would be helpful if you've published some reviews on one of the more well known game sites so you can claim some level of experience.

Most papers will pay $20 to $100 for a review (more like $20 than $100 so don't spend the money just yet). Most community/alternative weeklies will pay you $1,000,000 per article after the publisher wins the lottery. Until then, you'll make squat per article. If you're in college you might want to consider the local college newspaper. The pay sucks but the freebies can be good. You can take a few articles you've published, couple them with a letter explaining upcoming dates for new reviews, and some basics about the circulation, and send this to the PR folks at the studios and publishers to get some free games for review. Don't abuse this, though. You need to actually review the games you get as much as possible.

Finally, you can write books, like this one. Most game books are strategy guides. This is a brutal business. Honestly, being in The Perfect Storm (the actual storm and not the movie) could sometimes seem more appealing. The basics of the book business are you get hired to write a book, the publisher gives you a small advance—usually in portions based on completion dates that are established. Then, you earn a royalty on each book sold but not until the advance earns out. In reality you'll work really long hours, get yelled at by your editor to deliver on time (I always do), and maybe, just maybe, you'll eek out some extra cash if the book sells well. Some authors actually get really good at writing strategy guides. The best of them make some good dough. Unlike other books, strategy guides *must* to be on the shelf by the time the game ships. If you're late, you'll most likely sell a lot fewer copies. Your publisher will go to no ends to make sure you're not late. Torture wouldn't surprise me. The two biggest publishers of strategy guides are Brady Games and Prima Publishing. If you're interested in writing for Brady, send a writing sample to:

Acquisitions Editor
BradyGames Publishing
201 West 103rd Street
Indianapolis, IN 46290

If you're interested in writing for Prima, send a cover letter and resume to **freelance @primagames.com**.

Sybex, another publisher also produces some guides. To contact their acquisitions department you can send your proposal electronically to **proposals@sybex.com** or via mail at:

Acquisitions Department
Sybex, Inc.
1151 Marina Village Parkway
Alameda, CA 94501

For writing samples focus on a strategy walk-through for a favorite game, be it a special level of Doom III or how to defeat a particular map in Command & Conquer. Past writing experience (be it on the Web or otherwise) will also be critical. If an editor likes what they see, they'll be in touch. They'll probably ask you to write a portion of some book first to test you out, especially on your writing speed and accuracy. Don't be surprised if the first few contracts you see are piecework on a work-for-hire basis (i.e., you don't own the writing and you won't be paid any royalties). As you get better you'll get more work, and maybe some royalties. The business is really cutthroat so don't expect much.

The final way to write about games is on your own Web site. Don't laugh, there are a lot of well-written blogs and personal sites about gaming. Some even get enough of a following to attract attention from PR folks, and other larger sites such as GameSpy. Let's look at this activity in a little more detail.

Building a Gaming Web Site

Building your own gaming site may seem futile given the number of sits available. If you're smart about it you can create a cool site and carve out your moment of fame. You might not get your 15 minutes worth but you'll still get some gratification. The first thing to think about when developing a game-oriented Web site is the purpose for the site. This can also be thought of as what sort of category you want to place it in. I've helped you out by breaking down some of the various tracts you can pursue in Table 11.1.

Development Spec for a Site

There are more ways to build a Web site then there are to eat an Oreo cookie. However, there is an emerging way to build sites that seems to be the preferred approach. To help you out, I'm going to provide this spec to you and then I'll give some extra details about developing a good gaming Web site.

Good Web sites offer more than just plan vanilla HTML. They usually have some form of interactivity such as message boards, polls, and searchable archives. They tend to use some form of content management, and they are well organized and updated frequently. To do this, most sites use a combination of a Web page scripting language and a database. Content is stored in the database and then is drawn out by the scripting language and married to some form of design template and

TABLE 11.1
Categories of gaming web sites.

SITE TYPE	PURPOSE	COMPETITIVE OUTLOOK
General Gaming Site	Cover all things about games.	It's very hard to do this well without lots of resources. There are many professional sites that provide spectrum coverage and make it work well.
Genre Site	Cover a specific genre of games like real-time-strategy, role-playing or sports.	Less competitive but there are some great genre sites. If you create one make sure it's a genre that has a rabid fan base. For example, platform games don't really have a fan base like sports or role-playing.
Specific Game Site	Covers (to death and beyond) everything there is to know about a specific game or game-series.	The trick is finding a game that you love and isn't so popular that there aren't already 8M fan sites for it already. The world does not need another Quake or Half-Life fan site.
Tournament/ eSports Site	Specifically organizes and runs an online game server for tournament purposes.	These are popping up a lot lately as online gaming and tournaments grow. Best to focus on a few types of games and build a loyal following. Sometimes connected to a local LAN league or Gaming Café.
Game Blog	A personal site about games in a blog-like format.	Lots of these, but few are great. Easy to start, but hard to do really well. Can be lots of fun if you master the format.

served to the user. With a database it's also possible to create user login systems, collect and store input via forms, and much more. There are a number of technologies you can use to build this style of site but today many Web developers are using a basic suite of free or low-cost tools as follows:

- **Database**: MySQL is the database for most sites. It's free, easy to use, and integrates with PHP very easily. You can get a copy of MySQL at **www.mysql.com**. There are some good books on MySQL available as well as excellent online documentation.

- **Web Application Programming**: The most dominant Web scripting language for sites today is PHP. (ASP or PERL is also acceptable as is Python.) If you don't know any of these languages I suggest you become one of the many people who've learned enough PHP to develop simple scripts and database programs. PHP is available on **www.php.net** and there are a number of excellent books on PHP that'll teach you everything you need to know. There are also a number of PHP script archives, and lots of sites share code for features like user registration systems and more. Sites like Gamespy routinely use PHP for much of their development.

- **Graphics**: The three major products used for sites include PhotoShop, Paint Shop Pro, and Gimp. PhotoShop is the venerable graphics package from Adobe. It isn't cheap, though, so a lot of people on Windows systems opt for Paint Shop Pro, an inexpensive but powerful substitute (and a personal favorite). If you're going to use Linux, Gimp (a freeware PhotoShop clone) is a great product as well.

- **Editing Environment**: To edit your code and work on your pages you'll need some sort of editor. I recommend Homesite from Macromedia. It cost $99.00 and it's worth every penny. There are others though and you can find a pretty complete list at **phpeditors.dancinghippo.com**.

- **Message Boards**: If you want to have message boards for your site there are a number of board systems you can install for your site. Many of them use PHP and MySQL. The one I love the most is vBulletin (**www.vbulletin.com**) which offers a low price, and is available in a package or hosted form from vBulletin and other resellers.

- **Content Systems**: There are also complete content and community systems you can use to run a killer site. These systems which power sites like Slashdot.org and Joystick101.org take some time to install and master but can be the underpinnings of a great site. Many PHP fans use PHPNuke (**www.phpnuke.org**) as shown in Figure 11.1. The great thing about PHPNuke is that it is highly modifiable and the PHPNuke site maintains many of the hacks, add-ons, and modifications that you can use.

Easier Ways to Build Sites

If you've got the time and the skills to learn how to build a site on your own or with PHPNuke then you're going to have a great site. However, if you're not the most technical of Web heads you can still build a good site. First and foremost, you can always build a site with plain old HTML. Remember that in most cases it will be the design and content that make your site worthy first. Extra features like tips databases, user registration, message boards, and others only take good sites to the next level. They don't make bad sites better.

A great way to build and manage a great game site is to use one of the many blog tools available. Blog is short for Web Log, which is essentially an automated diary that lets you post thoughts, articles, and more to the Web in a systematic form. There are several major blog tools but the three most used are Blogger (**www.blogger.com**), Moveable Type (**www.moveabletype.org**), and Radio Userland (**www.userland.com**). Tripod.com, a long-time build your own site service, also offers a blogging system.

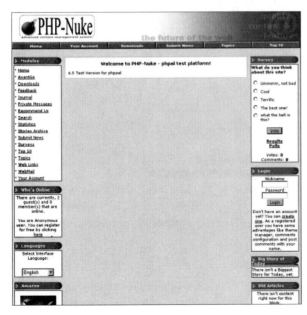

FIGURE 11.1
PHPNuke is a complete system for building user based community Web sites.

I recommend Blogger (Figure 11.2) and its free Blogspot hosting service. There are paid options that you can upgrade to for a fee including ad-free hosting. Once you log into the service you can edit entries and upload them to your own site, or one hosted on BlogSpot. You have a lot of control over the look and feel as well once you learn to edit the template structure.

Radio Userland (Figure 11.3) installs as a desktop application that integrates with a Web site. Userland is free for the first 30 days and then you need to fork out $39.95 to purchase the product. Userland has robust offline editing which makes it very nice for dial-up users.

Moveable Type is a Perl-based system and is very powerful but unless you know Perl and can easily install it, I'd stick with Blogger or Radio Userland.

If you doubt you can build a great and influential site with a blog-style site just check out BluesNews.com (Figure 11.4) which is basically a blog site and is one of the best and more influential hardcore gaming Web sites around.

Hosting Your Site

How you host you site depends, to a large extent, if you need access to a MySQL database and PHP scripting. If not, there are tons of services charging $10 to $20

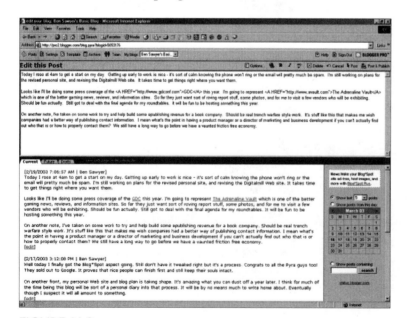

FIGURE 11.2
Blogger is a great system for maintaining a simple but powerful Web site on any topic.

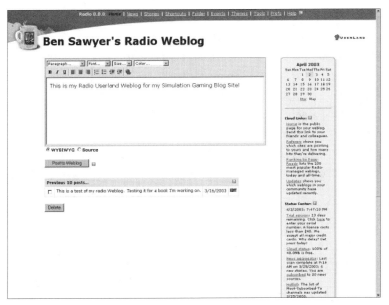

FIGURE 11.3
Radio Userland is another popular blogging Tool.

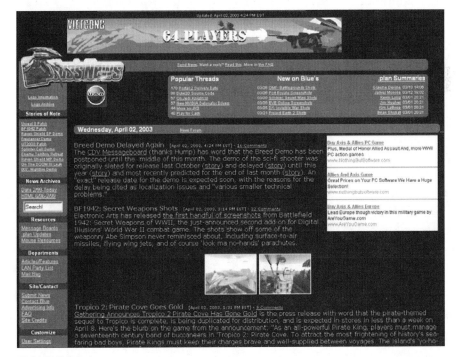

FIGURE 11.4
Bluesnews.com shows what a great, but simple styled game enthusiast Web site can be like.

a month. In terms of MySQL and PHP hosting, there are also tons of services charging from $30 to $70. There are cheaper plans but a quality hosting provider usually is going to cost you $20 or more a month. Since these are shared hosting environments (meaning you don't have direct control over the hardware), you'll need to use a Web based interface to setup and manage your database. You may want to familiarize yourself with a program called PHPmyAdmin (**www.phpmyadmin.net**) which many hosts use to let you administrate your PHP database in a shared environment. You may also want to install a local copy of the database and PHP for development as well.

Generating Content for Your Site

We've covered the tools and infrastructure for your site. Now lets get to the heart of the matter—assembling cool content worth publishing. There are several major types of content most sites use. Let's look at them and discuss how to acquire them:

News for Your Site

Most sites have some form of news on their site. Be careful not to become a hardcore news only site. The fact is between Bluesnews, GameSpy, Avault.com, Homelan, IGN, and others, the news is covered well. What you want to do is break news to your readers or to the overall community or maybe highlight something and add your own basic comments. If you're going to link to existing news, scan the other major sites and when you see something cool write a small note and link to it like this:

> Gamespy.com has a beta report on Warcraft III: The Frozen Zone game. Click here to read more.

You can break news by scanning all the headlines and press releases and being the first to mention a cool story. To help find news, you'll want to scan the best news sites and search engines. Table 11.2 provides the best list of sites to find gaming news other than the top game sites themselves. By searching basic terms like Videogame, Computer Game, Xbox, GameCube, and PS2 you should be able to find quite a bit of stuff that is worth linking to or regurgitating (in your own words!) on your site.

Another way to break news is to reach out to a developer, publisher, or hardware company and see if you can get them to tell you something new. This basically requires you to write the PR contact for the company, explain your site, send them some links, and ask them some questions. Ideally, you'll want to ask simple questions that might generate something new. That means not asking, "When is the

TABLE 11.2
News search sources.

SITE	COMMENTS
News.google.com	Google's news search engine is one of the best.
AsiaBizTech.com	Great place to search for Japan-centric gaming news.
DayPop.com	One of the places to search Blogs.
News.altavista.com	A good second choice to Google's news search.
RocketNews.com	News only search engine.
Annanova.com	Based in Europe, offers good news search.
Northern Light News www.northernlight.com/news.html	Has some sources others don't.
Newstrove.com	Searches 7000 sources.

game shipping?" Instead, try to get more creative and ask things like, "How many levels are being designed for the game?" or "Who is doing the soundtrack?"

Screenshots and Movies

The competition for screenshots of games in development is fierce. You should assume that you're going to be low on the totem pole until you build a following and some history. Screenshots are usually given out exclusively to various sites. They usually brand them and stealing shots from other sites is severely frowned upon.

Once a game is out you can generate your own screenshots of course. The best tool for generating screenshots of DirectX applications is Hypersnap DX from Hyperionics Software (**www.hyperionics.com**). I swear by it as do a lot of people. It costs $35. A trial version is available from their site. Hyperionics also markets Hypercam, a $49.95 program which creates .AVI movies that also works with DirectX.

Fan Kits

In response to the rise of fan Web sites, many developers and publishers are developing complete fan site kits or fan site networks to specifically coordinate content distribution to people building fan sites that cover their games. For example, for its upcoming Rise of Nations game, Microsoft created a 49MB fan kit that you could download.

In addition to downloadable kits there may also be special news distribution lists for fan sites to add your email too. Be sure to first look for these, and then contact the PR people for the game to see if there is more.

Increasingly, some publishers are actually running fan site contests. The best fan site judged by the publisher wins prizes. Westwood has run fan site contests for some of its games like Nox and CnC Renegade and Microsoft has run one for Crimson Skies among other games.

Other Content Ideas

News, screenshots, movies, and fan kits are good sources for your site but there is a lot more. I've created Table 11.3 to give you a bunch of ideas and examples about content on other popular sites you can use for your site.

TABLE 11.3
Content ideas for fan sites.

CONTENT IDEA	COMMENTS	GOOD EXAMPLE
Walkthroughs	Good game walkthroughs are excellent and sought after content by players.	www.planetquake.com/ quake2/q2guide/ spwalkthrough
FAQ	Creating a FAQ on a game is a great in-development and post-development feature. FAQs are usually best if they're the only one so be sure you're first.	http://wow.stratics.com/ content/faqs/phpfaq.shtml
Fan Art Section	Solicit fan art and post it in a gallery.	www.ffinsider.net/fanart.php
Forums	Good forums really build community well.	www.forumplanet.com/ planethalflife
Interviews	You don't have to just interview the development team. You can interview highly ranked players, people making mods, authors of the strategy guide, and others.	http://aoe.heavengames.com/ town/esteam/interv.shtml
Mailbag	Solicit letters and questions from visitors and then answer and/or post them.	www.bluesnews.com/cgi-bin/articles.pl?show=230
Links	Create a body of links to other sites and resources about the game(s) you cover. Be sure to check them for dead links every month.	http://ds.heavengames.com/ community/links
Previews	Provide an overview of a game before it's out. Just don't review it since so much can change even in the last few weeks of development.	www.avault.com/previews
Editorials	Get up on the soapbox but don't say something stupid!	www.avault.com/editorials
Ecards	Create Ecards users can send to one and other.	www.planetcnc.com/ features/e-cards/misc.shtml
Fan Fiction	Let fans submit stories based on a game universe.	www.planetcnc.com/ features/warstories
Game Glossary	Create a glossary of terms from a game or game genre.	www.planetcnc.com/ features/encyclopedia

Dealing with PR People for Your Site

When it comes to building a killer game site, be it a blog, a game fan site, or something bigger, the best sites provide some level of direct contact with the developers and publishers of a game. By contacting the PR people and being respectful, you can get questions answered, find some exclusive screenshots, and score review copies. Here are some tips on how to deal with game PR people:

✔ **Don't be a pest**: PR people are busy, and the developers are even busier. Sixty to eighty hour workweeks are not uncommon. This means you need to be patient. Don't email PR people every day. Don't ask for stuff until you look to see if the answer or stuff you want isn't already available. If you are patient, you'll earn the respect of PR people and they might even respond to you faster if you're not a pain.

✔ **Be clear as to what you want**: When you write a PR person don't just write "can I have some stuff for my site." Keep your request short, and be succinct as to what you want. Here's an example: "Hi, I'd like to get on the list to get an exclusive screenshot or two, and I'd love it if the five questions below could be answered by the development team at some point." If you want to be specific for a deadline then give them a specific date but don't ask for a date if you really don't need it.

✔ **Work through email**: Don't phone PR people or the developer. Don't ask for phone interviews. Leave everything to email because you're not going to get very far on the phone unless your site is getting one million visitors. Ninety-nine percent of the time you'll just get voicemail anyway.

✔ **Publish what you're given**: The surest way to make a PR persons enemy list is to not act on stuff you're sent. If you ask for a few questions to be answered or you get an exclusive screenshot and you sit on it for a while, or never publish it, don't expect to see much support after that. This goes double for review copies of games.

✔ **Promote your site**: PR people aren't dumb. They read all the same sites and travel to all the fan sites. If you're not doing much to cross-link your site, and earn links and other promotional pointers back to your site, they'll know. If you want to be taken seriously you need to get traffic and you can't get traffic without working for it.

✔ **Send a "thank you" note**: PR people and developers do like to get a thank you every once in a while. If they help you and you write an article, or post a screenshot send them a note eventually to thank them. If you can include your estimate as to how many unique people saw the content since it was posted. PR people thrive on being able to tell their bosses and clients numbers like "10,000 people read the preview on so-and-so's site."

Promoting Your Site

So you've built a site, stocked it with cool content, and you're on a first name basis with tons of PR people across the industry. That's awesome. You're probably having a good time yourself. Your next focus should be to promote your site. There are entire books written on Web site promotion and I'd definitely recommend getting one or two of them. The basics of search engine placement are important to know and I'm not going to reiterate that here and kill more trees needlessly.

Here are the three best tips for promoting a game site other than the normal search engine placement work:

✔ **Other Game Sites**: Get to know the other sites out there. Email them when you have something cool to share like an exclusive story, a new feature article, or tutorial. Cross promote stories on their sites too. The single best way to get traffic is from other game sites that link to you.

✔ **Publisher/Developer Sites**: When your site is done and looks right, email the PR people for the publisher and developer and see if they'll add a link to you. Many publishers and developers link to sites that cover their games.

✔ **Email Signature and Forums**: Put your site in the signature of your email. Include it in posts to the Usenet and other forums that exist on games, and any games you specifically cover.

Benefiting from Your Site

The most benefit you should expect from your site is the fun that comes from running it and interacting with its visitors. However, this isn't to say you shouldn't try to score something more from running a killer game site. First and foremost is to score some free stuff from various game companies. This is, of course, a delicate act. Game companies want to promote their games, but they can't give everyone a free copy or free t-shirts just because they've got some rinky-dink "I love this game" site.

Instead you need to do your work and be patient. First, make your site not only as good as possible but also well-trafficked. To demonstrate your traffic you could send a small letter to the company showing them a log report but honestly I'm not sure what they'd do with that. Better yet, add features to your site that show it's well read. This would be things like discussion boards, polls, user submitted comments, a guestbook, and articles from other writers. Also getting other sites to link to you is important. The more you're seen as a well-read integral part of a particular game or genre's fan community, the more likely your request to the PR department might get answered.

In terms of getting free stuff the best thing to do is write a nice email (and snail mail if you're organized enough, have the cash for stamps, and the time to stuff envelopes) to the PR department that tells them about your site and asks them for the basics. Here is a good sample letter:

> *Dear Melanie:*
>
> *I run SHIVEREDTIMBERS.COM, a fan site for games about pirates. We cover games like Tropico II, Galleon, and your game, Walk The Plank! My site gets about 5,000 visitors each month and has fairly active mailing lists and message boards. We'd love some support from your company. Here's how you can help us:*
>
> *Send us free stuff to give away.*
>
> *Send us review copies of Walk The Plank! I would love 2 to 3 copies if possible.*
>
> *Provide us some exclusive screenshots and maybe an interview with the developer.*
>
> *Keep us in the loop on all news.*
>
> *Thanks so much for your help. If you have any questions about the site, feel free to ask.*

Let the right person know about your site and make sure to ask for what you want. Then sit back and see if anything happens. Don't be afraid to pester someone once or twice but if you hit a brick wall then just deal with it. Not every PR person or company is going to be as perfect to deal with you as others. It's just the nature of the business.

Starting a Gaming Café

Another way you can put your habit to work is to start your own permanent LAN party or Gaming Café. This is not for the faint of heart because it involves creating a real business with real risk. If you ever thought of starting one of these establishments, here are some suggestions to help you get started.

The first thing to consider is whether your area can support a gaming café. In countries like Singapore, Korea, and China, gaming cafés are booming. These places have very dense populations where people spend most of their time either at home or at school. A game café gives young people a third place to go to. Countries like China also have a low-penetration of both Internet access and powerful PCs, indicating a demand for Internet or gaming cafés. The penetration rate for

PCs and the Internet is higher in North America and Europe. The population density is sometimes lower, and there are other more competitive pastimes for kids. While PC game rooms are booming in some places, they aren't necessarily going to boom in your backyard.

Assuming you think it can work, you need a basic recipe for a gaming café. First and foremost, you need to find a good space. You'll want a space big enough to support about 10 to 20 machines. You'll need furniture for these stations, decent enough machines, and a networking system. You'll also need Internet connectivity and not just a simple dial-up system—we're talking broadband here. Finally, you'll need some sort of system to charge for access.

The systems also can't be ultra cheap. They need to be capable of playing all the latest games (mostly first person shooters but also games like Command & Conquer) really well. If you can offer near state-of-the-art speeds and resolutions all the better because you will rival what most people have at their homes. This provides an extra incentive for players to frequent your location. Most places build their own custom systems themselves because they find it cheaper. Over time they will upgrade the parts, adding better graphics cards, sound cards, and memory. Some cafés, especially in the U.S., offer empty desk stations where gamers can bring their own PC in and set up.

Pricing

Most cafés offer a series of pricing plans and you'll need to do some experimenting to find the best mix for your neck of the woods. You'll need to consider the local economy and competition. Most cafés provide a basic hourly rate, discounted rate for memberships, bulk rates, tournament entry fees, and special rates for extra features like headphones or headsets. Not all places offer only games. Many offer basic Internet access, food, drink and sometimes games for sale. Table 11.4 offers what I found to be average pricing for key gaming services you can use as a reference to set your own pricing strategy.

Hours of Operation

In some places like Korea game centers will operate 24 hours a day. More typical hours of operation include:

Monday - Thursday:	11:00 a.m. - 8:00 to 10:00 p.m.
Friday - Saturday:	10:00 a.m. - 12:00 to 2:00 a.m.
Sunday:	10:00 a.m. - 10:00 p.m. (or later)

TABLE 11.4
Typical gaming café pricing.

SERVICE	DETAILS	PRICE RANGE
Internet Access	Basic access to the Internet for email and Web browsing.	$3 to $7/hr* but be careful here. If you have a gaming center you'd rather have everyone playing games. Some places offer 1 to 3 dedicated machines just for Internet access and the rest are for games only.
Game Access	Access to gaming PC, Console.	$3 to $7/hr*
Membership	Most places have one or more tiers of membership linked to either bulk hours or discounted hours.	$25 to $80 a year. Usually provides a 25% to 50% discount or some free hours.
Tournaments	Entrance in a local tournament.	$10 to $50 depending on prizes and time built into the support tournament.
Party	Allows rental of entire facility or portion at a discount.	Paid in advance, usually a fixed price per participant.
All Day Pass	Play as long as you want all day.	$20 to $35 depending on your hourly rate.
Headphone/ Headset Rental	Extra pricing for special feature.	$1/hr

* Some places will increase their rate after some point in the afternoon like 4 p.m. and others will offer discounts as low as $3/hr on slow days.

A typical café would be open just before lunch, stay open reasonably late (especially on Fridays and Saturdays), and open a bit earlier on the weekends. Most places will analyze their traffic of course and run discounts and tournaments on days that are slower to drum up traffic.

Rules of Conduct

Be sure to post and hand out distinct rules of conduct. Here is a good list to use:

✔ One warning, 30 seconds to respond or you're out.

✔ No alcohol, illegal drugs, or smoking.

✔ No loitering in front of our establishment.

✔ No rude or offensive language, fighting, or other forms of harassment.

✔ No surfing the Internet for PORN, WAREZ, or using the Internet for other illegal activities.

✔ Do not touch anyone else's equipment.

✔ No cheating. Cheaters will be banned for 30 days. This includes use of unauthorized scripts, configurations or hacks. If you are accused of cheating, staff will render a verdict, and you will be cleared or asked to leave immediately.

✔ Antivirus software is required. If you bring in your own machine prior to being connected to your computer our staff may request you run a virus scan on your machine in their presence and show proof of updated virus software.

✔ Do not touch any of our networking equipment without explicit permission from café staff. Touching any hub, switch, or other network gear will result in immediate expulsion.

✔ No food or drink near computers other than your own without explicit permission by our staff.

✔ If you are under 18 years of age, we reserve the right to ask your parent or legal guardian to sign a parent permission form.

✔ We reserve the right to change these rules (with or without notice) at any time.

Parental Permission

Since game cafés will appeal to kids, many cafés opt to make parents sign a parent permission and liability form. This form is meant to explain the rules of the café, and absolve it of liability for kids. While game ratings aren't a legal issue yet, game rooms can be reasonably expected to enforce access to games that are otherwise rated Teen or Mature by the ESRB. Furthermore, it's important to remind parents that your establishment is not a school, or a babysitter, and that you are not there to guarantee the complete 100% safety of their child. Ask parents and their children to sign the form and make sure you've got these all on file with the best contact information possible.

I've created a form for you that you can use as a starting point (show it to your attorney for further help since I'm not an attorney). You can find a word version on my Web site at **www.dmill.com/gamecafe**.

Game Café Software

From my simple analysis of all the café software, here are six of the best:

Cyber-Time:	**www.cybertimesoftware.com**
CafeSuite:	**www.cafesuite.net**
CiberControl:	**www.lucioperri.com/eng**
CyberCafePro:	**www.cybercafepro.com**
SmartLaunch:	**www.smartlaunch.net**
PAC Manager:	**www.pac-manager.com**

I like SmartLaunch and CyberCafe Pro the best. They seem the most robust. Most café software runs on a client-server basis. Most packages cost between $300 to $1,000 for up to 25 clients. If the software you use supports card readers (Smart-Launch does), you might try MagTek (**www.magtek.com**).

Another key product you'll need is a way for people to load games without the initial DVD or CD to be in the drive. I'm not talking piracy here. You'll need to own 25 copies of a game if you have 25 machines you want it on. However, you don't want DVDs stolen and you don't want to have to swap games in and out to make them work.

This is where GameDrive from Farstone (**www.farstone.com**) comes in. Game-Drive is a $20 product that lets you copy an entire CD/DVD into a single, compressed disk-image file that resides on your hard drive. It also provides a driver that fools Windows into treating the disk-image file as if it were a physical CD/DVD running in a physical CD/DVD drive. You can create up to 23 virtual CD/DVD-ROM drives and an unlimited number of CD/DVDs. You'll need a fat hard-drive to make it all work if you have several dozens of games for each station but once it's installed properly you'll be in great shape. A non-commercial alternative is a product called Daemon Tools (**www.daemon-tools.net**).

Working in a Retail Game Store

My first job was working in an independent computer store on the Upper East Side of Manhattan. This was before there were Electronics Boutiques or Software Etc. We specialized in game software. I had fun for a while and I scored lots of free games, or at least 50% off my games. We shut down the store at night and played the latest releases or previews for 30 to 45 minutes. The rest of the day I stood on my feet, worked long hours, unpacked boxes, and waited on mothers who didn't know Madden Football from Earl Weaver Baseball. I also had to deal with the occasional annoying kid who asked one million questions and never bought a thing. At the end of the day I swept up, vacuumed, emptied the trash, and figured out how to spend the $5/hour I was making. I still had loads of fun and it was a great way to learn more about games, and support what was easily the gaming equivalent of a 4-pack a day habit.

Today, however, games are retailed mostly at specific game-store chains not to mention big-box retailers like Wal-Mart, and price busters like Costco or BJ's Ware-house. There are still a few independents depending on your area. The biggest chains (at least in the U.S.) are GameStop (which owns Funcoland, Software, Etc., and Babbages) and Electronics Boutique. Both chains have about 1,000 stores in their chain. Most stores feature a single manager and several assistant managers/ clerks depending on the traffic and hours.

There are approximately several thousands game stores world-wide, each having an average of five to six employees meaning there are anywhere from 15,000 to 30,000 positions available in specialty game retailers. The average pay is peanuts for clerks, who might earn typical mall-rat salaries of $8 to $12/hour. Managers will make $30K to $45K depending on the market and district managers (i.e., overseeing a range of stores) will make $45K to $60K. Basic benefits seem to be the norm of most chains, although smaller chains and independents might not be so great. So there is a career path here if that's what you want.

 Aside from the major computer retailers, you can also try local LAN centers that are opening up. However, most of these are very small establishments paying very low-wages.

The good news about working in a game store is that you'll be surrounded by games all day and you'll get some sort of discount, which is half the reason to have such a job. The bad news is that the annoying kids, parents, and people who ask one million questions still come into stores. And last time I checked there weren't any chairs in the various GameStops or Electronics Boutiques I frequent. Turnover seems frequent enough on the assistant manager level. I'm betting that after a year or so (unless you really love what you're doing or are on track for a promotion) most people move on to other important stuff like finishing college.

To obtain a job at one of the major chains, you need to walk in and ask for an application and then speak to the manager. Loving games is a plus but savvy managers want people who are going to work hard. They want to know you'll show up on time, not B.S. with every customer too much, and stick around for a while. I recommend checking out the Electronics Boutiques employment page, which lists the qualifications and job responsibilities for assistant and full managers at their stores (**www.ebholdings.com/store.asp**). You can read their recruiting brochure and also search for job openings by state.

Have Fun First

The first thing about putting your habit to work is that you need to have fun. At times I've made it sound like some of the ways to use your habit aren't as much fun as they should be. Writing is harder than it looks, and working on your feet all day at the local game store isn't easy either. This isn't because they're intrinsically "unfun" jobs. It's because work is work. Work has special responsibilities, it puts you in situations you don't always want to be in, and more is expected of you than just finishing the latest level in Jack and Daxter.

That being said, working in a store, writing a book, building a site, starting a gaming café, can all be fun ways to integrate your love of games with you need for income. If you do any of these activities well and work with great people who also love games you'll have fun. If you get into anything related to games, be it writing, retail, or online and don't find yourself having fun, working with great people, or benefiting greatly from your gaming experiences, get out. That's not only good advice here, it's good advice about life in general.

chapter **12**

MODDING GAMES

Games have been released for many years with level editors. In ye-olden-times, gamers used hex editors to change elements of their favorite games like Ultima. I remember doing this with many Atari 8-bit games to put my name in a game or make changes to levels. So the basic practice of modding games has been around for a while. However, Doom (which was extensively modifiable) and the Internet took modding to a new level. Modding has now become an integral part of the games industry and the game playing community. CounterStrike, arguably one of the most popular games of the last two years, was created as a mod.

In this chapter I'll cover as much about modding, mutating, and level building as I can. Since I can't spend gobs of time on any single game, I have compiled good resources for specific games that are used by the bulk of the hardcore modding community.

Mods, Mutators, and Full Conversions

To become an avid modder, you'll first need to get the basic lingo straight. Mods represent any changes made to an existing published game and then made available to others. Mods cover the entire spectrum of game editing. Within the mod scene, you will see other terminology used including:

- ✔ **Mod**: Short for modification. It is used to describe any instance of modifying an original game in some fashion.

- ✔ **Total/Full Conversion**: This is basically a mod that goes all out. Such a mod creates a completely new game. As an example, CounterStrike is a total conversion of Half-Life.

- ✔ **Mutator**: Somewhat specific to Unreal, a mutator is the name some modders give to mods that make simple rule changes to existing parts of a game. For example, a mod that makes you impervious to your own rocket attacks is a mutator. This is what gave birth to the Rocket Arena mod that was popular in the early days of Quake.

- ✔ **Map/Level**: A level is a instance of a segment of a game be it a "level" in the game, a new game map, and so on.

- ✔ **Skin**: A skin is a new look and feel for an element of a game—usually the player (which is sometimes referred to as a player-skin).

- ✔ **Bots**: Bots are mostly a first-person-shooter phenomenon. They encapsulate fighting algorithms and patterns that are used to create a variety of opponents and other characters in modded first-person-shooters.

- ✔ **Prefabs**: These refer to pre-made maps and object models you can find and use in your games.

Games We Like to Mod

The number of games that are now "moddable" is numerous, and no doubt more are on the way. In the near future more games will ship with modding capability than those that don't have such capability. It's clear that some games have won the hearts and minds of the core modding community more so than others. Half-Life, Quake, Neverwinter Nights, Unreal, Dungeon Siege, Morrowwind, and eventually Halo certainly are leaders in the pack. Table 12.1 provides a listing of the top modded games. I adapted this list from the list presented at **www.moddb.com**. Later I'll present some specific resources for these games.

Half-Life is probably the most modded game available. I think that Half-Life II and Doom III will be the reining champs of the next generation of games released with modding capabilities. Quake is also extremely popular and Battlefield 1942 is gaining many modding fans. In other genres, Dungeon Siege, Neverwinter

TABLE 12.1
Game series and games we love to mod.

Alien vs. Predator 2	Half-Life I & II	Red Faction
Battlefield 1942	Halo	Return to Castle Wolfenstein
CnC Generals	Homeworld Series	Rise of Nations
CnC Renegade	Impossible Creatures	Savage
CounterStrike	Kingpin	Serious Sam
Day of Defeat	Knights of the Old Republic	Solider of Fortune
Deus Ex Series	Max Payne	Star Wars Jedi Knight II
Diablo II	Medal of Honor Series	StarCraft
Doom Series	Microsoft Flight Simulator	Team Fortress 2
Duke Nukem Forever	Morrowind	Thief Series
Dungeon Siege	Neverwinter Nights	Tribes
Enter The Matrix	No One Lives Forever Series	Unreal and Unreal Tournament
Ghost Recon	Operation Flashpoint	Warcraft Series
GTA 3	Quake Series	
GTA: Vice City	CnC Red Alert	

Nights, and Morrowind lead the pack in the world of RPGs. CnC Generals is the real-time-strategy game of choice to mod. Other great mods have been created for games like CnC Renegade and Tribes. The popularity of a game's modability is usually based on a combination of game popularity, community fervor, toolsets that debut with the game, support from the development studio, and overall ease of modding. Modding also benefits when supported by the game's developer. For example, look at what Valve has done with Half-Life and id Software has done with QuakeCon and QuakeC.

Core Modding Resources

Most modding resources are specific to a game itself. However, there are two sets of generic tools we need to discuss before moving on to specific mod tools. The first set of tools are generic game development tools that are as essential to the modding process as they are to game development itself. The second set is a class of tools that are somewhat mod-specific but are fairly generic to all games, or a large set of popular modifiable games.

12

Generic Tools for Modders

As they say on the Verc Collective (**http://collective.valve-erc.com**), modding tools can be arranged into six areas: mapping, coding, textures, sprites, models, and miscellaneous. This means you'll need 2D graphics tools, 3D graphics tools, a development editor, sound effects editor, and potentially some encoding tools plus whatever specialized tools there are for the particular game you are modding. Table 12.2 provides an assortment of tools to help in these areas. I haven't included every available tool because I've focused on freebie/low-cost tools, as well as the standard, widely used tools.

If you are a student, be sure to visit many of the sites for higher-priced software like 3D Studio Max and utilize the student discount pricing, which can be substantial.

TABLE 12.2
Generic development tools of importance to modders.

PRODUCT	URL	COST	COMMENTS
2D GRAPHICS			
PaintShop Pro Jasc	www.jasc.org	$90	Does almost everything you need from Photoshop for a fraction of the price.
Deeppaint Right Hemisphere	www.deeppaint.com	$199	Up and coming paint package.
Photoshop Adobe	www.adobe.com	$600	The big mama of 2D imaging programs.
3D GRAPHICS			
3D Studio Max	www.discreet.com	$3,495	The number one modeling package for PCs.
Rhino 3D	www.rhino3d.com	$895	Uses nurbs for modeling vs. polygons.
Lightwave	www.newtek.com	$1,549	After 3D Studio and Maya this is one of the most popular, and it's cheaper also.
TrueSpace	www.caligari.com	$585	Solid, low-cost modeling software for the PC.
Maya	www.aliaswavefront.com	$2,000-$7,000	Top of the line 3D design tool.
SoftImage	www.softimage.com	$1,500-$2,500	Major competitor to Maya and 3D Studio on the top end of the market.
Blender	www.blender3d.org	FREE	Open source modeling package.

(CONTINUED)

TABLE 12.2 (CONTINUED)
Generic development tools of importance to modders.

PRODUCT	URL	COST	COMMENTS
VIDEO ANIMATION			
Bink Video	www.radgametools.com	See site	The compression format favored for animated content by game developers.
SOUND EFFECTS			
Sound Forge	www.sfoundry.com	$400	The Photoshop of sound digitization and editing software
CoolEdit	www.cooledit.com	$69	Great low-cost sound effects editing system.
Goldwave	www.goldwave.com	$40	Another great lower-cost sound effects editing application.
DEVELOPMENT ENVIRONMENTS AND SCRIPT EDITING			
Codewarrior	www.metrowerks.com	$330	A well liked C++ development environment.
Visual Studio.NET	www.microsoft.com	$1,000	The C++ editor of many people use and which most products are built to compile with.
UltraEdit	www.ultraedit.com	$35	Major ASCII Editor offering lots of features for script programming.
NoteTab Pro	www.notetab.com	$0-$20	Great ASCII editor for Windows with a lot of powerful editing features. Less powerful free version available.
TextPad	www.textpad.com	$16.50	Good editor with syntax highlighting capability that can help with readability. You can find some packs that add syntax highlighting for game languages, such as Skrit—the Dungeon Siege scripting language.
OTHER TOOLS			
Deep Exploration	www.righthemisphere.com/products/dexp/index.htm	$249	A fairly inexpensive tool for importing, viewing, managing and exporting 3D models in a variety of formats.

12

Specific Modding Tools

There are two types of specific modding tools you will find: tools created directly by game developers and third-party tools from others. Originally, game developers didn't offer modding tools. Developers of some of the original modifiable games didn't release their hackneyed specialized tools because they didn't want to spend the time to make them extremely user friendly and so on. Today, though, more developers are building extremely robust tools, and then releasing them to the public. In addition, other independent developers are making tools once they understand the various file formats and other needs specific to a game. This makes the specific mod tool arena a mish-mash of cross-game utilities and game specific tools that you'll need to sort through. Table 12.3 provides a description of the most commonly used tools.

TABLE 12.3
Commonly used modding specific tools.

Tool Name	URL	Product(s) It Works With	Comments
3D Editors			
Milkshape 3D	www.swissquake.ch/ chumbalum-soft	Quake I-III, Half-Life, Unreal Tournament, plus others via custom exporters	Specialized low-poly 3D editor/ modeler. Also features "skeletal" animation capabilities. This allows you to export and morph target animation like the ones in the Quake model formats or to export to skeletal animations like Half-Life or Genesis3d. MilkShape 3D currently supports 37 different file formats from 27 different games or engines.
GMAX	www.discreet.com/ products/gmax	Quake III, CnC Renegade, Dungeon Siege, Flight Simulator, Impossible Creatures, Unreal Tournament & many others	GMAX has the potential to become the defacto 3D editing tool for a number of games, although specialized tools and editors may still be mainstays of this space as well.
QERadiant/GT Kradient	www.qeradiant.com	Quake II-III, Quake Engine powered games.	The main editor for Quake II-III based mods.
Hammer Editor	collective.valve-erc.com/ index.php?go=hammer	Half-Life	The official editor of Half-Life and Half-Life powered games.
GenSURF	tarot.telefragged.com/ gensurf/index.shtml	Quake II-III, Half-Life and other Quake born products.	Generates terrain and other outdoor environs.

(CONTINUED)

TABLE 12.3 (CONTINUED)
Commonly used modding specific tools.

Tool Name	URL	Product(s) It Works With	Comments
3D Editors			
Tread 3D	www.planetquake.com/tread	Quake, Half-Life	An older but solid editor for Quake.
PAK File Tools			
Pakscape	www.valve-erc.com/content/?page=utilities	Quake, Half-Life, and other Quake Engine based games.	The main pak file stuffer used today.
Texture Creation Tools			
Wally	www.telefragged.com/wally	Numerous	A great freeware texture editor.
Texmex	www.planetquake.com/texmex	Quake	Another texture tool but not as good as Wally or Texture maker.
Texture Maker	www.i-tex.de	Numerous	A great texture tool but sells for about $70.
Texture Studio	www.planethalflife.com/studio	Half-Life	Strong collection of textures.
Free Textures and Content			
3D Café	www.3dcafe.com/asp/freestuff.asp	Numerous	Good batch of free textures, models, and sounds.
Other Tools			
Quake 3 Arena Shader Editor (Q3ASE)	www.bpeers.com/software/q3ase	Quake 3 Arena	Good utility for creating shaders for use in Quake 3 Arena mods.

Server vs. Client

The modding landscape can also be thought of in terms of server-side vs. client side. A server side mod is one that enhances or changes the various server applications that are used to run multiplayer instances of various games like Half-Life, Unreal, or Battlefield 1942. Server side mods tend to deal with game administration, scoring, and rule sets. A client side mod, on the other hand, is one where you will more likely be changing the look and feel of a game but also potentially the rules as well. The core difference for these types of mods are that client-side mods usually require artwork, and sever-side mods involve programming (and maybe a

12

bit of data creation). What's also important is that server-side mods usually involve some level of administration. That means you would implement them using the server admin tools for the specific game. You should load them into the server and stack them (if you can) with other mods and mutators to get the desired effect.

Working with Mod Teams

It's not impossible to make a mod yourself, just as it isn't impossible to make a game yourself, or build a house, or fly a plane. It really comes down to your skills, resources (time and funds), and the scale of the project you take on. Mods can be small enough to be manageable by a single person. Some of the best mods aren't necessarily big endeavors. A good mod can even be as simple as a fantastic map or level that brings enjoyment to thousands of players or a mutator that changes the dynamics of play just enough to make something old entirely new again.

However, it's more likely you will want to form a team of two, three, or more to develop your mod. Teams form all the time and some actually do make it across the finish line as CounterStrike and Day of Defeat among others prove. Creating a team takes effort and leadership. Most team members will have other responsibilities like work, school, spouse, and kids. A good team will likely bond over time. This is where good leadership comes in. Someone, most likely the founder of the project, needs to be the type of person who can lead a group of volunteers. This means team leaders must possess a bit of charisma to inspire, but also the ability to push people with little to hang over their heads. It's a delicate balance. All I can say from my experience with similar situations is that it's all in the timing.

Forming a mod team is not unlike forming any sort of team for software development. Ideally, if the team can all physically meet every now-and-then, that can be a useful coordination and motivational tool. But most mod teams are dispersed teams. To make up for lack of physical presence, the core tools of mod development are really communication tools like instant messaging, IRC, email, and some sort of portal and asset management system. Sourceforge (**www.sourceforge.com**) is a good tool to use but it costs money for projects not deemed open-source. Setting up a CVS (**www.cvs.org**) server is also an option but it's not the easiest thing to do and requires access to a Linux box. Other people may just use a simple FTP site with a rigid directory structure and read/write privileges. Whatever system you develop, remember that at the heart of a good mod software team is a workable and organized communications system and file archive.

Make sure everyone is aware of how to contact each other and that multiple copies of files are being stored in multiple places. You should also have guidelines in place to communicate the time of day you can be reached. Also take time early on when forming a mod team to talk to each other about the project. Don't just rush into it. Take the time to get to know each other, and document (i.e., write-it-down!) what it is your team is going to build. Get the artists who are going to do the artwork to do concept sketches and have the programmers write a few paragraphs explaining what the scripts and extensions they'll write will do. The more you've talked to each other, held a few chats, or even a conference call to talk about your game ideas the better off you'll be because everyone will have bonded during this process.

Your team should consist of level/map builders, artists, and programmers. Depending on the game and the extent of the mod itself, the programming required might be as simple as writing scripts, or a combination of scripting and a language like C++. Many of the best Half-Life mods involve some form of C++ programming. QuakeC itself is a derivative of the C language so anyone on a team that can program in C is going to be a key member. Learning the scripting languages associated with most modifiable games shouldn't be terribly difficult to anyone who has done some level of programming. If you're forming the team be sure to test people who want to join. While it's fine to make a mod with your friends, you can't expect someone to just learn C++ in a weekend and be able to start programming on your mod team. Also, someone who isn't artistic already isn't suddenly going to become a great concept artist. So make sure that the people who join your team have the skills they need.

 I'm not going to knock artists or 3D artists, but I will say this, you don't have to be a world-class illustrator to be a great 3D artist. It's certainly a plus, but I know many 3D artists who are just that, great modelers and 3D animators. They've mastered the tools and techniques it takes to build all sorts of things in 3D. So just because someone can't draw to save their life, doesn't mean they can't model an axe, tank, flower, or building.

Setting Your Team Hierarchy

All good teams also need a hierarchy and rules. This is where leadership comes in. You'll need a leader who makes sure stuff gets done, that people respect their roles on the team, and yes, make hard decisions every now and then. Don't be scared if that's not your cup of tea; being a modder doesn't require you to be a leader. If you form a team, or join a team that is leaderless, expect the consequences. As part of your hierarchy you need to figure out who reports to who, who does what, and how conflicts will be resolved.

While most mods don't go on to get signed by Valve or id, consider early on to decide each persons "ownership" share of your project. Create a document for each person to sign and acknowledge that says what his or her share of the project is. A good team should be able to do this in ten minutes. A mod is not a form of retirement planning so if it's taking longer than a few emails to work out the details then the people you are working with are most likely behaving unrealistically. For what it's worth, if you created the next great mod, the company who wants it, will most likely hire people as employees rather than throw huge wads of cash at you. This means it's possible your mod efforts could lead to a job and not to huge riches.

When you join a team you should also get everyone to agree that the rights to the work you produce for the mod is exclusively yours if the project folds. At the same time, you should require that if everyone should quit a mod the people leaving should have a non-exclusive right to the work they left behind.

Finding Your Team

The best place to find modders is in the various forums, IRC channels, and on servers for the game your are devoted to modding. Most people mod the games they love. As you build up friends in these arenas you'll probably run across a few who have an interest in modding the game. They either have ideas for maps, or new motifs for the game—something different than what you've all seen already. There are also places like Moddb.com where you can post or reply to help wanted ads for a team.

Expect to be burned when you do modding. Teams often come and go. It's easy to put some effort into something and see it all fall apart if the team can't keep it together. While you can minimize your exposure to this by vetting a mod team thoroughly, you definitely can't sit on the sidelines either. If you approach each project as a chance to get better at your skills, you'll get the most out of your modding experience.

To show a team it helps to have some work to show other people, such as a demo map, player skin you've done, weapon model, or anything else that demonstrates your skills. Some of the best teams are made up of people who've previously done some level of lone-wolf modding. Recruitment of well-known and active modders and forum members is fairly constant. However, be warned. Good modders don't just join up with anyone. If you plan to recruit people of high-caliber you need some chops yourself. That means doing more than just ordering people around and stitching together a Web site.

Most positions on a mod team will be modelers, texture artists, skinners (texture artists who specialize enhancements post model application of a texture), coders, and general artists. However, teams usually need a bit more, including a Webmaster, PR specialist, documentation developer, and story editors. That means even if your game/mod development skills suck ass there is still a role for you to play to help a mod get made. Also if you're forming a team don't forget the importance of your site, and PR. A visible project is important. The more fan support you can build for your mod the more motivation you and your team will have to finish it. Even though I'm going to pull this figure out of my butt, over 80% of the mods that are started never get completed - so don't underestimate the power of PR and a solid Web site to push you over the finish line.

 The number one separation between good developers of any kind, and great developers is the great ones finish their projects good-or-bad as the reviews turn out. You can't get a review if the game isn't done.

The Basic Modding Process

Every game or strain of games (i.e., games based on a specific mother engine like Unreal or Quake) will require a different process of modding. The code, model formats, file formats, tools, and access to various game hooks will be different. The documentation can be good, bad, or apparently written by a five-year-old. However, there is sort of a basic process that the uninitiated must learn first.

Mods usually involve replacing levels, art, and code. Levels usually have a specific file format relevant to the game, while the formats for models, art, and textures may share enough similar traits that they are convertible between different engines. Elements for a game that you're replacing will usually have to be packaged into a unique resource file format that compresses and collects them for use by the game. For example, Quake uses a format known as PAK files. New code will have to be recompiled and organized based on the file structure of the game system, and games that use 3D maps may require the maps to be "compiled"—a process by which the editor creates an optimized map file for the game.

Modding Tutorials and Help

The great thing about the modding world is that there is a decent amount of information sharing that goes on. It's a pretty egalitarian sub-culture. The best places to find mod tutorials are on the various fan sites for each major game. Table 12.4 presents a list I compiled of some other major places worth visiting. In reality there are hundreds of tutorials you can find. While some of the ones I've focused on

12

TABLE 12.4
A batch of leads and top sites for modding resources and tutorials.

NAME	URL	COMMENTS
Skindom	www.planetquake.com/skindom/tutorials	The place to learn about skinning.
claudec's Lair of Quake 3 Arena Level Design	www.claudec.com/lair_of_shaders	One of the best sites for information about modding Quake.
Quake3World	www.quake3world.com/editing/guides.html	Extensive set of guides and links to important content for people creating Quake 3 based mods.
Code3areana	www.planetquake.com/code3arena	
Texture Studio	www.planethalflife.com/studio/tutorials.asp	Great set of basic tutorials on texture creation in Photoshop.
Polycount	www.planetquake.com/polycount	Modeling archive and tutorial center.
Qbranch	www.planetquake.com/polycount/cottages/qbranch/tutorials.shtml	Your keys 007 or better yet a series of tutorials on skinning and shaders for Quake 3.
Bubba's Arena	Planetquake.com/bubba	Under the Editing section you can find a plethora of beginner and advanced mapping tutorials for Quake.

are geared toward Quake and Half-Life their lessons can apply to other games you might choose to mod as well.

There are a few books out on modding as well:

Focus On Mod Programming in Quake III Arena
By Shawn Holmes and Andy Smith
ISBN: 193184156X

The book from Premiere Press is a good guide on modding Q3A and QuakeC. It's a compact design and covers the basics.

Introduction to Level Design for PC Games
By Andy Clayton
ISBN: 1584502053

This book isn't out yet but it should be halfway decent since Charles River Media makes pretty good game development books. It will be more of a general book, which is nice as well.

Distributing Your Mod

Before you can distribute your mod you might want to package it up for easy online distribution. This means creating some sort of installation procedure. If you want to build an installer for your mod there are two good recommendations I can give you. First you can use Winzip to create a self-extracting .exe which doesn't require a user to have Winzip installed. (Why they wouldn't have it is beyond me!) This product costs about $80 for the self-extracting license and the license for Winzip itself. In many simple cases the self-extractor is a decent choice.

A step up from the Winzip self-extractor is Nullsoft's SuperPiMP Installation System (**www.nullsoft.com/free/nsis**), which you can also find on SourceForge (**nsis.sourceforge.net**). This system was developed by the smart programmers of Winamp and is a very robust installation system that is completely *free*. I highly recommend checking it out if you want to create a really sweet and professional looking install for your mod.

Once you have your mod ready for distribution, don't just dump it on your site. You should try to get mirrors for your download, PR for it, and post it up on as many core download sites as possible. Like PR (see later), download sites for a mod will mostly come from the fan sites of the game you're modding. At the same time, don't forget about the core game sites and download sites like Download.com, Tucows, and Fileplanet.

Another potential outlet for your mod are the major gaming magazines. If your mod is truly cool you can expect them to want to distribute it with any cover mounted or polybagged CD. You can also submit your mod for consideration as well. There are usually two outlets for submitting. The first is to send an email to the editor who covers modding in general, or the genre of game you're modding. Tell them about your mod, and ask them about the chance to put it on a CD with their magazine. The second option is to talk directly to the CD editor for the magazine. As with other PR efforts, the critical thing here is don't pester these guys. Ask right and ask once. Then hope you hear good news. It also should go without saying that your mod should be good, which you will know once it's done and you get a good amount of downloads and buzz going on the various fan sites.

Promoting Your Mod

The first place to start with promoting any mod is the fan sites of the original game. Duh! Like that's some sort of epiphany. Seriously though, work all the community and Web pages that cover the core game and you'll be happy with the results.

Another form of custom PR is what is known as the *pre-release* PR. This is a widely adopted form of PR where you promote your product before it's out. If you deliver, then it's looking good but, like Duke Nukem Forever, and Daikatana before that, if you make a lot of noise and don't deliver you start to look really stupid.

Previews are the lifeblood of the game industry. As your mod takes real shape it can't hurt to get a little advance PR. Contact the various editors, or writers in-charge of the moddng sections and make them aware of your game. Work especially hard to attract the folks who run the fan sites devoted to the game. If you can release screenshots, in-game movies, or playable portions, this can help you get some attention.

Charging for Your Mod

You and your team have slaved for months to create a killer mod and now you want to see some payback. So you decide to charge for your mod right? Well, probably not, at least not yet. Most licenses for games state rules concerning mods, which includes selling them. Many games explicitly give you permission to modify them and use elements from the game to do it so long as your modifications only work with the retail product and you don't charge for it. Those same user licenses for games prohibit you from charging for any derivative products without express permission from the developer and publisher. This is to prevent others from creating a commercial product without the developer receiving some negotiated compensation beyond the fact that more games are sold. This entire issue actually went to court several times during the initial days of Doom and Duke Nuke'm. If you want to read more about this issue read It's a Mod Mod World on the IEEE Spectrum Careers site (**www.spectrum.ieee.org/careers/careerstemplate.jsp? ArticleId=i020203**).

At the same time most people don't want to charge for their mods, and depending on what you build, you'll be lucky if you could charge for it to begin with. I've long advocated, however, that charging for mods is not a bad proposition. My feeling is that if gamers could optionally charge for their mods there might be more incentive for gamers to mod, and even some reward for it. As Internet commerce and distribution infrastructure has improved, it seems very likely that the ability for you to charge for a mod may begin to exist.

Valve's Sream project is expected to create a monetizing environment for Half-Life mods that goes beyond their occasional support of mod teams like

CounterStrike. With Steam, mods deemed will be added to a repository where users can download them to their computer and pay for it in the process (or not, you're still free to make things free!) My guess is Valve will take a cut of the action and send the rest to the proper mod creator's bank account much like RealArcade does for small indie-game developers. When this happens (and if it works to generate real revenues for Valve), I fully expect there to be wider adoption of mod commercialization. For more on Steam visit **www.streampowered.com**.

MACHINIMA

Machinima is a derivative intersection between the world of digital filmmaking and games. Specifically, it uses 3D environments (many of them game based) to construct animated movies. It's ostensibly a mod medium because various game engines are usually modified in order for the movie capability to come about. Machinima basically started out with people creating fun Qmovies (Quake Movies) and the uploading them for others to watch. Some took it further and machinima was born.

Macinima at it's core is about the recording of live demos in these environments. The demo movies are then edited and recorded out to video, and perhaps mixed with other elements. Some machinima films are then replayed directly in the environment from which they are spawned, which is the most purest form of machinima or they form the root of a process that ends up as a video file. Tools mostly start with the same core SDKs, and editors used for traditional game mods, but can include specialized tools to do lip-syncing and more. I've not included a list of tools because frankly machinima.com does a really good job tracking it all so that I don't really need to.

You can learn a lot more about Macinima at **www.machinia.com** and it's sister site **www.machinima.org**. Table 12.5 lists some of the better sites to watch great Macinima and find tools to create your own machinima.

TABLE 12.5
Machinima links.

SITE	URL	COMMENTS
Machinima Glossary	www.z-studios.com/resources/references/mglossary.html	Great listing of the basic machinima lingo.
Open Demo Project	www.machinima.com/opendemo	An attempt to create an open file format spec for us in machinima production.
3D Filmmaker	www.3dfilmmaker.com	Covers more than machinima but has in-depth information on machinima as well.

12

Does this mean you'll be able to quit your day job and just mod all day? No. Most likely a few top mods will be very popular and self-supporting while others will merely provide some small extra income for a lot of hard work. The majority of mods will remain free though—either because they can't really generate revenue, or because their creators didn't do it for the money. Although selling your mods is cool, don't lose sight on the true ethic of modding. Do it because you love to do it and you want to create cool stuff for other gamers to enjoy.

Modding Is Not a Technology

The most important thing to know about modding is that it isn't a technology. There is no magic modding code that developers add to their games. There is no universal mod key on your keyboard. There isn't a single editor that does everything that you need to create a mod. Modding is a practice based on loving games, and of gamers becoming game developers. It began in earnest with Doom in 1993, spread with Quake, boomed with Half-Life, and now is beginning to permeate many major PC games. It's the true ascension of digital media. If we make media digital it becomes malleable, and if we start at the core of games being an interactive form of play then it's clear that true games will take the interactivity all the way through to the core of the game itself. In this chapter I tried to give you some of the knowledge to act on the practice of modding. It's your job to carry it forward and create some interesting things for other gamers to enjoy.

chapter 13

Becoming a Game Developer and Developing Your Own Games

The ultimate thrill for many monster gamers is to become developers and create their own games. This represents the Holy Grail for game lovers. But creating your own games doesn't mean that you have to go away to the programming monastery to become a hard core professional developer. Many monster gamers do this simply for fun. And some go all the way and reach nirvana—they actually get paid for creating games. In this chapter, I'll actually show you (with my cool crash course) how you can break into the game development industry by joining the ranks of one of the following groups:

✔ **Hobbyist Programmers**: Hobbyists programmers are developers because they enjoy the fun that comes from creating any game that could be enjoyed by themselves or others. They do not seek to become professional developers.

✔ **Amateurs**: These guys are like hobbyists except their ultimate goal is to advance up the food chain and become professional developers.

✔ **Professionals**: This group is dedicated to the art of developing games as professionals, either full time or as a part-time business. Professionals often work as independent contractors or as members of an established development studio or publisher.

Obtaining Da Skillz

So you really want to be a game developer? The prerequisite is a love of games. Fortunately, you qualify because you're reading this book. To succeed, however, you can't just sit on the sidelines and wear your badge stating, "I'm Cool, I Love Games." You must develop some specific skills to make you valuable as a developer. You also must invest time into developing these skills, and in most cases, you must be willing to work long hours (and I mean really long hours). Unless you are an extremely gifted programmer or artist, becoming a card carrying developer who makes games for a living will be harder than progressing through all of the levels in Rallisport Challenge on the Xbox. But hey, you're a monster gamer—you can deal with challenges.

So how can you acquire the skills needed to become a member of a game development team? One way is to teach yourself, but this takes a lot of discipline. (I know because this is the crazy path that I took years ago.) You can read a variety of books, magazines, and Web sites about game development and you'll learn a lot. The industry is now bursting at the seams with conferences, seminars, and lots of good documentation. (I'm even working on a new book—once I finish this one of course—titled *The Game Development Bible*, which would likely be a great source for you as a developer.)

The second way to acquire game development skills is in school. A school might sound weird but there are actually a number of schools that have special programs to train people for the game development industry. These programs aren't just for artists; some cover everything from programming, design, and production management. Table 13.1 lists some of the top programs but you can find a more exhaustive list at **www.gamasutra.com/education**.

The final way to acquire skills is to build a game yourself or obtain an entry-level job in the industry. Ask any developer and they'll tell you that learning by doing is probably the best training you can get today. We've already covered some ways to develop games by modding existing titles. So there is little excuse not to at least build a few maps, design a level, or even do a total conversion as an educational project. If you want to be an architect, you should tear apart or remodel a building. If you want to be a game developer, hack up a game. The nice thing is that by doing this you'll have something to show off.

TABLE 13.1
Major schools offering courses, certificates, or degrees in game development.

Alberta College of Art and Design 403-284-7617 www.acad.ab.ca admissions@acad.ab.ca	Georgia State University 404-651-2365 www.gsu.edu admissions@fsu.eduIndiana
Brown University 401-863-7600 www.c.s.brown.edu Thomas_dean@brown.com	University-MIMI Program 812-855-0661 www.indiana.edu inadmit@indiana.edu
California Institute of Technology 626-395-6346 www.caltech.edu gradofc@its.caltech.edu	Massachusetts Institute of Technology 617-253-3599 www.mit.edu cmscms@mit.edu
Carnegie Mellon University 412-268-5350 www.etc.cmu.edu etcadmit@cs.cmu.edu	Michigan State University 517-355-8332 www.admis.msu.edu admis@msu.edu
Centennial College 416-289-5000 ext. 8627 www.bccc.com knoble@centennialcollege.ca	Montana State University 888-678-2287 www.montana.edu admissions@montana.edu
DePaul University's School of CTI 312-362-8381 www.cti.depaul.edu ctiadmissions@cs.depaul.edu	New York University CADA 212-790-1370 www.scps.nyu.edu cadacada@nyu.edu
DigiPen Institute of Technology 425-895-4417 www.digipen.edu gcorpeni@digipen.edu	Northwestern University 847-491-3741 www.northwestern.edu cs-info@cs.northwestern.edu
Drexel University 215-895-1675 www.drexel.edu/comad/digitalmedia ddm22@drexel.edu	Palomar College 760-744-1150 www.edmagnin.com/palomar.html ed@edmagnin.com
Full Sail 407-679-0100 www.fullsail.com www.fullsail.com/admform	Purdue University 765-4947505 www.tech.purdue.edu cgadmissions@purdue.edu
Georgia Institute of Technology 404-894-4154 www.gatech.com admissions@success.gatech.edu	Rochester Institute of Technology 565-475-6631 www.rit.edu l.perlman@gccis.rit.edu

13

(CONTINUED)

TABLE 13.1 (CONTINUED)
Major schools offering courses, certificates, or degrees in game development.

University of Calgary
   Department of Computer Science
   403-220-5903
   www.cosc.ucalgary.ca
   discover@cpsc.ucalgary.ca

University of North Texas
   940-565-2767
   www.larc.csci.unt.edu
   ian@unt.edu
   interactive@cinma.edu

University of California, Berkeley
   510-624-6000
   www.cs.berkeley.edu
   oaurs@ucl4.berkeley.edu

University of Southern California
   213-740-8358
   www.usc.edu
   usc_interactive@cinema.usc.edu

University of California, Irvine
   949-824-6703
   www.uci.edu
   www.admissions.uci.edu

University of Texas, Dallas
   972-883-2016
   www.utdallas.edu
   dnajjab@utdallad.edu

University of Maryland, Baltimore County
   410-594-2282
   www.umbc.edu
   cctcinfo@umbccctc.com

University of Waterloo
   519-888-4567
   www.uwaterloo.ca
   www.askthewarior.ca

University of Michigan (EECS Department)
   734-764-1817
   www.umich.edu
   ugadmiss@umich.edu

Reading about Game Development

If you're going to develop your own game, you should read as much as possible about development. Table 13.2 lists the most notable books, magazines, and Web sites to help you spice up your reading list.

Conferences and Shows

I've written about conferences in other chapters but let me add a few things here. The biggest and best conference for game development is the Game Developer's Conference. It's held each year (in March) in San Jose, Calif. Going to GDC is expensive given the airfare, hotel, and entrance fees but it's worth it. This conference is amazingly useful to help you break into the industry. You can benefit from the sessions or the schmoozing. There are also volunteer opportunities that can help you get access to the show for free. You can find out more about volunteering at **www.gdconf.com/volunteers/index.htm**. As a member of the IGDA you also get discounts to conferences. If you haven't joined the IGDA, do so now by visiting **www.igda.org/join**. A membership is $100/year and student members can join for $35/year. If you attend GDC, bring your resume, demos, and business

WHAT TO STUDY IN SCHOOL

All this talk about schools may either scare your pants off or leave you wondering what the heck you should study so that you can get into the game development business. Well, it depends on your goal. If you want to be a programmer, you'll need math, physics, and programming. Math is really critical, especially for game developers. After all, those cool 3-D effects you see in most games aren't really done with smoke and mirrors. If you sat in the back of math class in high school, you'd better move to the front of the class now. In terms of actual programming, C++ is the language to master. Java is also useful. You should also consider learning something about languages like Python, Lau, Ruby, and PHP. These languages are good for people who might serve as designers and need to know how to use various game-scripting languages.

You also shouldn't skimp on studying topics like speech and writing. Having good communications skills is a must, especially in a team-focused industry like gaming. Developers also might consider taking creative-oriented courses like drama, music, art, and drafting. Basic liberal arts are useful also. Consider adding history, comparative media studies, art history, and literature. Some of the best developers and designers in the industry are actually history and drama majors. Game developers, as a group, are some of the most multi-skilled and diverse people you'll likely meet. Only a few careers mix the depth of technical engineering with the sheer creative side of the arts as gaming does.

TABLE 13.2
The basic reading list for any would-be game developer.

MAGAZINES

Game Developer Magazine www.gdmag.com	Available on newsstands and through qualified subscription. You can fill out a subscription form on their Web site. A must have. Lots of good articles, both technical and production oriented. Tons of want ads as well.
Develop Magazine www.develop.co.uk	Available only through subscription. An excellent magazine with a European focus and large production-oriented articles.

WEB SITES

Flipcode www.flipcode.com	Lots of news, resource lists, and forums to make this a great site for independent developers.
Gamasutra www.gamasutra.com	The sister site to the Game Developers Conference and *Game Developer Magazine*.
Gamedev www.gamedev.net	Gamedev.net is the most polished independent game development site on the net.
GDSE www.gdse.com	A large and well-stocked directory of game development related resources.

13

(CONTINUED)

TABLE 13.2 (CONTINUED)
The basic reading list for any would-be game developer.

BOOKS

The Game Development Bible ISBN 193211176X	By yours truly. A comprehensive look at the *full* game development process including design approaches, production methods, business models, resources, and much more.
Game Code Complete ISBN 1932111751	Written by a lead programmer for Origin Systems and Microsoft's casino games and produced by yours truly. This is a great book on programming and engineering quality game code. It's not a end-all be-all book on programming games but it ties everything together in a major way.
Premier Books Series www.premierepress books.com	Okay enough self-promotion. Premier Press's book series, edited by Andre Lamothe, has some winners (and losers) so check the reviews of their books on Amazon carefully. They've recently started a "Focus On" series that provides coverage of some niche topics that are pretty cool.
Wordware Publishing www.wordware.com	A small publisher with a lot of game books, some of them pretty decent.
Charles River Publishing www.charlesriver.com	Another publisher with a lot of game books but with a decidedly higher-end set of topics. Some are pretty good, although because of this their books may not be as adept at explaining stuff to newer developers..
GamaBooks www.gamasutra.com	A new publisher from the folks behind Game Developer Magazine and Gamasutra.com. Too early to tell what their books will be like.

cards. Don't be too pushy, and try to listen as much as possible. The roundtables are also great places to meet people and share your ideas and opinions.

Other shows worth checking out are E3 (which I covered extensively elsewhere), Millia in Europe, and Siggraph (**www.siggraph.org**) for artists. A European Game Developer's Conference just started and it will be held alongside ECTS (European Computer Trade Show) in the fall in London.

Don't Forget the Number One Skill: Finishing

The one thing I've learned in life (and not just in game development) is that *the* most important skill you can demonstrate is the ability to finish your projects. The software industry, and especially the game industry, is littered with unfinished projects. Projects remain unfinished because of poor planning, poor organization, lack of dedication, and lack of capital. The last 20% work of developing a game sometimes takes two or three times longer than the first 80% of the project. If you can learn to push yourself to finish your game, your level, your mod, and so on, and and get it out for others to see (or buy), you will be ahead of most wannabe developers.

If you can demonstrate the ability to finish a project (especially on time!) you will command some level of attention. Even a bad review is good news because it represents a game that made it to market and you certainly can't get a good review without a finished product. I've met a lot of promising developers in my work in the game development industry and the ones that have made it are the ones who somehow found a way to finish their work.

Successful Hobbyist and Amateur Development

Recall that amateur developers are different from hobbyists because they strive to become professionals at some point. They have a goal to land a job, get a publishing deal, or successfully self-publish a title. The great thing about hobbyists, on the other hand, is that their goal is to create something for fun. A hobbyist doesn't have to worry about developing a career or making money. Freeing yourself from those goals can be liberating, allowing you the time to do what you want, and the ability to pursue things that aren't as marketable. The challenging part is that the only thing driving you to finish a project is your ability to push yourself because little else is going to. This is why most hobbyist efforts fizzle after the initial "idea bliss" and reality sets in.

Fortunately, there are some tips I can offer to help hobbyist and amateur developers become more successful:

✔ **Don't bite off more than you can chew**. Keeping things simple is the name of the game here, especially when it comes to artwork. Artwork is what causes a game budget to spiral into the stratosphere. If you keep you design simple you won't blow the budget and you'll be able to finish the damn thing. This is why most successful hobbyist games are either 2D puzzle type titles, or are modifications of existing titles.

✔ **Building a game is hard enough but selling it is even harder**. Unless you've got an insanely great game (think Serious Sam, Max Payne, Never-Winter Nights, or better), think about self-publishing it. There are numerous outlets for self-publishing but look at opportunities provided by Real Arcade (**www.real.com**) and Valve's Steam product (**www.steampowered.com**) which integrate distribution and e-commerce into a seamless delivery system. Some Real Arcade games have done exceedingly well in this channel.

✔ **Other good outlets for independent and hobbyist developers include Web based games in Shockwave and Wild Tangent's Web Drivers**. Great Shockwave games can earn revenue via Real Arcade and Shockwave.com and Wild Tangent's (**www.wildtangent.com**) products enable some incredible Web delivered products to reach a wide audience.

✔ **Utilize the Mod forums to find other developers and team members for your project**. Start small here and look for people who can help you on small projects so that you can test them out. There are lots of willing people on the Web who will work on independent efforts but the team dynamics are tougher to work out so build slowly and carefully. Over time, you'll find a core group that is dependable and responsible.

✔ **If money is involved in a team-based project, work out the details up front**. If you might eventually sell or publish your product then money is involved, get everyone on the team to agree in writing to a simple bulleted list of points about who owns what, and what each person has rights to should money enter the picture. This includes proposed percentage divisions of the royalties, proposed salaries, titles, ownership of the code and other assets. You don't need a room full of expensive lawyers or fancy contracts to put a deal together, but at least put something in writing that covers the big points.

✔ **Proceed carefully if someone is interested in publishing or distributing your game**. Retaining a lawyer isn't a bad idea but making them the negotiator is. Take your time, be considerate, and listen more than talk. Don't be afraid to talk to other developers for advice, and don't sign anything until you have to. If things get really serious, I suggest you ask your lawyer to research and find a software industry lawyer with game industry experience.

✔ **Try to be as professional and organized as possible. Use project management software like MS Project or Excel**. Utilize a code versioning system like CVS or Perforce. Write an actual development plan, design document, and technical spec. And most of all, try to follow some sort of schedule.

✔ **Most of all have fun**. If you can't enjoy the process, why bother? If the process of developing your game turns out to be a pain in the ass, your game probably won't be fun to play.

Game Development Kits and Software

One thing amatuer and hobbyist developers should look at are the growing number of tools and kits for developing games that are easier to handle than a "from-scratch" approach. These tools aren't for everyone and in some cases they're limited in the scope of games they can produce but overall for newbie developers, or people just dabbling they can be quite useful and fun.

Torque Game Engine
www.garagegames.com/pg/product/view.php?id=1
Developed by the guys behind well known former studio Dynamix, this is a cool game engine with a lot of power, aimed at garage developers. Garagegames.com offers support and a publishing outlet for the best-of-breed games you might develop.

Dark Basic
www.darkbasic.com
Dark Basic is a special game development system based on Basic but it's hardly basic and can do quite a bit of stuff. Dark basic includes unique language features that make it easy to do 3D programming, sprites, sound, music and multiplayer action. There are two flavors of Dark Basic a regular and Pro version with advanced 3D features.

The 3D Game Market
www.the3dgamemaker.com
From the people who brought you Dark Basic comes this low-skill level 3D game creation kit.

The Game Creation System
www.pieskysoft.com/prod__gcs.html
This is a game creation system that has been around for quite some time. It's not going to let you create Doom but it can be a fun first place to go if you're totally new and just want to experiment. A game using this system was a finalist in the Indie Games Festival a couple years. That game Pencil Whipped can is made by Chisel Brain Software and can be found at **www.chiselbrain.com**.

Linux for PlayStation 2
www.us.playstation.com/hardware/more/SCPH-97047.asp
If consoles are your thing don't forget the Linux for PS2 development kit. You have to order this directly from Sony but once you've got it you can create non-commercial games for the PS2. For more on the community of PlayStation 2 Linux developers check out playstation2-linux.com.

Distributing and Selling Your game
Once you have a finished game (and assuming you haven't received a letter of intent from Electronic Arts or Activision to publish your game), you're going to

want to distribute, promote, and sell your game. This can be a fun experience, or it could be a nightmare. How it turns out depends a lot on your attitude and how methodical you are. I don't have enough pages to cover all of the ins and outs of distributing and selling games, but I'll devote a little space to giving you my sure-fire five-step plan.

Step 1: Finish the Packaging

Even electronically distributed games need documentation, help files, a professional installer, readme.txt docs, and more. Don't skimp on these things because they can really round out your overall product.

 Make the installer include the registration for the product. Ask users to fill out a few pieces of optional information about themselves, where they obtained the game, and how they obtained it. Upload this information to a database on the Web. It will give you crucial statistics and opportunities to follow up with users. Wise Installer and Installshield have the capability to do this pretty easily.

Step 2: Build a Great Web Site

All good independent game marketing starts with a good Web site for a game. Take the time to build a good one ahead of the development, stock it during development, and certainly make as much use of it after development as possible. Visit the sites of other good independent developers to get an idea of what a good site looks like.

Step 3: Build ecommerce Capability

If you're selling your game, or upgrades to it, then Web-based commerce is essential. There are some great ways to do this including PayPal, Shareit.com, and Authorize.net. If you choose to take credit cards you'll need to qualify for a merchant account. Then, you can hook up a Web gateway to that reseller. Authorize.net is a great gateway and I personally use them. Qualifying for a merchant account, however, is a laborious process (which is why PayPal is so big) but a reseller can walk you through it and help you qualify if you can. Visit Authorize.net's reseller page for more help: **www.authorizenet.com/reseller/directory.php**.

Step 4: Distribute Your Game (or Demo) as Aggressively as Possible

Getting your game available for download isn't just a matter of putting it on your Web site. You should submit it to various archives like download.com, Simtel (**www.simtel.net**), and Tucows (**www.tucows.org**). Look for other download sites as well. Not everyone is going to randomly find your site and download

INDEPENDENT GAME DEVELOPERS FESTIVAL
www.indiegames.com

Looking for a cool way to have fun, get a crack at some notoriety, an maybe even earn some cash? Consider the Indie Games Development Festival. It's sort of the game industry's answer to Sundance. It was started by Gamasutra publisher, Alex Dunne, when he was editor of *Game Developer* Magazine. Every year at the Game Developer's Conference, ten finalists that were selected in the preceding months by a panel of judges get to compete for a variety of awards including best overall, best art, best sound, and best design. Prizes range up to $10,000 so it's not just a vanity competition. Teams winning finalist slots get free passes to the GDC as well as a ton of publicity. To qualify, your project can't receive any funding from a commercial game publisher.

I've been both a judge and a finalist so I can attest that the Indie Games Festival is an incredible outlet for hobbyist and amateur developers. My project that qualified as a finalist was a non-profit foundation-supported project called Virtual U (**www.virtual-u.org**), which is a simulation game of university management. Because of the exposure, we easily received over 4,000 visits to our Web site. Several of my peers that year actually got publishing deals, helping them to fulfill their own dreams.

As a judge, I can offer you a few pointers that might help you make it to the finals:

- Mark the entry dates on a calendar early so you can use it as a milestone for your development efforts. The entry deadlines can sneak up fast and you want to put your best foot forward when it's time.

- Don't be scared to submit an unfinished project. While you don't want to submit a project that's half-baked, it's okay to submit a project that's nearly done. If you make it past the first cuts, you will get opportunities to submit further upgrades to the judges so it pays to get in under the deadline if you have enough to be competitive.

- Documentation is important. Judges don't have a lot of time to judge your game. Good start-up docs and an install that actually works are *musts*. Including some saved games, and walk-throughs are a smart idea.

- The interface, especially the game controls, is probably the biggest mistake I witnessed and penalized good games for so pay particular design attention to those. In the year I judged, I saw some incredible graphics doomed by games that were literally unplayable because of poor control layouts or ridiculous control combinations.

- The simplest games often rule the day. Because of the rules of the competition, there are always going to be a few games that have capital behind them. Capital can do a lot to help someone create incredible entries. Don't be too discouraged, though. Often simple, yet insanely great games like Kung Fu Chess from Shizmo Games (**www.kungfuchess.com**) which was nothing more than real-time chess can win.

- If you're a student in school, consider the special slots open for student entries. You don't get a chance for the big prizes but this is an additional outlet for games that aren't capable of cracking the Indie finalist round. Be sure to submit to both! In 2002 some of the student entries were pretty amazing.

13

your game and you probably won't have the bandwidth available to support every download as well?

You can also submit your game for various covermount or polybagged CDs that come with popular magazines. These aren't always easy to obtain but a nice email to the disc editor will help. Make sure you've got a place for them to download it and you might pick one per country for an exclusive (no one wants to be in with the crowd). Covermount editors are more aggressive overseas and not all are game magazines either.

Step 5: Promote Your Game Properly

Build a small press list of sites devoted to games like Avault.com, Gamespot, and so on. Send them a nice note or formal press release announcing your game. Provide them a link to download it, and a link to screenshots as well. If your game isn't super-top-quality don't let this hold you back but don't be surprised if they choose not to cover it. Some magazines and sites have a section devoted to independent developments or mod games. By targeting an editor or writer specifically, you will increase your chances of getting covered. Whatever you do, don't pester or whine to the editors and writers. Take what you can get and move on. Send a new note when a significant (and I mean significant) new version is released. If you stick around long enough, someone will give you some coverage.

This is the basic outline for self-publishing and independent development. Most of the successful independent developers build a library of titles overtime to diversify their income and provide them with a growing customer base. To be successful, you need to become a tireless promoter and marketer since getting people to find out about your game is half-the-battle.

Obtaining a Game Industry Job

Getting a job in the game development industry involves two paths. The first is to somehow land a publishing deal and start your own development squad. Good luck! That's so rare that you might have better odds buying a few lottery tickets and winning the daily grab-ass double (or whatever they call it in your state). The other path is to follow the crowd and apply for a job, rock the interview, and get the corner office with the view of the parking lot. (Well, don't set you're expectations too high just yet.) There are thousands of people who work in the game industry and with a little bit of luck, sacrifice, and smarts (and a little schmoozing now and then), so can you.

In the game development industry, you'll find two tracks of employment: the business side and the development side. I bring that up because some people like being a sales guy, customer service rep, packaging designer, or HR manager. For them, such a job cold be as fulfilling as being the guy who models the main character, programs the AI, or produces the title. While we all like to make fun of the marketing weenies, there are a lot of other jobs that go into running a successful game publishing firm like EA. Even Id software has several staff members who don't develop games and I bet they like their jobs. Besides, the next time you go to a cocktail party what would you like to tell the hot chick who comes up to you sloshing a pink martini? Your choices are, "Well, I'm the Marketing Director of the water treatment plant down the street," or "Like, wow, baby, I do marketing shit for this really cool game company." Let's run through the key positions you'll find at most development studios and publishers. I'll lump most of the non-development categories together at the end.

Game Tester

Most major publishers have dedicated in-house testing positions. These people play games all day long (what a dream) looking for bugs or other problems that could upset players. Finding problems with a game is really a scientific process for most companies. You may think that Nintendo just throws a bunch of games into a room and comes back three days later to hear what happened. Fat chance. Testing involves very targeted analysis derived from written testing plans. Play testers play a game over and over looking for ways to trip it up, find imbalances in play, or outright mistakes like misspellings and poor grammar. In some cases, they may play a game well beyond the point where they're bored by it. They may replay the same sequence twenty times trying it a different way each time to see if they can find mistakes in a level or make the game do something no one on the development team intended.

Testing jobs are usually entry-level so they don't pay very well. The average salary for a first year testing job is probably no more than $30,000. People who manage testing processes can make more. In larger companies people in testing can rise up to become production managers. After you've spent the greater part of the last two or three years doing nothing but looking for mistakes and other problems, you start to develop a pretty good sense of what works and what doesn't.

Skills Needed for Testers

For this job you need to understand PCs and consoles left and right and you need to be really organized. Table 13.3 shows a posting for a typical testing job. Good testers should play as wide a range of games as they can, and become adept at

---

TABLE 13.3
A typical game testing position (LucasArts).

MAJOR RESPONSIBILITIES:

- Test upcoming LucasArts computer and console games for bugs by playing and running functionality tests.

- Work with testers and programmers to isolate conditions for repeating found bugs and verifying fixed bugs.

- Proofread or provide content for product documentation as requested.

- Maintain notes and database on any found problems.

- Excel as a team player and strive to maximize team/department performance. Assist in special projects as necessary.

QUALIFICATIONS:

- Strong familiarity and experience with gaming consoles, Windows based PC's and MAC OS.

- Excellent verbal and written skills.

- Computer game familiarity required, previous game testing experience recommended.

- Database experience recommended.

- Must be willing to work 50+ hours per week.

---

looking for or noticing bugs. After that just apply for jobs. However, before you accept such a job, find a few roommates so you can pay the rent. At the salary you'll be pulling, you'll need subsidized housing.

 Many companies use TestTrack Pro from Seapine software to track and organize their testing process. If you want to learn more about this product go to **www.seapine.com**. Even if a company doesn't use TestTrack, chances are their home-brewed system is somewhat similar. Excel is also a tool utilized a lot by testing departments.

Game Programmers

The game industry offers a lot of programming positions but many of these positions are support ones. Only a few lead programmers are needed. Projects are not produced in the "lone-wolf" style they once were. Many programming positions involve creating support tools, such as editors, resource compilers, and so on. Programmers also specialize in specific components of a game including configuration screens, installation systems, specific mini-games. or portions of a game, and so on. A large project could have 8 to 12 programmers working on various pieces of the game. If you don't make the mistake of thinking you'll be the guy programming the heart of a game, you'll be one step ahead. (You might even get hired.)

Game programmers are hired for positions based on their experience and capability (That's right; these guys definitely don't get hired for their good looks.) As with most software projects, you'll find senior programmers, junior programmers, programmers who develop technologies, and those who work on shipping products. Most projects have a single lead programmer whose job it is to decide or single-handedly set the formats, and specifications of the game system. That person is also responsible for the various builds of a product when all the various elements of a game are brought together and compiled into some early playable form.

Most programmers earn good pay, and the best-of-the-best can command very good salaries. It is not uncommon, though, for similarly skilled programmers to make better money in non-game industries. There are a lot of young people who love working on games so the demand is high-enough that there are developers willing to take cuts to work in an industry they love. After all, wouldn't you rather program games than sling code for some really boring corporate financial application. The salary range for programmers in the game industry can range from $40,000 to $200,000 but salaries do get skewed to the lower-end of the scales.

Skills Needed for Programmers

Don't apply for a programming job unless you are a kick-ass programmer. What else can I say? It doesn't matter if you are self-taught or you went to MIT. You can either make pixels fly around the screen at 60 fps or you can't. Programming is a skill that you can do only if you've acquired the specialized knowledge and others will know right off the bat if you have the skills. To work in the game industry there is really only one language you need to know—C++ (although it helps to know others). Ninety-five percent of all games are written in C++ and the only way to write a game for any of the consoles is with C++. Table 13.4 lists the qualifications found in a typical job listing.

Game Artists

You must be a good artist to get work. If you can't create amazing art and animations, you can't talk your way into a job. You must have good artistic skills but just being able to draw isn't enough in the games industry. You have to have some technical talent. Games require certain constraints such as tight resolution, lower-polygon counts, color specifications, and so on. Technical capability at programs clearly involves 3D modeling and animation packages.

13

TABLE 13.4
Typical programming job listing example (Gas Powered Games).

SYSTEMS ENGINEER

- 4 years of game engine programming.
- Demonstrated success with large-scale code architecture.
- Experience with scripting language implementations.
- Intimate understanding of PC performance issues.
- Demonstrated ownership of process and tools outside the game engine black box, with a focus on team productivity.

GRAPHICS ENGINEER

- 4 years of full time game programming experience.
- Minimum 2 years working with D3D, (recent years; DX7 or better.)
- Solid grasp of Linear Algebra and Computational Geometry.
- Deep understanding of PC rendering pipelines and performance issues. · Exposure to the 3DStudio MAX SDK.
- Working knowledge of Physics, Calculus, Statistics, and other scholarly pursuits.

REQUIRED PERSONAL TRAITS FOR ALL POSITIONS:

- Strong communication skills.
- Flexibility, an open mind, and a love of learning.
- Persistence.
- Patience.
- A sense of humor.

Artists jobs are usually sub-divided in a game studio. Some studios will want you to be a jack-of-all-trades while others will hire you based on a demonstrated specialty. The categories of artist jobs include:

✔ **2D Artist and Animator**: Unlike 3D artists who may just be good architects and animators, a 2D artist is a skilled pen and paper illustrator who can produce the same work for game purposes be it an interface, background screen, or two-dimensional artwork.

✔ **Texture Artist**: This is a specialized 2D artist who is focused on creating refined and realistic textures to be placed on 3D objects (organic and inorganic).

✔ **3D Artist**: This is an artist who must be able to model and animate any number of objects utilizing 3D modeling and animation software.

✔ **Character Artist and Animator**: This is a specialized 3D artist focused on creating human, animal, or beasts in 3D software and then realistically animating them.

✔ **Concept Artist**: A "designer artist" who's job it is to pre-conceive on paper a basic look and feel for key game areas, scenes, characters, and so on. This person may also work on the implementation of the game.

✔ **Lead Artist**: A nifty name for the artist who is in charge of the art team and its production work. This artist may also serve as the overall concept artist, and may create some key pieces.

Skills Needed for Artists

Good game artists are illustrators; they can produce any scene required by a design specification and work within the technical constraints of a project. This could mean producing a killer beast with less than 400 polygons that looks like a cross between a lion, alligator, and eagle. Artists also need to be able to work very quickly. Beyond that, they need specific skills with whatever art tools are used. Most shops demand that their artists use their standardized tools but most skilled artists should be able to make the jump from one 3D product to another. Table 13.5 lists the skills required for a artist job posting.

Tools for Artists

Table 13.6 lists the important tools that artists use in their work. I've also included some information to help you find the tools and some useful comments.

Game Designers

Higher level jobs like designer and director are earned through years of experience. You can't just drop in and say, "Give me the job." You might have to work for years

---

TABLE 13.5
3D artist job list example (Firaxis Games).

• 4+ years industry or related experience	• Photoshop proficiency
• Two full projects' worth of creating real-time 3D assets for strategy games	• Real-time modeling and/or animation experience required
• Lead or Senior Artist credit on at least one project	• Ability to work well as part of a team and solo
• Must be well-versed in real-time production process	• Excellent traditional skills desired
• 3DS Max proficiency	• NetImmerse experience a plus
	• Passion for making games a must

TABLE 13.6
Important tools artists should have experience with.

Tool	Place to Get It	Comments
Photoshop	www.adobe.com	You need to know Photoshop upside down and left-to-right. Paint Shop Pro is a cheap alternative to cut your teeth on as well.
Maya	www.aliaswavefront.com	There is a personal learning edition for Macs and Windows you can download for free so there is little excuse not to have played with it.
3D Studio Max	www.discreet.com/ products/3dsmax	Probably the most used program around. No learning edition available but you can check out gMax which is derived from 3D Studio Max. You can order a set of manuals for $40.00 and some schools can get highly discounted versions.
SoftImage	www.softimage.com	There is a free download or CD you can order called the Softimage XSI Experience CD. Search their site for it.
LightWave 3D	www.lightwave3d.com	No learning edition but qualified students can get the entire product for $395. Documentation is available for free online.

in QA (sweeping floors), testing, production, or as a junior designer to move up the ladder. Sometimes programmers are able to move into a director-level or designer job as well. A clever statement about game designers that really puts things into perspective was written by the well-known designer, Ernest Adams. Writing for a special jobs and careers issue of *Game Developer* Magazine, he said that a designer's job is not to design the game he or she wants, but the game the collective leadership of the studio or publisher needs to sell. As a designer your job is to build a product people will buy. Truly successful game designers are team players, and learn to use their creativity within the constraints of the company they work for.

Level Designer

Many games have distinct levels and maps. This is where a game's puzzles and challenges are presented. This is also where most of the design work occurs. Level designing used to be simple enough that one or two designers could do it. One of them might even be the game's overall designer. Today, many game levels are so big and complex that they require a team of designers working under an overall senior or lead designer.

Skills Needed for Level Designer

Depending on the game, a level designer will need some understanding of 3D modeling and, in the cases of studios which have licensed specific engines, they might want need skills with specific editors like UnrealEd. Some programming background can also help level designers because many level and scenario design editing tools implement some sort of scripting language that is used to enhance the interactivity of a level. Quake C is a good example of a scripting language. Another language that can help you cut your teeth on scripting (game or otherwise) is Python (**www.python.org**). Python is used for scripting Web sites among other things and is used in some games today. Lua is another scripting system that has gotten some interest from game developers. You can find information on Lua at **www.lua.org**. Table 13.7 presents a sample job listing for a game designer position.

Writers

Not every game needs a writer but many do. Opportunities include writing documentation, character dialog, stories, and more. If a game is particularly text heavy it may employ an in-house writer. Other games may utilize an in-house writer or freelancer made available via a publisher. Often a designer or producer may serve as a writer with an outside copyeditor and proof reader being employed as part of the testing and QA process.

TABLE 13.7
Level Designer sample job listing (Amaze Entertainment).

Amaze Entertainment is seeking experienced Level Designers for high visibility game production. The ideal candidates have 2+ years of experience as a Level Designer with a strong understanding of UnrealED.

JOB RESPONSIBILITIES AND REQUIREMENTS:

- Experience building single player game maps in the Unreal/Unreal Tournament engine using UnrealED. Having shipped games using the Unreal/Unreal Tournament engine a huge plus.
- Strong skills in level design, architectural design, problem solving, intuitive, creative mind.
- Implement level functionality including sounds and music. Ability to collaborate as a team to achieve a great game play experience.
- A love and passion for games of all genres. (interest in developing games for kids a big plus).
- Excellent verbal communication skills.

Skills Needed for Writers

A degree in English or some other proof of writing capability is usually required.

Producers

People often confuse producers with designers. While it's common for producers to help with the design of a game, they're job is not to be the game's designer. They are the project manager and their job is to be the top-dog, supporter, and cheerleader for a game. That involves setting and managing the schedule, budget, and progress for each stage. If something goes wrong (which is common), they get put on the firing line. Producers must work with marketing, QA, packaging, and the other groups who are involved. Producers track the game from beginning to end as if they are the glue that keeps everything together. Producers rise through the ranks usually from testing and QA but anyone who is deemed "management" material may find themselves plucked for the position.

Skills Needed for Producers

Producers must pay their dues and work through the entry level positions. Most of all they need to have real leadership and organizational skills. Familiarity with basic tools the industry uses is typically required. There are also some production management oriented tools that producers might want to become proficient in as well, especially Excel and MS Project. Larger development shops also use version control and asset management software like NXN's AlienBrain (**www.nxnsoftware.com**) and Perforce (**www.perforce.com**). Table 13.8 shows a listing for a typical producer position.

Musicians and Sound Guys

Musicians and sound effect artists either have the inherent skills or they don't. However, those with those skills need to compliment them with the technical specifics that enable their work to be "game compliant." This includes having knowledge of the various digital music formats, file size issues, and 3D positional audio, as well as the subtleties of what makes a good game music score or a great sound effect. Talent in this area is often treated as contract labor. Breaking in is tough but with demo tapes, hard work, and savvy marketing (and a lucky break or two) you might become the next Tommy Talirico, Fat Man ,or Jeremy Soule.

Industry Salaries

No one works for free in the game industry. Peanuts maybe, but not for free. So you're wondering what do the people who bring you your favorite games make.

TABLE 13.8
A typical job description for a game Producer (The Collective).

We're looking for an experienced producer with a solid track record in delivering high quality titles that will relish the opportunity to work alongside the best in the industry managing the production of a truly incredible title.

REQUIREMENTS

- 3+ years experience in the production of console, PC, and/or arcade games.
- Self-motivated and detail-oriented.
- Experience in managing/scheduling large development teams.
- Excellent interpersonal and organizational skills.
- Excellent written and oral communication skills.
- Familiarity with game design.
- Ability to contribute innovative and original ideas towards all aspects of game production and development.
- Willing to accept and provide direction, work well under pressure, and handle multiple tasks.
- Passion for making and playing games.

PLUSES

- Technical and/or art background

While a few game developers have made some amazing amounts over the year, the majority earn a comfortable living so they can pursue their dream like working in a tollbooth or stocking shoes at a department store! The ones who often make larger amounts do so from cashing out on some sort of ownership of their studio, receiving a lucky bonus for an incredible selling product, or because they have a much in-demand talent. All three cases are the *exception* to the basic salary bell curve, however. The great thing about the game industry is there is quite a bit of salary history to draw from thanks to annual surveys conducted by the International Game Developer Association (IGDA). Table 13.9 shows the salaries for various positions that I've adapted for the most recent survey.

Creating a Resume and Demos

The two basic ways to demonstrate your talents so you can get hired is to either create a killer demo or game or prepare a good resume. Creating a killer demo is harder than it sounds so let's focus on the resume. (A killer demo reminds me of that old line about pornography: You can't say exactly what it is in words, but you know it when you see it.) A resume may sound too formal for the games industry

TABLE 13.9
Game development positions and salaries.

POSITION	SALARY RANGE	COMMENTS
Programmer	$40-$120K	A few exceptional talents can break the $100K barrier but these are gifted programmers with lots of experience and a track record of on time, quality, delivery.
Artists	$40K-$75K	Don't be shocked to see a bit less depending on the local or for entry level positions. Aside from pure talent factors higher-end salaries are usually complimented by more management responsibility.
Designers	$40K-$75K	Lower level jobs represent level designers, assistant designers, writes, etc. and entry level positions can break below this scale depending on the locale as well. Higher up salaries usually include project management and lead duties.
Producers	$45-$120K	There are a number of junior level producers. Higher-ups can earn more for bigger projects or by managing multiple products or a product line. Climb is long and arduous and you must be truly able to manage the production of a team and not just hurl cool ideas and run for coffee.
Audio	$30K-$75K	Wide range is indicative of the business. Great scores cost money, while entry level sound engineers can expect to make slightly less than their artist brethren. Most jobs are contract jobs.
Tester and QA	$20K-$60K	The majority of jobs are low-end. This is the job you take to get in the door and don't expect it to pay much. Higher up jobs with management responsibility will pay a more healthy salary. Others switch over from this into design and production tracks as well.

but the fact is the biz has become much more traditional than it was in its early days. In the early days you could demonstrate some fast 2D graphics that didn't flicker on the screen to get you an interview. Today, degrees are preferred and employers typical look for three to five years of experience. Imagine someone asking for five years experience in 1981!

I don't want to tell you how to write a resume (there are way too many books on this topic) but here are a few pointers to help you land that interview with a games-related company:

✔ Keep it short and sweet. A good resume fits on a single page. If you need more than one page you better be able to justify it. If you need more space, provide a link to a Web page or something. People who work in HR departments can't really read, anyway.

✔ Don't put an objective or mission on your resume. Contrary to what you read, this just makes you look like a moron who went to some stupid resume writing workshop. That's what your cover letter is for anyway. Let's face it; your mission is to just get a bloody job, have fun, work more hours than there are in the day, and pull in some dough to pay the rent even though you'll be living at your job most of the time anyway.

✔ Don't sell non-gaming experience short. Obviously, having any sort of game-related experience is a plus, even if this experience amounts to a few articles you wrote for a Web site or a magazine. But don't hide what you've done elsewhere (unless it's really bad like hacking into the IRS computers or modding games with your fellow inmates at the state prison). Savvy recruiters want really well-rounded responsible people. If you managed a team of eight people that built a killer Intranet procurement system for a 1500 person company, that's cool too. Beat your drum.

✔ Don't write a cover letter that's too sappy about having wanted to work in the game industry all your life. Keep the letter short and simple and highlight your biggest interest and selling point. Your cover, if you're lucky, will get read in 30 seconds by an assistant. You probably get half that time to make your point. Here is some suggested text to consider (assuming you don't have any experience):

"I'm am interested in being considered for a [job type/ or specific opening here] at your company. I have attached my resume to this letter detailing my work experience [optional: and relevant experience concerning games]. Among my experience, the work I've done/I'm doing at Some Company, Inc. gives me a good background for this position. During my work at Some Company, Inc. I was responsible for overall deployment of a 50 person networked database application including all user testing, bug fixes, as well as serving as a key staff programmer. The application included a custom client, written in C++, that directly linked to a SQL database running on Linux servers.

I've been a hardcore game player for many years, and given the right opportunity would love to move into this industry from my current work. In addition to my specific work experience I have highlighted some key skills relevant to the position I'm applying for which includes extensive knowledge of C++, Windows programming, and network development.

Thank you for considering my resume. In the resume will find links to some relevant graphics demos that demonstrate more game-specific work I'm capable of producing."

13

You might also consider building a Web version with links to downloadable copies of your work. If you've worked on a number of titles, you should include a "softography" on a separate page outlining the games you've worked on and what achievements those titles have had.

For more on resumes, careers and tips visit **Mary-Margeret.com** a leading game job recruitment agency. Their site has lots of help and useful information.

Demo Reels

Good demo reels are a must for artists, level designers, and even programmers. A demo reel could be a video tape showing your sample work, or it could be a CD with digital copies or executables of your work. Online demo reels are also common. A good demo reel should show off your skill set in five to eight minutes time. Be sure to include as many things as you can that show off your real game-related skills. If you're an artist show some stills, texture samples, several polygonal characters, and animations of characters showing walking, talking, jumping, and fighting. Perhaps some architectural and vehicle structures as well and maybe some scans of your pencil and concept art capability. (Leave out the crap about the perfect girlfriend or boyfriend you are looking for. This isn't a dating service!) If you're a level designer, try to include more than one level. I'd also recommend including a few paragraphs explaining your philosophy about the work you are submitting, and how long (in hours) it took you to complete.

Programmers will want to show a demonstration of their skills either through a completed game or some sort of quality graphics demo. This could be some really fast and fun 2D effects and animation, as well as some 3D programming. You needn't recreate Quake; a program that loads a mesh from 3D Studio and animates it could be just good enough. Include you're source code as well. In most cases, your demo needn't prove every skill you have; if it's sufficiently good, you should earn an interview. An interview for most programmers is going to involve some sort of test as well.

Interviews and Tests

A studio or development team can't afford bad hires. You can expect, because of this, any interview to be really tough, so be prepared. Newbie applicants will also find that tests are given to see how well they work under pressure and to ensure that their skills (or potential talents) are solid. Anyone can build a decent level but it's another thing to do it fast. And anyone can make a great demo program but few can spot bugs in some other guy's code and demonstrate core knowledge of the OS or DirectX that you didn't rip out of some book, tweak to bits and call it your own.

Don't get too worried about these tests, however. If you're good enough to develop the demo reel that got you the interview, chances are good that you'll pass the tests and interviews. Even then don't expect that you'll be offered every job you interview for. (You might be a star but the guy interviewing you might not like your hair color.) Eventually, you'll get the job you want.

Distributing Your Resume

There are four things you can do with a resume and demo reel. The first is to look on the Web for jobs at the various studios and companies and apply for them. The second is to go to the Game Developer's Conferences, ECTS, and E3. These conferences, especially GDC, offer a chance to talk to HR departments and contacts about potential job openings. Resumes and business cards are often taken. You don't need anything more than an expo pass to get to the HR tables at GDC so there is little cost other than the travel involved. The third route is to talk to a recruiting agency for the industry such as Mary-Margeret.com These agencies specialize in recruiting and placing talent in the industry. However, understand, that they are usually most beneficial to established developers. Some development houses also don't use recruiters so don't count on them to be you ace-in-the-hole for your job search. The final outlet is the Web. Many people post their resume and demo-reel on a well-constructed homepage because yes, recruiters, developers and HR managers do troll the Web looking for fresh meat (I mean new hires).

To help with your networking, you should consider joining the International Game Developer's Association (see Figure 13.1) and attend one of their local meetings held near your area. By building a Web-based resume and demo reel and putting the URL on your business card, you can make your resume available just by sharing your card. However, when going to a meeting or conference, it's a good idea to actually take some copies.

Before you jam out your resume, apply to your favorite game development degree program, or polish up your demo reel, you might want to take five seconds to see some of the dark underbelly of the game development industry. You can do this by visiting Fatbabies.com (see Figure 13.2). This site is a combination rumor and industry gripe site for the game development industry. As with any mature industry, there are bound to be sad stories of employee woes. Fatbabies provides an outlet for these stories. After you read a few you might be thinking that the super boring

13

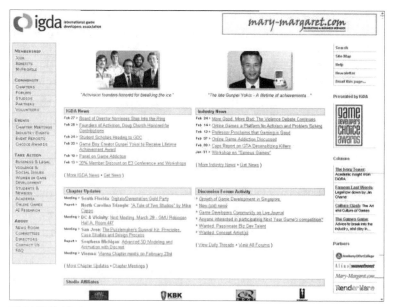

FIGURE 13.1
The IGDA located at www.igda.org.

FIGURE 13.2
Fatbabies.com presents a darker side of the game industry.

job at your father-in-law's bank might be a good career move. But keep in mind that not all of the stories and posting on Fatbabies are perfectly true. Take what you read with a "grain of salt." Oh and if you find out who the Fatbabies are, let Trip Hawkins of 3DO know. I'm pretty sure he'd love to meet up with them in a dark alley someday!

Parting Words

You should now have an appreciation for the types of skills it takes to create games. Making games on any level is a labor of love because it's hard to get rich making games. The industry, being as fickle as it is, never guarantees anything, much less your job. If you get a career going in the industry, you need to keep in mind that you will make games you love, and some you don't. Every creative career poses this challenge because sometimes you must work on projects that others want you to do more than you want to. Hopefully, you can make great games by day (and night) and play great games by night (and day). There's something to be said for 24×7 gaming that is both fun and tax deductible. This is the ideal that all monster gamers should strive for.

13

Index